>> 美语从头学

赖世雄
高级美语

> 赖世雄 著

外文出版社
FOREIGN LANGUAGES PRESS

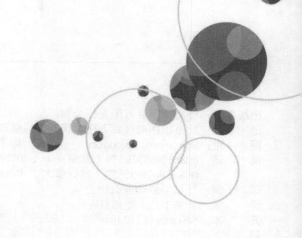

图书在版编目（CIP）数据

高级美语 / 赖世雄著. — 北京：外文出版社，2014（2018年重印）
（美语从头学）
ISBN 978-7-119-08686-6

Ⅰ.①高… Ⅱ.①赖… Ⅲ.①英语－美国－教材 Ⅳ.①H310.1

中国版本图书馆CIP数据核字(2014)第024155号

选题策划：知语文化
特约编辑：贾志敏
责任编辑：李春英
装帧设计：郭海亭
印刷监制：冯　浩

高级美语

作　　者：赖世雄

出版发行：外文出版社有限责任公司
地　　址：北京市西城区百万庄大街24号　　邮政编码：100037
网　　址：http://www.flp.com.cn　　　　　电子邮箱：flp@cipg.org.cn
电　　话：008610-68320579（总编室）　　008610-68995964/68995883（编辑部）
　　　　　008610-68995852（发行部）　　008610-68996183（投稿电话）
印　　制：北京华创印务有限公司
经　　销：新华书店 / 外文书店
开　　本：880 mm×1230 mm　　　1/32
印　　张：9.75　　　　　　　　　　字　　数：250千字
版　　次：2018 年 6 月第 1 版第 14 次印刷
书　　号：ISBN 978-7-119-08686-6
定　　价：32.00元（平装）

序

这套《赖世雄美语从头学》系列丛书是专为英语初学者以及想重新学好英文的人士所编写的。

本系列丛书其实是我一生学习英文的缩影。1961 年,我在台北念初一起就接触英文,6 年的中学生涯中,由于语法的艰涩用语不易了解,背单词又太累,懒散的我索性放弃了学习,结果在大学联考中名落孙山,英文竟只得了 7 分(满分是 100 分)! 和很多联考失利的年轻人一样,我选择了当兵,我的英文就是在当兵期间重新学习的。这段期间我扭转了学习态度,按照自行摸索的方法,竟然让我全凭自修学好英文,后来也考上了公费赴美留学,在美国明尼苏达大学攻读大众传播及英语教学的硕士学位。可惜在念博士课程时内人罹患尿毒症,不得不中断学业,赶返台北照顾内人迄今。

从一个原本对英文一窍不通的我,到今日热爱英文并以英语教学为终身职业的我,这个转变全在于我在学习英文的路途上一路坚持。1990 年,时任中央人民广播电台科教部主任的张力先生请我在该台向全中国推广英文听、说、读、写的全向式教学。面对这项既光荣又艰巨的挑战,我随即召集台北常春藤出版社所有的中外编辑,按照我学习英文的切身经验,历经数年辛苦编写以及反复斟酌修改,这套《赖世雄美语从头学》终于问世。

为了让读者真正学懂学透这套丛书,我特别邀请发音纯正的 Jennifer 以及在台湾大学外文系任教的美籍老师 Bruce 一起逐课录制讲解。这些内容早年在中央人民广播电台播出以来就一直深受好评。阅读本套丛书时若能配合这些有声课程的使用,学习效果会远超出读者的想象。

这套丛书自从上市以来就一版再版,由此可见广大读者对这套书的信任和喜爱。这些年我们在全中国不知培养了多少因为学习本套丛书而成功的人士。例如知名的李阳老师。有一年李老师邀请我去他的广州集团总部访问时,就当面跟我说:"我就是看了您的书才有今天!"这套书上市以来,无数读者纷纷感慨相见恨晚。他们直言这套书充满了"正能量",帮助他们少走了很多弯路。一位读者通过微博告诉我们他大学四级没过，很是沮丧，经同学推荐开始学习这套书，结果一发而不可收拾，半年苦读后在研究生考试中英语取得出人意料的高分，顺利考上了研究生。还有一位同学在跟着这套教材学习之后，凭借优秀的英语能力获得了在联合国机构工作的机会。他们虽然都是普通的学子，但他们的这些进步让我们倍感欣慰。如果这套丛书能够帮助海峡两岸超过四亿的英语学习者重拾丢掉的英语，让流利的英语成为大家自信的资本，点亮以后的人生，那是一件多么荣幸的事！我本人愿以此为终身职志。

随着时代的进步，大家对英语学习资料的要求也更加多元化。我们编辑团队也在不断努力为大家提供更加便捷的学习途径，我们也在手机、网络等方面做着全新的尝试。对于本套丛书我们也一直努力改版升级。此次改版除了让版面更加赏心悦目外，重点在于我们又增加了辅助大家学习的新内容。

1. 增加了朗读音频。除了详解的讲解音频外，我们力邀美籍专业老师录制了纯正的美语朗读音频。标准的语音一定能够让你更加自信地讲英文，迅速在人群中脱颖而出。

2. 随书附赠学习手册。每册书我们都附赠一本实用手册。内含本册书的单词表、短语表以及根据读者学习程度精心设计的"对症"学习锦囊，包括生活口语、职场口语、实用写作、成语妙解等。我们希望这些锦上添花的学习资料能够将读者打造成为真正的英语全能王。

本人在人生最黄金阶段编写及讲授本套丛书，愿将它献给所有想学好英文的朋友！

学英语，其实有方法

由于我学英文时，听、说、读、写并重，使我多次在国际性会议中担任同声传译及在大学教学时，皆能游刃有余。我是怎么学好英语的呢？ 我天赋平平，起步也就是当年的英语七分，只不过在后来的英语学习中秉持了以下三个学习态度，经历了三个学习阶段而已。

三个学习态度：

1. 善用零星时间：我在走路、等车、坐车、休息的时间都在说英语或看英文书籍。

2. 少就是多、慢就是快：我英文程度差，所以每天只看一两句英文，勤查字典，了解句意后，就利用零星时间慢慢地念，一遍遍地重复念，我最后竟然能够凭声音记住单词、短语或句子，不知不觉中说英语的速度也愈来愈快了。

3. 持之以恒、永不放弃：学习语言贵在勤加复习，每日不间断地练习，终有成功的一天。

三个学习阶段：

第一阶段：学习音标

我善用零星时间，每天只学三至四个音标，配合胶质唱片随着外籍老师灌制的录音跟着念，一遍一遍重复地念。元音学完后，再学辅音，约两个星期为一周期，如此反复练习三个月后，我打开字典就可以凭音标念出每一个英文单词的正确发音。

第二阶段：学习入门会话

我的做法是：先查字典以了解每一课会话的字词内容，再慢速将会话内容利用零星时间反复念出来。到了下午我会找个无人的地方，以一人分饰两角的方式把会话反复表演出来，并不时加入自己曾学过的词汇以扩大会话内容，如此才能活学活用。经过三个月后，我在路上见到外国人时竟然敢开口，更因为自己对发音的挑剔及自信心，常获得老外的称许。

第三阶段：大量"阅读"

我深知仅从会话学英语，所学得的词汇及常识是有限的，于是我在自修学会基础会话的能力后，便转而注重英文阅读能力的培养。

我的做法是看到文章就念出来，这才是真正的"阅读"：我选择内容生动、文字浅显的文章入门。一旦选定文章后，我本着"少就是多"的学习态度，每天只精读一小段。我会先以慢速朗读这一小段（愈慢愈好），以粗略了解这一小段的内容。再以字典勤查每一个单词，并将字典内的相关短语或例句一一抄写在笔记本上。最后，我再将该小段的英文译成中文，然后将此中文以口译的方式翻成英文。之后，就以自己的英文叙述该小段的内容，直至我当天深夜上床睡觉为止。这个做法有助于我对字词运用的了解及口译能力的培养。时至今日，我可以在阅读英文报纸或杂志之后，随即用英文说出报章杂志的内容！

读者不难发现，《赖世雄美语从头学》就是我学习英文的过程。读者购买这套丛书时，马上会发现不论哪一本书，我们都本着"完全解析"的态度将读者学习英文可能遇到的疑难杂症全都以系统而又完整的方式解说，读者在看这些书时会觉得我就在您身旁一样，不时鼓励您向前迈进。

我们都想把英文学好，我做到了，你当然也可以做到！如果你现在的程度比"七分"好，那你就可能比我做的更好。

目录
CONTENTS

Lesson 1

Let's Visit New York!

参观纽约！

New York, New York. The city so nice they named it twice.
纽约州的纽约市，这城市好得人们称呼它两次。

1   *Reading* 阅读

These words were used to describe New York when it was by far the largest, richest, and most developed city in the United States. New York still remains the largest and most famous city in the U.S. today, but some of its "nice" reputation has fallen over the past thirty years with stories of rampant crime making headlines around the world. How true are these stories? Is New York still a "nice" place to visit? If so, what can a tourist do in New York? Let's take a closer look at America's premier city.

First, as personal and social security are always uppermost in the minds of travelers, just how "dangerous" a city is New York? Despite the glaring headlines, New York, located in the northeastern U.S., is one of the safest cities in the U.S. In fact, New York state (which includes New York City — thus, "New York, New York, the city so nice they named it twice") ranks below other big-population states like California in both violent

1

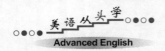

crime (of much concern to the tourist) and property crime. Other major cities have higher crime rates, too. Thus, the foreign traveler to New York City can feel more secure here than in most other large metropolitan areas of the U.S.

Besides safety, why do more foreigners visit New York than any other American city? The answer lies in the character of New York itself. No other city in the world is more cosmopolitan. A walk through its hundreds of residential neighborhoods is like walking around the world itself. Place names like Chinatown and Little Italy can be found on any map of New York, but smaller ethnic neighborhoods also abound. Also, all these groups sponsor annual or seasonal festivals, so that nearly every week one or more of these peoples will share their cultural experiences (and food!) with other New Yorkers.

Because of this unsurpassed ethnic diversity, the restaurant goer will feel that he has died and gone to heaven while in New York. There is hardly a cuisine on the planet that is not represented here. Even better, many of these exotic restaurants are reasonably priced. One is never far from a restaurant in New York. There are thousands of Chinese restaurants alone.

Besides the internationally famous sight-seeing attractions — mostly in the borough (district) of Manhattan — such as the Statue of Liberty, the World Trade Center with its two 110-story towers, Wall Street, the United Nations, and

Broadway, many other interesting places await the curious traveler. The Bronx Zoo in the northern borough of the Bronx is one of the world's best. The borough of Queens offers a great variety of ethnic residential neighborhoods. Brooklyn contains the Botanical Gardens, Coney Island (a beach with an amusement park), and J.F.K. International Airport. Finally, Staten Island, the smallest borough, still affords a look at what New York used to be like, including a farm!

For culture lovers, New York has more museums than any other city, but some of these are not internationally known. A visit to any of these historical, technical, ethnic, or academic museums is well worth the time. New York's art, music, dance, and fashion scenes are a mecca for the young and professional alike. The Internet website for specific information on New York City and state tourism is www.iloveny.state.ny.us. A toll-free number for tourists already in the U.S. or Canada is also available at 1-800-CALL-NYS.

No matter what your interest is, if it can be found in an urban environment, it can be found in New York. Its eight million citizens hail from every corner of the globe, but they are united in the love of their challenging but rewarding city. As the locals there say, "Sure, you have to be a little crazy to live in New York, but you'd be nuts to live anywhere else!"

过去人们总是用这些字眼来描述纽约,当时它是美国最大、最富有和最繁华的城市。今天纽约仍然是美国最大最有名的城市,但是过去 30 年来,由于犯罪猖獗的报道在世界各地成为头条新闻,使得它的一些"好"名声直线下降。这些报道可信吗?纽约仍是观光的"好"地方吗?如果是的话,游客在纽约能做什么呢?咱们这就仔细来探访一下这个美国首屈一指的城市吧。

首先,个人和社会安全向来是游客心中最关切的事,那么纽约到底有多"危险"呢?尽管有那么多触目惊心的头条新闻,位于美国东北部的纽约仍是美国最安全的城市之一。事实上,纽约州(包括纽约市——于是有"纽约州的纽约市,这城市好得人们称呼它两次")在暴力犯罪(这是观光客很关心的)和财物犯罪上的排名比其他人口众多的州——如加州,还要低些。其他主要城市的犯罪率也比它高。因此,比起大部分其他的美国大都市,来纽约市的外国游客在此地能够觉得比较安全。

除了安全外,到纽约的外国人为何比到美国任何其他城市多呢?答案在于纽约本身的特色。世界上没有任何一个城市比它更国际化。 走一趟它数以百计的住宅区就像走过全世界一样。诸如"唐人街"和"小意大利"等地名在纽约市的任何地图上都找得到,但较小的种族小区也有很多。此外,所有这些团体每年或每季都会赞助举行庆典活动,因此几乎每个礼拜都会有一个或多个民族和其他纽约人共同分享他们的文化经验(和食物!)。

由于这种无与伦比的种族多样性,经常上餐厅的人到了纽约会觉得仿佛死后上了天堂一般。地球上几乎没有一道菜在这里找不到。更棒的是,诸多异国风味的餐厅消费价格都很公道。在纽约到处都是餐厅,而光是中国餐厅就有几千家之多。

除了国际闻名的观光胜地——大部分在曼哈顿区——例如自由女神像、由两座110层大楼组成的世贸中心、华尔街、联合国总部和百老汇等，还有其他许多有趣的地方等着好奇的游客去参观。位于东北部布朗克斯区的布朗克斯动物园是世界上最棒的动物园之一。皇后区则有各个不同种族的住宅区。布鲁克林区则包含植物园、科尼岛（一座有游乐场的海滩）和约翰·肯尼迪国际机场。最后还有史坦登岛，这最小的行政区仍保有纽约市往昔的风貌，包括一座农场在内！

对爱好文化的人来说，纽约的博物馆比其他任何城市都要多，但其中有些并非国际知名的。不管是参观历史、科技、种族或是学术博物馆所花的时间都很值得。纽约的艺术、音乐、舞蹈和流行服饰圈对年轻人和专业人士同样都是心所向往之处。有关纽约市的详细信息和纽约州的观光旅游可在下列网址找到：www.iloveny.state.ny.us。而人已经在美国或加拿大的游客则可打免付费电话，号码是1-880-CALL-NYS。

不论你有什么样的兴趣，只要是在都市环境中可以找到的，在纽约就一定找得到。它的800万市民来自全球各个角落，因为爱上这个要拼才会赢的城市而相聚在一起。正如那儿的当地人所说："当然，居住在纽约你必须有点疯狂，但除非发疯了，否则你不会搬到其他任何地方去住！"

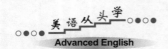
② *Vocabulary & Idioms* 单词短语注解

1. **by far + the +** 最高级形容词 **+** 名词 最……的……
   This is by far the most wonderful thing that has ever happened to me.
   这是发生在我身上最棒的一件事了。

2. **over / during / for the past +** 数字 **+** 表时间的名词
   过去……（时间）以来
   * 上述短语多与现在完成时或现在完成进行时连用。
   We're having a drought because over the past seven months it has rained only twice.
   过去七个月以来只下过两次雨,所以现在正在闹旱灾。

3. **headline** [ˈhɛdˌlaɪn] *n.* (新闻报道等的)标题
   make (the) headlines / hit the headlines 成为报上的头条新闻
   The news of the earthquake hit the headlines immediately.
   有关地震的消息立即成为头条新闻。

4. **Despite + N/V-ing, S + V** 尽管 / 虽然……, ……
   = In spite of N/V-ing, S + V
   Despite the fact + that 从句, S + V 尽管 / 虽然……, ……
   = In spite of the fact + that 从句, S + V
   注意
   由于 despite 及 in spite of 均视为介词, 故其后不可直接置 that 从句作宾语, 而须先在其后加 the fact 作其宾语, 然后再接 that 从句, 此时的 that 从句乃其前 the fact 的同位语。
   Despite the drizzle, we decided to go for a walk anyway.
   = Despite the fact that it was drizzling, we decided to go for a walk anyway.
   尽管正下着毛毛雨,我们还是决定出去走走。

5. **rank** [ræŋk] *vi.* 位居,列于
   Germany ranks as the richest country in Europe.
   德国名列欧洲最富裕的国家。

6. **lie in...** 在于……(= consist in...)

The answer to why he is so popular lies in his courtesy.

他会那么受人欢迎，是因为他待人总是彬彬有礼。

7. **cosmopolitan** [ˌkɑzmə'pɑlətn] *a.* 世界性的；来自世界各地的

8. **abound** [ə'baund] *vi.* 大量存在；充满，富于

abound in / with... 充满 / 富于…… ；盛产……

The Great Plains of North America abound in grain crops.

北美的大平原上盛产谷物。

9. **sponsor** ['spɑnsɚ] *vt.* 赞助

The big company sponsored many runners in the marathon for cancer patients.

那家大公司赞助许多选手参加那场为癌症病人而举行的马拉松比赛。

10. **unsurpassed** [ˌʌnsɚ'pæst] *a.* 无人能比的，无法超越的

surpass [sɚ'pæs] *vt.* 胜过，超越，凌驾

Alexander's achievement in anthropology surpassed his predecessors.

亚历山大在人类学方面的成就超越了他的前辈们。

11. **diversity** [daɪ'vɜsətɪ] *n.* 多样性，变化

12. **One is never far from a restaurant in New York.**

= Restaurants are everywhere in New York.

= Restaurants are all around in New York.

13. **await** [ə'wet] *vt.* 等待，等候(= wait for...)

The children awaited their mother to pick them up from school in their classroom.

那些小孩子在教室里等他们的妈妈来接他们放学。

14. **a great / wide variety of +** 复数名词　各式各样的……

Department stores offer us a wide variety of consumer goods to choose from.

百货商店提供我们各式各样可选择的消费品。

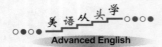
15. **mecca** ['mɛkə] *n.* 向往的地方，希望一游之地

16. **A and B alike** A 与 B（ = both A and B ）

Juvenile crime is of concern to parents and law enforcement officials alike.

少年犯罪对父母和执法人员来说都是他们所忧虑的事情。

17. **hail from...** （人）来自于……（ = come from... ）

Ed hails from Chicago，so he can be our tour guide when we go there on business.

艾德来自芝加哥，所以我们去那里出差时他可以当我们的导游。

Lesson 2

The Amish

亚米希人

1   *Reading* 阅读

In the land of rock and roll, the space shuttle, and computerized living, who could imagine that about 50,000 Americans do not use telephones, electric lights, or cars, not because they are poor, but out of choice? As hard as this may be to imagine, the Amish, or more properly, the Amish Mennonites, still live a traditional, rural lifestyle direct from 17th century Europe!

To understand these unique Americans better, it is necessary to understand their history. Beginning with the revolution started by Martin Luther, leader of the Protestant Reformation in Germany in the 16th century, Europe was wracked by religious wars for several hundred years. Modern Europe is a product of these wars and of the political and religious philosophies of those times. The main figures in this tragic period were the Roman Catholic Church and the Protestants, those who rebelled against papal rule from Rome. Among the thousands of splinter groups formed outside of Rome's religious rule were the Mennonites, a group of particularly conservative, rural Christians situated in what

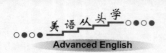
is today Switzerland, part of eastern France, and southern Germany.

To make a long story short, the Mennonite Amish were so conservative that they made more enemies than friends. In order to preserve their peculiar lifestyle, they began to immigrate to the British colonies in North America in about 1720 (before Canada and the United States were formed as independent countries). There they found the religious freedom they had sought. Amish settlements sprang up in the colonies and territories of Pennsylvania, Ohio, and Indiana as well as in Ontario, in what is today Canada. Surprisingly, there are no Amish groups today in Europe.

Little has changed about their lifestyle since then. Just how conservative are the Amish? A group of Amish looks like a cast from a biblical movie set. All the men wear large brimmed black hats, beards (but not mustaches), and clothes made by their wives. The women wear a hair covering called a bonnet, long dresses, and black shoes. Even though all Amish men and women marry, you will not see a wedding ring, for even this simplest type of jewelry is banned among them. The Amish are primarily farmers, and good ones, despite the fact that they do not use modern farm machinery. Their children are educated in local primary schools, but secondary education is in the home. Sundays are spent mostly in church. An old dialect of German mixed with English is used in church and at home. Their lives are uncomplicated and few Amish leave their homes to enter the mainstream American society.

Rural Pennsylvania where most of the Amish live is beautiful countryside. If you have the opportunity to drive through the gentle, rolling hills amidst lush farmlands, perhaps you will see a horse and buggy driven by a family dressed mostly in black. These are the Amish, an enduring and endearing people.

在摇滚乐、航天器和电脑化生活的国度里,谁会想到有大约 5 万名美国人不用电话、电灯或汽车,不是因为他们穷,而是出自于选择呢? 同样令人难以想象的是,亚米希人,或更正确的称呼——亚米希·门诺那特人,如今仍过着 17 世纪欧洲延续下来的传统乡村生活方式呢!

想更进一步了解这些独特的美国人,我们必须了解他们的历史。在 16 世纪德国新教徒改革领袖马丁·路德发起革命之后的数百年间,欧洲饱受宗教战争的摧残。现代欧洲是这些战争和当时政治和宗教哲学的产物。这段悲剧时期的主角是罗马天主教会和反罗马教皇统治的新教徒们。在数以千计脱离罗马宗教统治而形成的支派中,门诺那特人是其中特别保守、属于乡间基督徒的一支,他们当时聚居在今天的瑞士、法国东部的一部分和德国南部一带。

长话短说,亚米希·门诺那特人由于太过保守以致树立的敌人比交到的朋友还多。为了保存他们独特的生活方式,他们于 1720 年左右(在加拿大和美国成为独立国家之前)开始移居到北美的英国殖民地。在那儿他们找到追求已久的宗教自由。亚米希人的新建村落出现在宾西法尼亚州、俄亥俄州和印第安纳州以及现今的加拿大安大略省等殖民区和领地。令人惊讶的是,欧洲现在竟没有亚米希人的团体。

自从那时候开始,他们的生活方式几乎没有改变。亚米希人到底有多么保守?一群亚米希人看起来就像圣经电影中的一个场景。男人都戴着有帽檐的黑色大帽子、留胡子(但不留八字胡)以及穿妻子亲手做的衣服。女人都戴着一种绑带子的包头软帽,穿连衣裙和黑鞋。尽管亚米希人也男婚女嫁,你却看不到一枚结婚戒指,因为即使这种形式最简单的珠宝在他们当中也是被禁止的。亚米希人主要是农民,虽然不使用现代农耕机械,他们还是把农活做得很好。他们的孩子在当地的小学受教育,但中等教育却在家里教授。他们的礼拜天大多在教堂里度过。上教堂和在家时,他们使用一种混合德语和英语的古老方言。他们的生活不复杂,而且很少有亚米希人离家进入美国主流社会。

田园式的宾西法尼亚州有着美丽的乡间,大部分的亚米希人就居住于此。如果你有机会开车穿过那些绿油油农田中静谧、逶迤的山丘,也许你会看见驾着四轮马车大部分都穿着黑衣的一家人。这些就是亚米希人,一个屹立不倒又令人喜爱的民族。

2 *Vocabulary & Idioms* 单词短语注解

1. **out of choice** 出于自由选择
   We did not clean the school yard out of choice, but because we were being punished by our teacher.
   我们清扫校园并非出于自愿,而是因为被老师处罚之故。

2. **As hard as this may be to imagine, the Amish, or more properly, the Amish Mennonites, still live...**
   = Though / Although this may also be hard to imagine, the Amish, or more properly, the Amish Mennonites, still live...

3. **traditional** [trəˈdɪʃənḷ] *a.* 传统的

4. **rural** [ˈrʊrəl] *a.* 乡村的

5. **wrack** [ræk] *vt.* 折磨;损坏;破坏
   Sam wracked his brain late into the night until he thought of the answer to his problem.
   山姆绞尽脑汁直到三更半夜才想出问题的答案。

6. **religious** [rɪˈlɪdʒəs] *a.* 宗教的

7. **political** [pəˈlɪtɪkḷ] *a.* 政治的
   The evening TV news often begins with the day's national political events.
   电视晚间新闻通常先播报当天国内的政治新闻。

8. **rebel against...** 反抗……
   Teenagers often rebel against their parents' authority.
   十几岁的青少年常常会反抗父母的权威。

9. 句型分析
   The main figures in this tragic period were the
         (1)   (2)   (3)
   Roman Catholic Church and the Protestants,
                 (4)

those who rebelled against papal rule from

(5)　　　　　　　(6)

Rome.

(1) 主语

(2) 介词短语，作形容词用，修饰 (1) 中的 figures。

(3) 不完全不及物 be 动词的过去式

(4) 名词，作表语。

(5) 指示代词，作 (4) 中 the Protestants 的同位语。

(6) 关系代词 who 引导的定语从句，修饰其前的名词(亦即先行词)
those。

10. **splinter group** [ˈsplɪntɚ ˌgrup] n. (从大团体中分裂出来的)小派别

11. **conservative** [kənˈsɜvətɪv] a. 保守的

12. **Among the thousands of splinter groups formed outside of Rome's religious rule were the Mennonites, a group of...**

= The Mennonites, a group of...were among the thousands of splinter groups, formed outside of Rome's religious rule.

13. **to make a long story short** 长话短说

Dad came home after work, shopping, and visiting his colleague; to make a long story short, he came home late.

老爸下了班又去购物和拜访同事后才回家；长话短说,他很晚才回到家。

14. **preserve** [prɪˈzɜv] vt. 维护, 保存

The leaders in many Arabic countries are trying to preserve their traditional lifestyle from Western influence.

许多阿拉伯国家的领袖都致力于维护其传统生活方式不受西方影响。

15. **peculiar** [prˈkjulɪɚ] a. 特有的

16. **immigrate** [ˈɪməˌgret] vi. 移民;(自外国)移入
emigrate [ˈɛməˌgret] vi. 移居(外国)

Hoping to earn more money and provide a better education for his children, Mr. Lin immigrated to Germany.

林先生希望多赚些钱以供子女接受更好的教育，于是便移民到了德国。

17. **spring up** 兴起，出现

A wind suddenly sprang up. 突然刮起了一阵风。

18. **A as well as B** A 和 B

Jupiter and Saturn as well as Uranus have been shown to have rings.

木星、土星和天王星一直都显示具有星环。

19. **ban** [bæn] *vt.* 禁止

Smoking is banned in this hotel, so you'll have to smoke outside.

本旅店禁烟，所以你必须到外头抽烟。

20. **despite the fact + that** 从句 尽管……（的事实）

Despite the fact that Marshall is married, he still enjoys looking at girls.

尽管马歇尔已婚，他还是很喜欢看女孩子。

21. **machinery** [məˈʃinərɪ] *n.* 机器（集合名词，不可数）

22. **uncomplicated** [ʌnˈkɑmpləˌketɪd] *a.* 不复杂的

complicated [ˈkɑmpləˌketɪd] *a.* 复杂的

Don't worry. This problem is uncomplicated at all.

别担心，这个问题一点也不复杂。

23. **enduring** [ɪnˈdjurɪŋ] *a.* 持久的

Legends are very enduring; they often last for many centuries.

传奇故事历久不衰；它们常常可以持续好几个世纪之久。

24. **endearing** [ɪnˈdɪrɪŋ] *a.* 可爱的

Lesson ③

Indoor Pollution
室内污染

① Reading 阅读 📖

So you think that by staying at home you are safe from all the terrible kinds of pollution present outdoors, such as in or near factories, roads, and garbage dumps? Do you think that by staying in your office you are breathing cleaner, safer air than when you go outside for lunch or are on the way back home from work? Think again. Recent research done at the University of Texas has shown that staying indoors may actually be more harmful to one's health than being outdoors even in smoggy cities.

Apparently, we are safe neither at home nor in the business office. We use water in both places, but the above-mentioned research shows that chemicals added to our local water supply to kill harmful bacteria can have unwanted side effects. These chemicals can cause potential harm through drinking and in seemingly harmless activities as cleaning one's house. These additives are released from water by daily actions like water running out of faucets, spraying from garden hoses, or splashing in dishwashers and washing machines. As the water is agitated, these chemicals are released into the air and then breathed in. Once inside our bodies, they start to affect our health adversely.

Does this mean we should stop bathing? No, say the scientists, but we should put all pollution into perspective. Activities at home such as the burning of propane, coal, cooking oil, or even candles and incense release carbon monoxide and particulates such as soot which have been proven as harmful to health as working or living near high-density traffic. New rugs, bedding, and even clothing give off that "new smell," which is a sure sign of chemicals. In the office, newly applied paint, newly purchased telephones and other telecommunications equipment, and computers and their peripherals release polluting chemicals, too. As offices and homes often have inadequate ventilation, these chemicals can build up to become health nuisances. Their toxic effects are only now being slowly recognized.

These facts suggest that, at a minimum, proper airing of newly purchased goods with an obvious chemical smell is a wise precaution. Home and office windows should be opened during good weather to allow a flushing of stale air. Even one's car needs to be ventilated as well as the garage.

We need further research to understand better other potential health hazards, too. For example, the effect of overcrowding of schools (carbon dioxide build-up), factory work environments (an endless list of potentially dangerous

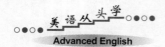
substances), and even home heating and cooling (the furnace and air conditioner may be our enemies, not our friends) have only recently started to come to light. Until we understand the effects of our new technological environment better, we can only hope that "there is no place like home."

你是否认为待在家里就可以摆脱户外诸如工厂、马路及垃圾场附近种种可怕的污染？你是否以为待在办公室内，你所呼吸的空气就比你外出吃午餐或下班回家路上干净、安全呢？再仔细想想吧。最近得州大学所做的研究显示，即使是在烟雾弥漫的城市里，待在室内可能比待在户外对个人健康的危害更大。

显然，我们在家里或办公室内都不安全。我们在这两个地方都会用水，但上面提到的研究指出，为杀死细菌而添加在我们地区用水中的化学药剂会带来不良的副作用。这些化学药剂会经由饮用以及清扫屋子等看似无害的活动而引起潜在的危害。经由水龙头流出、从花园水管喷出或是在洗碗机和洗衣机内溅起水花等日常使用，这些添加物从水中被释放出来。当水被搅动时，就会将这些化学物质释放到空气中然后被人体吸入。一旦进入体内，这些化学物质便开始对我们的健康产生不利的影响。

这是不是说我们就应该停止洗澡呢？科学家们说不必，但我们应该要洞察所有的污染。居家活动如燃烧煤气、煤炭、食用油甚至蜡烛和香，所产生的一氧化碳和烟灰等的微尘已被证实对健康的危害不亚于在高密度交通流量区附近工作或居住所造成的危害。新地毯、床罩甚至新衣服散发出来的那股"新味道"无疑是化学物质的一种迹象。在办公室里，新刷的油漆、新买的电话和其他通讯装备、计算机及其外围设备也释放出污染性的化学物质。由于办公室和住所往往通风不良,这些化学物质会愈积愈多进而成为危害健康的物质。它们有害的影响如今才慢慢被注意到。

就这些事实看来,对于新买而有明显化学味道的东西,最少要有适当的通风才是明智的预防措施。天气好的时候,家里和办公室的窗户应该打开,让污浊的空气能流通出去,即使是车子和车库也需要通风。

我们还需要进一步的研究以便更加了解其他潜在的健康危险。例如,学校过于拥挤(形成二氧化碳累积)、工厂工作环境(数不完的潜在危险物质),甚至家庭的冷暖空调(暖炉和冷气机可能是我们的敌人,而不是朋友)等所造成的影响直到最近才开始被发现。在我们更了解新科技环境所造成的影响之前,我们只能期盼"世上没有一处像家一样"(原意为"世上只有家最好")。

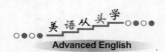
2 *Vocabulary & Idioms* 单词短语注解 ✍

1. **garbage dump** 垃圾场
   dump [dʌmp] *n.* 垃圾堆 & *vt.* 倾倒(垃圾等)；抛弃
   Sally just dumped her lousy boyfriend.
   萨莉刚刚把她那差劲的男友给甩了。

2. **breathe** [bri ð] *vt. & vi.* 呼吸
   breath [brɛθ] *n.* 呼吸
   take a deep breath 深呼吸
   hold one's breath 屏息，屏住呼吸
   catch one's breath 喘口气，喘过气来
   If we don't do anything about the air pollution, we won't be able to breathe fresh air anymore.
   如果我们不对空气污染采取任何行动的话，就再也呼吸不到新鲜空气了。
   David took a deep breath before diving into the water.
   大卫深深吸了一口气才跳到水里。
   She held her breath in anticipation as the judge began to announce the names of the winners.
   当裁判开始宣布优胜者的名字时，她屏息以待。
   After running eight hundred meters, he could hardly catch his breath.
   跑完 800 米后他差点喘不过气来。

3. **be on the way** + 地方副词 往……的途中
   to + 地方名词
   While I was on the way to work, I saw two traffic accidents.
   我在上班途中看到两起交通事故。

4. **be harmful to...** 对……有害
   harmful [ˈhɑrfəl] *a.* 有害的
   harmless [ˈhɑrmlɪs] *a.* 无害的
   Smoking when one is pregnant is harmful to the baby's health.
   怀孕时抽烟有害婴儿的健康。

5. **side effect** 副作用

effect [ɪˈfɛkt] *n.* 影响；效果

have an effect / influence / impact on... 对……有影响（力）

His high school English teacher has had a great influence on his achievements.

他的高中英文老师对他的成就有很大的影响。

6. **potential** [pəˈtɛnʃəl] *a.* 潜在的；有可能的 & *n.* 潜能，潜力

There are a number of potential problems in this plan.

这项计划有一些潜在的问题。

7. **seemingly** [ˈsimɪŋlɪ] *adv.* 看来；似乎，好像

He is seemingly generous, but actually he counts every cent he spends.

他看来似乎很慷慨，但实际上他对所花的每一分钱都斤斤计较。

8. **additive** [ˈædətɪv] *n.* 添加物；添加剂

9. **release** [rɪˈlis] *vt.* 放出，释放

10. **splash** [splæʃ] *vi.* （水等）溅起，飞溅

Don't splash so much when you swim. 游泳时水花别溅得那么高。

11. **agitate** [ˈædʒəˌtet] *vt.* 搅动，摇动（液体）

After being agitated, the colors of the liquid in the test tube blended into one.

经过搅拌之后，试管中液体的颜色便融合成一个颜色。

12. **adversely** [ədˈvɜslɪ] *adv.* 不利地

13. **perspective** [pəˈspɛktɪv] *n.* （对事物的）正确判断，合理观察

put sth in perspective 就某事予以仔细考虑

When Bob put his problems in perspective, he realized that he didn't really have too much to worry about.

当鲍勃仔细考虑他的问题之后，他认识到自己其实没什么好担心的。

14. **propane** [ˈpropen] *n.* 丙烷（即煮饭用的煤气）

15. **carbon monoxide** [ˌkɑrbən məˈnɑksaɪd] *n.* 一氧化碳

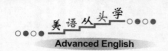

carbon dioxide [ˌkɑrbən daɪˈɑksaɪd] *n.* 二氧化碳

16. **particulate** [pɑrˈtɪkjəlet] *n.* 微粒状物质，微尘

17. **high-density** [ˈhaɪˌdɛnsətɪ] *a.* 高密度的
    low-density [ˈloˌdɛnsətɪ] *a.* 低密度的
    density [ˈdɛnsətɪ] *n.* 密度；稠密，浓密
    Country people are free from high-density traffic.
    住在乡村的人免受交通拥挤之苦。

18. **give off...** 发散 / 放出…… (气体、液体等)
    Her new perfume gives off a subtle，lovely scent.
    她的新香水散发出一股淡淡的迷人香味。

19. **telecommunications** [ˌtɛləkəˌmjunəˈkeʃənz] *n.* & *a.* 电信(的)

20. **peripheral** [pəˈrɪfərəl] *n.* (计算机的)接口设备

21. **ventilation** [ˌvɛntəˈleʃən] *n.* 通风设备
    ventilate [ˈvɛntəˌlet] *vt.* 使通风
    Open the window so that we can ventilate this room we are painting.
    把窗户打开好让我们正在油漆的房间空气流通。

22. **build up (...)**
    (使)增进 / 增加；加强 / 建立(……) (及物与不及物均可)
    If you don't do anything about these problems as they arise，they'll just build up.
    如果问题发生时你不去处理，那问题就会越来越多。
    It's unfair of you to build up her hopes by making her impossible promises.
    你给她无法实现的承诺来增加她的希望，这样做是不对的。

23. **come to light** 显露，披露；被发现
    Many new clues came to light when the detective investigated the murder victim's apartment.
    那名警探调查该谋杀案被害人的公寓时发现许多新线索。

24. **There is no place like home.** 世上无处比家好。

注意

"There is no place like home." 本是一句谚语，表示"世界上没有任何一处地方像家里那么好。"但本文取其相反意思，表示作者希望"没有任何一个地方会像家里一样有那么多危险的污染源。"

Lesson 4

Pizza, Please!

请吃比萨吧！

1 Reading 阅读

One of the world's most popular foods along with the hamburger, fried chicken, and milk shakes is pizza. Although the origin of the first three foods is well understood, that of pizza — until recently, anyway — was for a long time an international controversy.

The word pizza has always been known to mean pie or cake, and is an Italian word. This fact alone might suggest pizza's origins. However, some years ago in New York City, a Chinese restaurateur challenged the Italian ethnicity of pizza by declaring that pizza was originally a Chinese food, but was then taken along with pasta by Marco Polo back to Italy. It seemed the question would never be solved.

The case actually made itself into court (only in America!). Italian restaurateurs challenged the Chinese businessman's view, but when all the evidence was in, the result was announced by a judge: as early as the Roman Empire, pizza was baked in ovens there and eaten. Chinese normally steam or fry their foods, not bake them. Bread and other baked goods to which pizza belongs were developed from India through Europe where they are still enjoyed today. Besides, cheese is an essential element of pizza, and the Chinese traditionally did not produce cheese. The case was closed, and pizza's paternity has now been established.

For pizza lovers, of course, their favorite food might have been invented in Argentina or Indonesia. Who cares? Indeed, pizza has changed as it has spread around the globe, so that when ordering a pizza in Honolulu, New York, Paris, Istanbul, New Delhi, or Tokyo, you are sure to receive a slightly different version in each city or country. Pizza known to Italians and New Yorkers (where pizza was first introduced into the United States by the many Italian Americans living there) is a round, thin-crusted baked dish covered with tomato sauce and cheese. To improve the taste, pieces of Italian sausages such as pepperoni and salami, and vegetables like onions, green peppers and olives are added. Occasionally, anchovies, small, salty fish, are also used. However, Asians enjoy pizza with corn, cucumbers, and other vegetables, not to mention assorted seafood. Hawaiians, perhaps predictably, developed a pizza with a pineapple and ham topping. Today, nearly every country has its favorite local variety of pizza. Worldwide, there must be more than 1,000 varieties of pizza.

Some people are not so fond of pizza. They classify it as a junk food, along with greasy French fries, potato chips, and hamburgers. On the contrary, say defenders of pizza, it

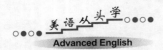
is indeed a healthful food. Carefully chosen fresh ingredients can ensure the quality of any food we eat, and pizza is no exception.

Others protest that pizza is too fattening to be eaten regularly. Not true, respond those enamored of pizza's charms. It all depends on the ingredients and how well they are prepared. For example, the meats which are used as toppings on pizza are often first fried to remove excess fat. The cheeses used can be selected for their high protein but low milk fat. Sparse rather than generous addition of spices such as salt ensure that pizza need not be considered junk food. A well-made pizza not only looks, smells, and tastes great, but it is a wise choice for everyone as a regular food source. Indeed, it seems the only disadvantage to pizza is that when dropped, it causes a mess!

Children enjoy pizza because it's fun to eat and delicious. Workers enjoy it because it is inexpensive and quick to order, too. Families enjoy the convenience of carrying home a whole meal from the many vendors of this world-famous food. With its many advantages, no one needs to resist the allure of one of the world's most popular foods. Come to think of it, let's have pizza for dinner tonight!

和汉堡包、炸鸡以及奶昔一样，比萨是世界上最受欢迎的食物之一。虽然前面三种食物的起源甚为明了，比萨的起源——总之一直到最近——长久以来在国际间一直引发争议。

比萨这个词向来被认为是派或蛋糕的意思，而且它是意大利文，光是这一点也许就暗示了比萨的起源。然而几年前纽约市有一家中国餐馆的老板对比萨的意大利"血统"提出质疑，他宣称比萨原本是中国食物，但后来和面食一起被马可·波罗带回意大利。当时这个问题似乎永远也解决不了。

实际上，这场官司还闹上了法庭（也只有在美国才会！）。意大利餐馆的老板们质疑那位中国商人的看法，而在取得所有证据后，法官宣布了以下结果：早在罗马帝国时代，人们就把比萨放在火炉上烘烤来吃。中国人通常把食物拿来蒸或炒，而不是烘烤。面包和比萨所属的烘焙食品早先在印度发展而后传到欧洲，至今在当地仍广受喜爱。此外，奶酪是做比萨不可或缺的材料，而传统上中国人并没有生产奶酪。本案终结，比萨的法定身份如今已然建立。

当然，对比萨爱好者而言，他们最喜爱的比萨或许是从阿根廷或印度尼西亚发展出来的，谁在乎呢？的确，比萨流传到全球各地时已经有了改变，因此当你在檀香山、纽约、巴黎、伊斯坦布尔、新德里或东京点比萨时，每一个城市或国家的比萨做法一定都会有些许不同。意大利人和纽约人所熟知的比萨（住在纽约的许多意裔美国人首先将比萨引进美国）是一种圆形的烤薄饼，上面撒满蕃茄酱和奶酪。为了增加美味，可加上几片美式腊肠和萨拉米香肠等意大利香肠，以及洋葱、青椒和橄榄等蔬菜。有时候也会添加鳀鱼，一种很咸的小鱼。然而，亚洲人喜欢吃加上玉米、黄瓜和其他蔬菜的比萨，什锦海鲜更是不用说。夏威夷人，或许一想就知道，发展出一种上面覆着菠萝和火腿的比萨。如今几乎每个国家都有当地最受欢迎的比萨口味,而全世界必定已有超过1000种的比萨了。

有些人不喜欢吃比萨,他们把它归为垃圾食物,和油腻的炸薯条、薯片以及汉堡一样。相反地,为比萨辩护的人则说它确实是一种健康食品。慎选新鲜的配料可确保我们所吃的食物质量,而比萨也不例外。

其他反对的人则说比萨太油腻,不能常吃。迷恋比萨魅力的人回答说不对,那完全要看配料以及准备功夫的程度而定。例如,放在比萨上面的肉类通常会先炒过以去除多余的油脂。所使用的奶酪可以选择高蛋白但低奶油的;添加少许而非大量盐之类的调味料便可确保比萨不被视为垃圾食物。制作精巧的比萨不仅色、香、味俱佳,而且是大家日常食物来源的一个明智选择。的确,比萨似乎只有一个缺点,那就是当它掉到地上时会弄得一团糟!

儿童喜欢吃比萨,因为它吃起来好玩又美味可口。工人喜欢吃,因为它不贵而且订购快速。家庭则享受从许多食品店把这举世闻名的食物带回家当作一餐的便利。因为有许多好处,任何人都不必抗拒这种全世界最受欢迎食物之一的诱惑。现在想一想,不如咱们今天晚餐就吃比萨吧!

2 *Vocabulary & Idioms* 单词短语注解

1. **along with...** 和……，以及……
   Patty and Henry along with their parents came to our family's barbecue.
   贝蒂和亨利随同他们的爸妈来我们家烤肉。

2. **origin** ['ɔrədʒən] *n.* 起源

3. **controversy** ['kɑntrə,vɜsɪ] *n.* 争论，辩论
   Abortion is a continuing controversy with passionate supporters and detractors on both sides of this issue.
   堕胎这个议题在强烈支持和反对者之间是一个无止尽的争论。

4. **restaurateur** [,rɛstərə'tɜ] *n.* 餐厅老板

5. **ethnicity** [ɛθ'nɪsɪtɪ] *n.* 血统

6. **It seemed the question would never be solved.**
   = The question would seem (to be) unsolvable.

7. **announce** [ə'naʊns] *vt.* 宣布
   The mayor announced water-rationing during the second month of the drought.
   市长在干旱的第二个月宣布限水政策。

8. 句型分析

   Bread and other baked goods to which pizza
   　　　　　　　(1)　　　　　　　　　　(2)

   belongs were developed from India through
   　　　(3)　　　　　　　　(4)

   Europe where they are still enjoyed today.
   　　　　　　　　　(5)

   (1) 名词，作主语。
   (2) 关系代词 which 引导的定语从句，修饰 (1)。定语从句中的介词 to 亦可放在从句句尾，而成 "which pizza belongs to"。
   (3) 及物动词 develop 的过去式被动语态。

(4) 介词短语, 作副词用, 修饰 (3) 中的 developed。

(5) 关系副词 where 引导的定语从句, 修饰 (4) 中的 Europe。

9. **essential** [ə'sɛnʃəl] *a.* 必要的;基本的

10. **element** ['ɛləmənt] *n.* 要素, 成分

11. **paternity** [pə'tɜnətɪ] *n.* 父系,(本文指)身份起源

12. **be sure to V** 一定会……

You are sure to freeze if you don't take a sweater with you to San Francisco.

如果你没有带毛衣到旧金山去的话,你一定会冷死的。

13. **assorted** [ə'sɔrtɪd] *a.* 各种各样混杂在一起的

14. **be fond of...** 喜爱……

My wife is fond of strawberry icecream. 我太太喜欢草莓冰淇淋。

15. **classify** ['klæsə,faɪ] *vt.* 分类, 归类

Biologists classify animals into groups based on similar physical traits.

生物学家将动物按照相似的身体特征分门别类。

16. **ensure** [ɪn'ʃur] *vt.* 确保

Only hard work and a good plan can ensure your success.

只有努力工作和完善的计划才能确保成功。

17. **be no exception** 没有例外

All the students wanted to go outside for class, and the teacher was no exception.

所有这些学生都想上户外课,老师也不例外。

18. **Not true, respond those enamored of pizza's charms.**

= Those who are enamored of pizza's charms respond, "Not true."

be enamored of... 迷恋……

= be very fond of...

* **enamored** [ɪn'æməd] *a.* 珍爱的

19. **depend on...** 依赖……

We depend on our parents when we are young; they depend on us during old age.

我们小时候依赖父母；他们年老时则依赖我们。

20. **disadvantage** [ˌdɪsəd'væntɪdʒ] *n.* 不利，弊端

advantage [əd'væntɪdʒ] *n.* 益处，好处

21. **resist** [rɪ'zɪst] *vt.* 抗拒

If you want to lose weight, you'll have to resist all these delicious desserts!

如果你想减肥，你就必须抗拒所有这些甜食！

Lesson ⑤

Hot Animals Around the World: Chameleons

世界热门动物：变色龙

① Reading 阅读 📖

Every few months this program will feature an animal which has caught the eye of the world's public to become a favorite or "hot" animal. In the first of this unusual series, we will look at the chameleon, one of nature's strangest creatures.

Perhaps no other group of animals has caught mankind's imagination like reptiles. Among the several subclasses (or "orders" in biology) of reptiles are snakes and lizards, turtles and tortoises, crocodiles and alligators, and the tuatara, a marine lizard in New Zealand. The dinosaurs, too, belonged to the class of reptiles. Was it a snake, lizard, or crocodile that caught the fancy of some Chinese in times gone by to create the dragon? A perennial theme, reptiles have been featured over the past ten years in box-office hits and bombs alike as dinosaurs (*Jurassic Park* and *The Lost World*), crocodiles, and snakes (*Anaconda*). Though not nearly as large as these mighty reptiles, the lowly chameleon nonetheless has amazed countless generations with its special talents and skills.

What is a chameleon? Its unusual name fits this unusual animal perfectly, for it translates from the ancient Greek as "lion on the ground." This is unexpected, since chameleons spend most of their time in trees, and as for looking like a lion, a chameleon looks like a...well, a chameleon! No other animal in Nature's zoo looks quite as bizarre as they do. Where do they live? True chameleons are found only in the tropical forests and jungles of the Old World, and nearly half of its species live on the African island of Madagascar.

What's so special about the chameleon? Plenty! From its tongue to its tail the chameleon offers a storehouse of specialities. The tongue of this modern-day dinosaur look-alike can be extended more than twice the length of its body. This type of tongue, also present in frogs and toads, is called an extensile tongue. The eyes of the chameleon are even more remarkable. Its eyes are turreted and can be moved independently so that it can view two different objects simultaneously! This comes in especially handy as it is tree-dwelling. The chameleon can keep one eye on its prey and the other on its footing. Its head is often helmet-shaped, and some species have horn-like structures growing out of this scaly helmet.

The feet and tail of the chameleon are also special. Both are prehensile; that is, they are both perfectly adapted to their sylvan environment. The toes of the chameleon's feet are bunched into inside and outside groups of two or

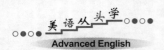
three to enable this reptile to grasp tree branches tightly. The chameleon can thus climb extraordinarily well while using its tail to grab objects for further balance.

The above inventory of natural selection specializations would be remarkable enough, but what really separates the chameleon from its fellow reptiles is the fact that its scales contain the ability to change color. Though many people think the chameleon can change its color at will and that it can blend into any color, these are misconceptions. In fact, chameleons can blend into many natural colors and even patterns, but they cannot do this at will. Instead, this happens naturally according to temperature, emotional state of the animal, and the triggering of certain hormones within its body.

It is hard to imagine an animal more interesting than the chameleon, with its weird appearance and special abilities. We should always remember, however, that these animals require their native habitat to flourish in, not zoos or individuals' terrariums. If you want your grandchildren to see this gift of nature, do not collect it as a pet. These natural treasures evolved over millions of years without mankind's help; they will continue to survive better if left alone.

每隔几个月本节目将专题报道一种受世人瞩目而成为最受喜爱或“热门”的动物。在这个特别系列中，首先我们将介绍大自然中最奇特的生物之一——变色龙。

大概没有其他种类的动物像爬虫类那样引发人类的想象力。在几个亚纲（或生物学的“目”）的爬虫类中，有蛇和蜥蜴、乌龟和陆龟、鳄鱼和短吻鳄以及虫蜥蜴——一种现存于新西兰的海蜥蜴。恐龙也同样属于爬虫类。到底是蛇、蜥蜴还是鳄鱼使远古时代的中国人有所联想而创造出龙的呢？大家对爬虫类这个主题的兴趣一直没有断过，过去10年来以爬虫类为主角拍成的卖座电影和票房极差的电影包括有恐龙的（《侏罗纪公园》和《迷失的世界》）、鳄鱼和蛇类的（《狂蟒之灾》）。虽然和这些巨大的爬虫类在体型上相去甚远，低姿态的变色龙仍然以它特殊的才能和技巧让无数个世代的人感到惊奇。

变色龙是什么样的动物呢？它特殊的名字还真符合这只特殊的动物，因为它从古希腊文翻译过来是“地上的狮子”之意。这真叫人意想不到，因为变色龙大部分的时间都在树上，至于说看起来像狮子这点，变色龙看起来就像一只……呃，变色龙！在大自然的动物园里，没有其他动物长得像它们一样古怪。那它们住在哪里呢？真正的变色龙只有在旧世界的热带森林和丛林中才找得到，而几乎有半数的种类住在非洲的马达加斯加岛上。

变色龙有何特别之处呢？那可多了！从舌头到尾巴，变色龙有一大堆特点。这种像是现代恐龙的动物，它的舌头可以伸到比它身体的两倍还要长。这种青蛙和蟾蜍也有的舌头叫做伸缩舌头。变色龙的眼睛则更加了不起。它的眼睛是旋转式的，能够个别转动，如此一来它可以同时注视两个不同的物体！这对它这种住在树上的动物特别有用。变色龙可以一眼盯着它的猎物,另一眼看着它立足的地方。它的头形状通常像盔甲,有些种类的变色龙还会从多鳞的甲胄长出角状的结构来呢。

变色龙的脚和尾巴也很特别,二者皆适于抓握;也就是说,二者皆极为适合森林的环境。变色龙的脚趾卷曲成里外两组各两只或三只,使这种爬虫类能够紧抓住树枝;因为变色龙可以利用尾巴抓住物体来增加平衡,所以格外善于攀爬。

以上在物竞天择下发展而成的种种特长实在是了不起,但真正使变色龙不同于其他爬虫类的是它的鳞片拥有变色的能力。虽然很多人以为变色龙可以随意变换颜色,且能够融入任何颜色,但是这些都是错误的观念。事实上,变色龙可以融入许多自然的颜色,甚至形状,但它们却不能随心所欲。相反地,那是根据温度、自身的情绪以及它体内某些荷尔蒙机制而自然发生的。

很难想得出比拥有怪异外表和特别能力的变色龙更有趣的动物。然而,我们要时时记住,这些动物需要原居住地来繁衍,而不是动物园或个人的小型饲养园。如果你想让子孙看到这大自然的恩赐,那就不要搜集它来当宠物。这些自然奇珍在没有人类的帮助下演化了数百万年;如果不受打扰的话,它们将更能继续生存下去。

2 *Vocabulary & Idioms* 单词短语注解

1. **chameleon** [kəˈmiljən] *n.* 变色龙

2. **catch the eye of...** 引起……的注目
   The pretty girl caught the eye of all the boys on the beach.
   那个美少女吸引了海滩上所有男孩子的目光。

3. **catch the fancy of sb** 投合某人的心意；讨某人的喜欢
   = catch sb's fancy
   The Italian dress on sale in the department store caught Maria's fancy,
   so she bought it.
   百货商店里那件打折的意大利时装很合玛丽亚的意，所以她就把
   它买了下来。

4. **perennial** [pəˈrɛnɪəl] *a.* 永久的，持久不断的
   A perennial problem for teachers is too many students in a class.
   班上学生人数太多一直是老师们长久以来的问题。

5. **box-office hit / bomb** 非常卖座 / 票房惨淡的电影

6. **bizarre** [bɪˈzɑr] *a.* 怪异的，奇异的

7. **extensile** [ɛkˈstɛnsl̩] *a.* 可伸长的

8. **turreted** [ˈtʊrɪtɪd] *a.* (像炮塔般)旋转式的
   turret [ˈtʊrɪt] *n.* (战车、坦克等的)炮塔

9. **simultaneously** [ˌsaɪmlˈtenɪəslɪ] *adv.* 同时地
   simultaneous [ˌsaɪmlˈtenɪəs] *a.* 同时(发生)的
   The children dropped their ice creams simultaneously, so their father
   could only catch one.
   因为那些小孩子同时弄掉了冰淇淋，所以他们的爸爸只能接住其
   中一个。

10. **come in handy** 派得上用场
    A dictionary always comes in handy in my English class.
    我上英文课时字典总是派得上用场。

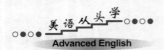

11. **scaly** [ˈskelɪ] *a.* 有鳞的，鳞状的

12. **prehensile** [prɪˈhɛnsl] *a.* （身体的一部分）能卷缠和抓牢（某物）的

13. **be adapted to + N/V-ing** 适应于……
Although mammals, whales are perfectly adapted to living in the sea.
鲸鱼虽然是哺乳动物，但却非常适应生活在大海里。

14. **sylvan** [ˈsɪlvən] *a.* 森林的

15. **bunch** [bʌntʃ] *vt.* 使成一束
Arnold was so angry that he bunched up his fists when talking to the policeman.
和警察说话时，阿诺德气得握起了拳头。

16. **extraordinarily** [ɪkˈstrɔrdṇˌɛrɪlɪ] *adv.* 格外地；极端地

17. **inventory** [ˈɪnvənˌtɔrɪ] *n.* （详细的）表，目录，清单

18. **natural selection** 自然选择

19. **separate A from B** 将 A 与 B 分开
Miss Anderson separated the boys from the girls and had them sit opposite each other.
安德森小姐将男生和女生分开来并要他们面对面坐着。

20. **at will** 任意地，随心所欲地
As male college students, we can leave our dormitory at will, but the girls have a curfew.
身为男大学生，我们可以任意离开宿舍，但是女孩子则有门禁。

21. **blend into...** 与……融合，融入……
After we let it go, the crab blended into sand so well that we could no longer see it.
我们放手后，那只螃蟹便钻进沙中让我们再也看不到它。

22. **misconception** [ˌmɪskənˈsɛpʃən] *n.* 错误的观念，误解

23. **trigger** [ˈtrɪgɚ] *vt.* 引发，激发（本文中为动名词作名词用）
The earthquake triggered a landslide, which buried the village.

那场地震引起了山体滑坡,掩埋了这个村庄。

24. **flourish** [ˈflɜːɪʃ] *vi.* 繁衍;活跃;兴盛

   Although Amy was depressed in high school, she flourished in college.
   虽然艾米在中学时不得志,但她在大学却很活跃。

25. **terrarium** [təˈreəriəm] *n.* 小动物饲养园

26. **evolve** [ɪˈvɒlv] *vi.* 逐渐发展 / 演变

   Life on Earth is evolving all the time; this is the law of evolution.
   地球上的生命不断在演变,这就是进化论。

Lesson 6

Table Manners in Anglo-America

英美餐桌礼仪

 Reading 阅读

"Oh, no! Here I am at an American family's home at the dinner table. There are all kinds of plates, saucers, cups, and silverware at my place. Which should I use for which food? Should I sit down first or wait for the host to invite me? Should I have brought a gift? Someone please tell me what to do!"

Have you ever been in or had a nightmare about this situation? Don't worry! This article will help steer you through the rocks and reefs of Anglo-American table manners so that if you are ever abroad in Canada or the United States, or at someone's home from one of those countries, you will feel right at home.

It is important to distinguish what kind of occasion you will be attending before you plan for a pleasant evening. Most Anglo-Americans enjoy entertaining at home, but they don't enjoy stuffy, formal dinners. They invite their friends over for a fun evening, not as a test of one's knowledge of cultural traditions. If, however, you are invited to a formal affair, such as a so-called "sit-down" dinner, you may want to know in advance some basic rules of "black tie" etiquette.

The first thing to remember when attending a dinner at a Western home is that you are the guest and that you are a foreigner. No one will invite you if he does not really want you to enter his "castle," so you can be sure that you are wanted. Additionally, as you do not come from the same country or culture as your host, he or she or they will surely be aware of this, and will be very forgiving if you unintentionally do or say something which would otherwise offend them. Keeping these two simple tips in mind should greatly ease your concern about being present at a dinner in someone else's home.

Before arriving at your host's home, you may want to make sure of three things. First, be a few minutes late, say, about five to ten minutes if possible. Never be early, as the host may not have everything prepared yet. Nor should you be more than 20 minutes late. Your host may begin to worry about whether you are able to attend the dinner or not. Next, as to whether to bring a gift, in most informal gatherings, it is not necessary. If you like, you can bring some fruit or sweets, or, especially if there is a hostess, some flowers. These are thoughtful, cheerful gifts sure to please. Do not bring alcoholic beverages unless you are sure of your host's or hostess's preferences in drinks. Above all, do not spend a lot of money, and never give money. As we say in English, "It's the thought that counts." Finally, wear comfortable clothing. One can overdress as well as appear sloppy. For a special occasion or religious holiday,

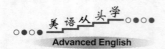

such as a retirement party or Christmas, a tie and jacket would be suitable for the gentlemen and a dress or sweater and skirt for the ladies.

For more formal affairs, you will probably be told what to wear, such as "formal dress requested," etc. A tie and jacket or tuxedo for the gents and an evening gown for the ladies would be in order here. If you are unsure what to wear, you can always ask the host. Gifts are seldom appropriate for these affairs, unless for a wedding reception, at which gifts are more customary than cash.

Your host in his home will usually motion you where to sit. At formal gatherings, name cards are sometimes provided, or you will be told where to sit. Do not be alarmed by a great deal of cutlery: simply start from the outside and work your way in. Formal affairs often have several courses of food with the appropriate cutlery for each dish. There is no harm in checking with your neighbor to see what implement he is using. After all, "When in Rome, do as the Romans do." It is customary to ask others to pass dishes to you for self-serving; at a formal dinner party, there is usually catering (service). Again, do not hesitate to ask others for information or advice. They are usually pleased to help you.

The most important piece of advice is this: enjoy yourself. No host enjoys seeing nervous or fearful guests who are struggling to "do the right thing" at his home or expensive formal dinner party. Watch others or ask for their advice, and join in the conversation and good times as best as you can. If you do, after the first such evening out, you will certainly look forward to the next!

"哦,糟糕!此刻我坐在一个美国人家里的餐桌前吃晚餐。在我眼前有各式各样的盘子、碟子、杯子和银制餐具。该用哪种餐具盛哪一道食物呢?我应该先坐下来还是等主人来招呼呢?我是不是应该带了礼物才来呢?有谁来教教我该怎么做!"

你是否曾经置身于或经历过这样可怕的情形呢?别担心!本文将助你破除英美餐桌礼仪的重重障碍,如此一来,以后如果你出国到加拿大或美国,或到这两国人士的家中做客,便能怡然自得了。

在计划过个愉快的夜晚之前,先分清楚要参加的是哪一种场合非常重要。大部分英美人士喜欢在家里招待客人,而不喜欢沉闷的正式晚宴。他们邀请朋友到家里来是为了过个快乐的夜晚,而不是要测试一个人的传统文化知识。然而,如果你应邀参加一个正式场合,例如所谓的"安排就座"晚宴,也许你会想事先知道一些正式宴会礼节的基本规范。

当你参加西方家庭的晚宴时,首先要记住的是:你是客人,而且是个外国人。如果不是真要让你进入他的"城堡",人家不会邀请你,所以你可以确定你是受欢迎的。除此之外,因为你来自和主人不同的国家和文化,他或她或他们当然会明白这一点,所以哪怕你无意间做了或说了某些冒犯他们的事时,他们也会非常宽宏大量的。记住这两个简单的准则应该就能大大消除你到别人家用餐的忧虑。

在到达主人家之前,你可能要先确定三件事情。首先,要晚到几分钟,譬如说 5 到 10 分钟左右,如果可能的话。千万不要提早到,因为主人可能尚未一切就绪。但你也不要迟到超过 20 分钟,否则人家会开始担心你是否能来赴宴。其次,关于要不要带礼物,在大部分非正式的聚会中是不需要的。你若高兴的话,可以带一些水果或甜点,或者,尤其是有女主人的话,可以送一些花。这些都是体贴、令人愉快的礼物,一定会讨人喜欢。不要带酒类饮料,除非你确知主人或女主人偏爱什么酒。更重要的是,不要花太多钱,而且绝不要送礼金。就像我们在英文中说的"It's the thought that counts."("礼轻情意重")。最后,穿着舒适的衣服。过度打扮以及显得邋遢都不好。在特别的场合或宗教节日,如退休宴会或圣诞节时,男士宜穿西装打领带,女士则穿连衣裙或毛衣加裙子。

在较正式的情况中,你可能要照规定穿着,例如"请着正式服装"等等。此时,男士宜穿西装打领带或穿燕尾服,女士则穿晚礼服。如果你拿不准该穿什么服装,问主人就好了。在这些情况送礼通常不适当,除非是结婚宴席,在习俗上大多是送礼物而非现金。

屋里的主人通常会招呼你就座。在正式的聚会中,有时会摆出写上名字的卡片,要不然人家会告诉你座位。不要被一大堆刀叉餐具吓着了:只要由外往内按顺序使用就行了。正式宴会常会有几道菜须使用特定的刀叉餐具,这时不妨咨询一下邻座的人看他用什么餐具。毕竟,人总要"入乡随俗"嘛。习惯上可以请别人将菜传给你自己来盛;在正式晚宴上则通常会有分菜(服务)。同样地,不要犹豫不敢向他人请教,他们通常都会很乐意帮助你。

最重要的一个忠告是:好好享受。主人都不乐于见到客人在他家中或昂贵的正式晚宴上紧张害怕得努力要让自己的举止得当。观察别人或向他们请教,尽可能地融入谈话和欢乐当中。如果能做到这样, 初次尝过甜头之后, 你就一定会很期待下一次的晚宴了!

② *Vocabulary & Idioms* 单词短语注解 ✎

1. **saucer** [ˈsɔsə] *n.* 小茶碟

2. **steer** [stɪr] *vt.* 引导; 使前进
   We all like our math teacher because she helps steer us through difficult algebra problems.
   我们都很喜欢我们的数学老师, 因为她帮助引导我们弄懂了艰深的代数问题。

3. **the rocks and reefs** 岩石和暗礁; (引申为) 重重障碍
   rock [rɑk] *n.* 岩石
   reef [rif] *n.* 暗礁

4. **distinguish** [dɪˈstɪŋgwɪʃ] *vt.* 使有别于; 区别 & *vi.* 辨别
   distinguish A from B   区别 A 与 B
   = distinguish between A and B
   = tell the difference between A and B
   = tell A from B
   = tell A and B apart
   Parents should spend extra time and effort on teaching children how to distinguish right from wrong.
   做父母的应该多花时间和功夫教导子女如何分辨是非对错。

5. **stuffy** [ˈstʌfɪ] *a.* 沉闷的; 空气不通的

6. **in advance** 事先, 预先
   Those black clouds are telling us in advance that it is going to rain hard.
   那些乌云在预示我们快要下大雨了。

7. **etiquette** [ˈɛtɪkɛt] *n.* 礼节，礼仪（不可数）

8. **...some basic rules of "black tie" etiquette.**

   = ...some basic rules of high society manners.

9. **be aware of...** 留心 / 注意……

   Be aware of killer bees when you enter the forest.

   进入那片森林时要留心杀人蜂。

10. **thoughtful** [ˈθɔtfəl] *a.* 体贴的，设想周到的

    It is thoughtful of sb to V　某人很体贴(做)……

    It was certainly thoughtful of our neighbors to watch our house for us
    while we were away on vacation.

    当我们外出度假时，邻居帮我们看家真的是很体贴。

11. **It's the thought that counts.**

    重要的是心意。(即中国人讲的"礼轻情意重"。)

12. **overdress** [ˌovəˈdrɛs] *vi.* 过度打扮，穿着太考究

    You'll overdress if you wear a suit to a casual party.

    如果你穿西装去参加非正式的派对，那你就太过于盛装了。

13. **appropriate** [əˈproprɪˌet] *a.* 合适的

14. **customary** [ˈkʌstəˌmɛrɪ] *a.* 惯例的

15. **motion** [ˈmoʃən] *vt.* 以姿态或手势示意

    Paul motioned me to cross the street by waving his arm.

    保罗挥舞着手臂示意要我过马路。

16. **cutlery** [ˈkʌtlərɪ] *n.* 刀叉类餐具(集合名词)

17. **There is no harm in + V-ing** ……无害 / 无妨

    There is no harm in teasing your friends if you mean only to amuse
    them.

    如果你只是想让朋友高兴，那么开开他们的玩笑也就无伤大雅了。

18. **implement** [ˈɪmpləmənt] *n.* 器具

19. **hesitate** [ˈhɛzəˌtet] *vi.* 犹豫

Children often hesitate to tell their parents that they did something wrong.

小孩在告诉他们父母自己做错事时通常会犹豫不决。

20. **look forward to + N/V-ing** 期望 / 盼望……

All Chinese children eagerly look forward to Chinese New Year hong baos!

所有的中国小孩都急切地盼望收到压岁钱！

Lesson 7

The Delights of South Island

南岛之乐

Reading 阅读

One of the odder coincidences of physical geography is the fact that there are two double islands, roughly the same size, positioned at each other's antipodes, or farthest-distant point. The islands of England and Ireland in the Northern Hemisphere and the islands of North Island and South Island in the Southern Hemisphere are just such a coincidence. The first two islands comprise the United Kingdom and the Republic of Ireland (or Eire), and the second two islands comprise New Zealand. Among these four islands, there can be no doubt that South Island is the least polluted and most spectacularly scenic of them all.

There is much competition to make such a claim. The island of England, politically constituting England, Scotland, and Wales of the United Kingdom, is dotted with country villages set alongside rivers and lakes. There are not very tall but nonetheless rugged mountains in the north, and endless miles of rocky coastline that seem mystical. Ireland, too, is a paradise of greenery, with far fewer people than populous

England and even more quaint villages scattered among its low-lying hills and forever green fields. North Island in New Zealand sports a balmy climate and the beaches to make use of it; one beach alone is more than 150 kilometers long, and with relatively few people on its shores, one can pretend one is at the very end of the earth. Volcanoes, large lakes, and quickly flowing rivers traverse the land. Given the beauty of these three islands, what makes South Island so special?

Plenty. For those who like mountains, South Island is sure to please. Mt. Cook at 3,764 meters is its highest peak, with 16 others above 3,000 meters. Naturally, many local and foreign mountain climbers come here for the challenge of these Southern Alps. In addition, there is an extensive glacier system, endless forests, and innumerable lakes throughout this highland area. Some of the world's best mountain scenery is available within the 500-kilometer long chain of the Southern Alps.

Perhaps you prefer the sea? South Island is not only an island, but many tiny islets can be found off its coastline. Great deep-sea fishing, scuba diving, and snorkeling can be had, though the waters here are cooler than those of North Island. (Remember, in the Southern Hemisphere, as we go north, it gets warmer.) As fewer people live on South Island than on North Island, those who crave solitude and pristine beaches will be amazed at their luck here. With almost no heavy industry on South Island, the air, water, and land are all free of

pollution. The local seafood is therefore clean, plentiful, and never-ending.

Do healthful climates interest you? South Island is the place to be. Its temperate climate sees little snow except in the highlands and mountainous areas. Like Ireland and England, there are no extremes of temperature, either. Summers are warm, not hot, and winters are brisk rather than freezing. The fresh air is sometimes humid from the abundant rainfall of this area. Every season invites the nature lover to get out and be active in the countryside.

Of course, South Island is not for everyone. For those who need busy, crowded, noisy, and polluted cities, this Southern outpost will surely disappoint. For those who enjoy pressure and stress, South Island will leave them empty-handed. And for those who would rather stay at home or in an office in front of a computer screen or in the thumping, smoke-filled dance floors of discos, some of the world's best natural scenery will never entice them away. For the rest of us, though, South Island is the world's best-kept secret. If Nature's paradise sounds alluring, make a point of visiting South Island.

　　自然地理上较为奇特的巧合之一是地球上有两组大小约略相同、位置相对或者说相距最为遥远的双岛。北半球的英格兰和爱尔兰群岛以及南半球的北岛和南岛就是这样的一种巧合。第一组的两座岛构成英国和爱尔兰共和国,第二组的两座岛则组成新西兰。四个岛中,南岛无疑是污染最少且风景最秀丽的。

　　这样说势必经过一番竞争。在政治版图上构成英国的英格兰、苏格兰和威尔士的英格兰本岛,沿着河岸湖畔的乡村星罗棋布。北部的山虽不高但崎岖不平,而绵延不绝的岩岸则展现出神秘的风情。爱尔兰也是个绿色天堂,人口远不及人烟稠密的英格兰,却有更多古意盎然的乡村散布在低洼的山丘和常绿的田野间。新西兰的北岛以拥有温和的气候和可享受这宜人气候的海滩为傲。仅一个海滩就超过 150 公里长,而岸上人口相当稀少,可以让人假装自己是在世界的尽头。火山、大湖和湍急的河流横亘着全岛。既然这三个岛如此美丽,南岛又有何特别之处?

　　那可多着呢。对那些喜爱大山者来说,南岛一定能取悦他们。南岛的最高峰库克山高 3764 米,另外还有 16 座超过 3000 米的山峰。自然而然地,许多国内外的登山家来到此地挑战南半球的阿尔卑斯山脉。此外,还有一个广大的冰河系统、绵延不绝的森林和数不胜数的湖泊遍布在这个高原带。人们可以在这绵延 500 公里长的南阿尔卑斯山脉之间欣赏到一些举世无双的湖光山色。

　　也许你比较喜欢海?南岛并不只是一座岛屿,它的外海还散布着众多小岛,可以从事深海钓鱼、深海潜水和浮潜——虽然这里的水温比起北岛的水温要低。(记住,在南半球愈往北走海水愈温暖。)由于南岛的人口比北岛少,喜爱独处和原始海滩的人将会对于他们有幸来到这里而惊奇不已。南岛上几乎没有重工业,空气、水和土地都未曾受到污染。因此,当地的海鲜干净、丰富且取之不尽。

你对健康的气候感兴趣吗? 来南岛就对了。除了在高原和山区地带,这儿气候温和,很少降雪。就像爱尔兰和英格兰一样,气温也不严酷。夏天暖而不热,冬天则凉爽而不寒冷。清新的空气有时会因这地区充足的降雨而潮湿。这里一年四季都适合爱好大自然的人出门到乡间去活动一番。

当然,并非每个人都会喜欢南岛。对那些需要繁忙、拥挤、嘈杂和受污染城市的人而言,南半球的这个边陲之地必定会让他们感到失望。对那些喜欢压力和紧张的人而言,南岛将使他们空手而返。而对那些宁愿待在家里或办公室计算机屏幕前,或是窝在音乐震天响、烟雾弥漫的迪斯科舞池内的人而言,世上最棒的一些自然景色永远也无法诱使他们离开。但是对我们其余的人而言,南岛是世上最棒的秘境。如果大自然中的天堂听起来让你觉得有吸引力,那么别忘了到南岛去玩一玩。

2 Vocabulary & Idioms 单词短语注解

1. **coincidence** [koˈɪnsədəns] *n.* 巧合（的事件）

2. **antipodes** [ænˈtɪpəˌdiz] *n.* 对跖地（地球上正相对之两个地区）

3. **comprise** [kəmˈpraɪz] *vt.* 包括 / 含；由……组 / 构成
   = consist of...
   The solar system comprises the sun, eight planets, comets, and many space rocks.
   太阳系由太阳、八大行星、彗星以及许多太空岩石所构成。

4. **There is no doubt + that 从句** 毫无疑问地……
   There is no doubt that health is more important than wealth.
   健康无疑比财富更重要。

5. **spectacularly** [spɛkˈtækjələlɪ] *adv.* 壮观地，华丽地

6. **be dotted with...** 布满 / 点缀着……
   dot [dɑt] *vt.* 星罗棋布；点缀（常用被动）
   After the earthquake, the village was dotted with crumpled houses.
   地震过后，那座村庄到处都是残破的房舍。

7. **quaint** [kwent] *a.* 古怪有趣的；(由于老式而) 奇特的

8. **scatter** [ˈskætə] *vt.* 使散开 / 分散；撒播
   The farmer scattered the seed into the wind to plant his crops.
   那个农民迎着风撒播谷物的种子。

9. **sport** [spɔrt] *vt.* 炫耀，夸示
   Edwin sported his new suit and tie for the wedding party.
   埃德温向人炫耀他要穿去参加婚礼的西装和领带。

10. **balmy** [ˈbɑmɪ] *a.* 和煦的，温和的

11. **the very + N** 正 / 就是(那一个)……(= just the + N)
    注意
    此处的 very 为用于加强语气的形容词，表 "正 / 就是(那一个)的" 之意，置于定冠词 the 之后，用以修饰名词。

At the very end of this lane on the right side you can find my house.
就在这条巷子底右手边你可以找到我家。

12. **traverse** [trəˈvɜs] *vt.* 横越, 穿过, 横贯
The skier traversed the side of the mountain during his descent.
那名滑雪者沿着山边滑下坡。

13. **innumerable** [ɪˈnjumərəb]] *a.* 数不清的, 无数的
Innumerable mosquitoes greeted us by the lake, so we had to leave quickly.
我们在湖边一眼望去都是蚊子,因此只得赶紧离开。

14. **scuba diving** 借水肺而做的潜水活动
scuba [ˈskubə] *n.* 水肺(潜水者所用的一种水中呼吸装置)

15. **snorkeling** [ˈsnɔrkḷɪŋ] *n.* 浮潜, 使用呼吸管潜泳
snorkel [ˈsnɔrkḷ] *n.* (潜水者使用的)呼吸管

16. **crave** [krev] *vt.* 渴望, 热望
Many pregnant women crave certain foods.
许多孕妇都会特别想吃某些食物。

17. **be amazed at...** 对……感到惊讶
I was amazed at how much German Jane had learned after staying one year in Munich.
我很惊讶简在慕尼黑待了一年就学会了那么多德文。

18. **Its temperate climate sees little snow...**
注意
此处的 see 表"经历"、"遭遇"、"有……的经验",即等于 experience 之意。
We didn't see much rain here last year, but this year the rain has been ample.
我们这儿去年没下什么雨,但今年则雨量充沛。

19. **abundant** [əˈbʌndənt] *a.* 丰富的, 充裕的
be abundant in... 富于……;盛产……

South Africa is abundant in diamonds and other important minerals.
南非盛产钻石和其他重要矿物。

20. **outpost** [ˈaʊtˌpost] *n.* 边远地区

21. **thumping** [ˈθʌmpɪŋ] *a.* 砰砰响的

22. **entice** [ɪnˈtaɪs] *vt.* 引诱，诱惑
    Mary <u>enticed</u> Robert <u>into</u> marrying her by cooking him delicious meals.
    玛丽为罗伯特烹调美味的三餐诱使他娶她。

23. **alluring** [əˈlʊrɪŋ] *a.* 诱惑人的；迷人的

24. **make a point of + V-ing** 必定／照例……；总是要做(某事)
    On the first day of each month I make a point of paying my rent in person.
    每个月一号我总是会照例亲自付房租。

Lesson 8

Ireland's Contribution to English

爱尔兰对英语的贡献

1 ***Reading* 阅读**

Nearly everyone knows that countries such as the United Kingdom, the United States of America, Canada, Australia, and New Zealand are primarily English-speaking countries; that is, English is the mother tongue used in these countries. What is less well known is that English is also the mother tongue in countries such as the Republic of Ireland (officially called Eire), Barbados, Jamaica, Trinidad, and Guyana. Among these latter few, the Irish have made contributions to the English language in both its lexicon and literature which can be considered second to none.

Virtually every aspect of English literature has been graced by the writings of the Irish. This fact is all the more amazing because Ireland is a relatively small country, with never more than four million people throughout its long history. Yet many great "English" writers were indeed born and often raised in Ireland, though many, too, emigrated to the United Kingdom at some point in their lives. Among these pillars of English literature were Jonathan Swift, William Butler Yeats,

James Joyce, Samuel Beckett, Oscar Wilde, George Bernard Shaw, and Edmund Burke. Many other lesser-known figures have punctuated English literature as well. These men's contributions to the English language and to Western thought in general are immeasurable. A review of two of these writers' major works will reveal why.

Jonathan Swift (1667-1745) by most reckoning is the best English-language satirist ever, and one of the world's greatest as well. Born in Ireland of English parents, Swift went to school there through his bachelor's degree (Trinity College, Dublin, capital of Ireland). Thereafter he frequently traveled between England and Ireland, including years spent at Oxford College, where he earned his master's degree. Swift wrote a great deal of poetry, but he is best regarded as a prose satirist. He wrote prolifically both in Ireland and England, nearly constantly shuttling from one to the other. In Ireland he worked on *Gulliver's Travels*, which he later had published in England in 1726. Already famous by that time, Swift would become immortalized with this last great work. What child does not know the story of the brave sailor Gulliver as he travels through lands in which he is at turn both a giant and a midget? Yet most readers are not aware of Swift's intent to satirize the political, academic, and religious leaders of his time. Read either way, Swift's genius as a writer of English cannot be denied.

Advanced English

A giant of English theater was George Bernard Shaw (1856-1950). Born in Dublin, Shaw moved to England with his family when he was 20 and stayed there for most of the rest of his long life. His early fiction writing was so poor that he could not find a publisher. Only when he began to work as a playwright did his fortunes improve. Among the many, many plays for which Shaw is famous, perhaps his most lasting (though not his most critically acclaimed) is *Pygmalion* (1916), the story of a language teacher who attempts to "civilize" a young prostitute by training her to speak correctly. If this story sounds familiar, it should: *Pygmalion* was later filmed winning an Oscar for Shaw and later again transformed into the highly popular Broadway musical *My Fair Lady* (1956). A good story never dies: the original *Pygmalion* has since been updated in the hit movie *Pretty Woman* (1990) starring Richard Gere and Julia Roberts. As with Shakespeare, many of Shaw's plays are continually restaged or rewritten into new media because Shaw wrote on many themes which touch on the human condition, independent of time and space.

Among the constellation of Irish talents, perhaps Swift and Shaw are two among the more brilliant stars, but much more could be written of those mentioned above and many others. Though English literature written by the British suffices as an eternal and shining canon of literature, it would be nonetheless dimmer without the considerable talents of its Irish contributors.

几乎每个人都知道,英国、美国、加拿大、澳大利亚和新西兰等国都是说英语的主要国家;也就是说,英语是这些国家的母语。较不为人所知的是,英语也是爱尔兰共和国(正式称呼为 Eire)、巴巴多斯、牙买加、特立尼达和圭亚那等国的母语。在后面这几个国家中,爱尔兰人在英语词汇和文学上的贡献可说是无人能及。

英语文学几乎在各方面都因为爱尔兰人的作品而变得多姿多彩。这一事实则因爱尔兰是个相当小的国家,其人口在漫长的历史上从未超过 400 万而更加令人惊讶。然而许多伟大的"英语"作家的确是在爱尔兰出生且通常都在爱尔兰长大,即使当中也有很多人在他们人生某个时期移居到英国去。在这些英语文学的巨擘中有乔纳森·斯威夫特、威廉·巴特勒·叶芝、詹姆士·乔伊斯、塞缪尔·贝克特、奥斯卡·王尔德、乔治·萧伯纳以及埃德蒙·伯克。其他许多较不知名的作家也不时出现在英语文学中。这些人对英语和西方一般思想的贡献是无法估量的。在这些作家中挑两个出来回顾其主要作品就可了解原因了。

乔纳森·斯威夫特(1667-1745)一般都认为是历史上最好的英语讽刺作家,也是世上最伟大的讽刺作家之一。斯威夫特出生于爱尔兰,父母是英国人。他在那儿接受教育直到完成学士学位(爱尔兰首府都柏林的三一学院)。此后他经常往返于英国和爱尔兰之间,包括他在牛津大学攻读硕士学位的那几年。斯威夫特写过许多诗,但却以散文讽刺作家著称。他几乎不断穿梭于爱尔兰和英国之间,并在两地写出大量作品。《格列佛游记》是他在爱尔兰写的,稍后于 1726 年在英国出版。当时已经成名的他,因为最后这本巨著而得以名垂不朽。哪个孩子不知道勇敢的水手格列佛周游各地,一会儿变成巨人,一会儿又变成小人儿的故事呢?然而大部分的读者却不知道斯威夫特是想借此讽刺当时的政治、学术和宗教领袖。不管读者怎么看这本书,斯威夫特身为英语作家的天分是不容置疑的。

乔治·萧伯纳(1856-1950)是英语戏剧上的一位巨人。他出生于都柏林,20岁时随家人搬到英国,从此以后他大部分的时间都呆在那儿。他早期的小说作品很差劲,以致于没有出版商愿意出版他的书。一直到他开始写剧本,命运才得到改善。在他诸多赖以成名的戏剧当中,传颂最久的(虽然不是最受批评家赞扬的)也许是《卖花女》(1916),故事描述一位语言教师试图通过正确的说话训练来"教化"一名年轻的妓女。如果这故事听来耳熟,那并不奇怪:《卖花女》稍后被拍成电影为萧伯纳赢得了一座奥斯卡奖;后来又被改编成极受欢迎的百老汇音乐剧《窈窕淑女》(1956)。好故事绝不会被遗忘:《卖花女》原剧之后又被改编为理查·基尔和朱莉亚·罗伯茨主演的卖座电影《风月俏佳人》(1990)。和莎士比亚一样,萧伯纳的许多戏剧作品不断被重新搬上舞台或改编用在新的媒体上,这是因为他所写的主题触及人生百态,不因时间和空间改变而有所不同。

在爱尔兰群星中,也许斯威夫特和萧伯纳是其中较为耀眼的两颗;但上面所提到的其他那些人和另外许多作家还有更多可供介绍之处。尽管英国人写的英语文学足以当作永久且闪亮的文学标准,但若没有爱尔兰这些人才的众多贡献,它将会逊色许多吧。

2 *Vocabulary & Idioms* 单词短语注解

1. **lexicon** [ˈlɛksɪkən] *n.* （某语言的）全部词汇

2. **be second to none** 无人出其右；不亚于任何一个
   When it comes to skyscrapers, Chicago is second to none.
   说到摩天大楼,芝加哥不亚于任何城市。

3. **virtually** [ˈvɜtʃʊəlɪ] *adv.* 几乎,简直

4. **Yet many great "English" writers were indeed born and often raised in Ireland,...**
   = Despite this, many great "English" writers were born and often raised in Ireland, ...

5. **pillar** [ˈpɪlə] *n.* 巨擘,中坚分子

6. **punctuate** [ˈpʌŋktʃuˌet] *vt.* 使插入
   European history is punctuated with religious wars.
   欧洲历史上间或有宗教战争发生。

7. **immeasurable** [ɪmˈmɛʒərəbḷ] *a.* 不可估 / 测量的
   measurable [ˈmɛʒərəbḷ] *a.* 可估 / 测量的
   There is an immeasurable number of stars in the universe.
   宇宙中有数不清的星星。

8. **reveal** [rɪˈvil] *vt.* 揭露；显示
   His worried face revealed that his son had not yet been found.
   他焦虑不安的神色透露出他的儿子还没被找到。

9. **reckoning** [ˈrɛkənɪŋ] *n.* 计算
   By the captain's reckoning, we are still 100 kilometers away from port.
   根据船长的计算,我们离港口还有 100 公里。

10. **bachelor's degree** 学士学位
    master's degree 硕士学位
    doctoral degree 博士学位(= doctorate [ˈdɑktərɪt])

11. **a great deal of** + 不可数名词 许多 / 大量……

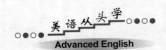
We have a great deal of work yet to do, so let's go back to our desks.
我们还有许多工作得做，所以咱们回工作岗位吧。

12. **be regarded as...** 被视为……
Christopher Columbus is regarded as one of the world's most important explorers.
哥伦布被视为世界上最重要的探险家之一。

13. **prose satirist** 散文讽刺作家
prose [proz] *n.* 散文
satirist ['sætərɪst] *n.* 讽刺家

14. **shuttle** ['ʃʌtl] *vi.* 穿梭般（往返）来回
Before Mr. Carner could clinch the business deal, he had to shuttle between New York and London several times.
在卡纳先生能敲定那笔生意前，他必须在纽约和伦敦穿梭往返好几趟。

15. **at turn** 交替，轮流
My mother is at turn a housewife and the boss of her own publishing company.
我妈妈一方面是家庭主妇，另一方面又是她自己出版公司的老板。

16. **satirize** ['sætə,raɪz] *vt.* 讽刺，讥讽
Many cartoons satirized the social and political life there during the Depression.
很多漫画讽刺了大萧条时期那儿的社会政治生活。

17. **Only when he began to work as a playwright did his fortunes improve.**
= It was not until he started working as a playwright that he began to meet with success.

18. **civilize** ['sɪvl,aɪz] *vt.* 使开化，教化
A university education helps to civilize students.
大学教育有助教化学子。

19. **transform** [trænsˈfɔrm] *vt.* 改变；化作

The ugly caterpillar was transformed into a beautiful butterfly in only one week.

那只丑陋的毛毛虫在仅仅一个礼拜中就破蛹成为一只美丽的蝴蝶。

20. **constellation** [ˌkɑnstəˈleʃən] *n.* 星座，星群；(喻) 灿烂的一群

21. **suffice** [səˈfaɪs] *vi.* 足够

suffice as... 足够作为……

Your essay is so good, Catherine, that it can suffice as your final term paper.

凯瑟琳，你的论文非常优秀，足以作为期末论文。

Lesson 9

Why Is Basketball So Popular?

篮球热

1 *Reading* 阅读

Soccer and baseball have more fans, but no other sport has increased in popularity so quickly over the past 30 years than has basketball. What accounts for the sudden meteoric rise in a sport which, after all, is played best by people who are unusually tall? The secret to basketball's success lies in three particular sources: the celebrities in the game; commercial sponsorship of those players and the game itself; and the mushrooming of crowded, urban environments around the world.

All sports have their heroes. Currently, baseball has Mark McGuire and Sammy Sosa, the home run-hitting kings. Tennis has Martina Hingus and Pete Sampras, the darlings of the courts. Soccer has players so popular that they are mobbed by fans wherever they appear, especially in Europe and South America. Only basketball, however, has celebrities who have caught the attention of the world like no others. Michael Jordan is so popular even after having officially retired from the game that there is talk of his running for public office in the

United States. Dennis Rodman, the muscular, tattooed, and much ballyhooed player formerly of the Chicago Bulls, makes headlines whenever he pulls another of his crazy but fun-loving publicity stunts. Former players like Larry Byrd and Magic Johnson continue to command respect for their personal integrity and unparalleled sportsmanship. Basketball shoes, T-shirts, and even movies are made with these basketball superstar icons. No other sport figures can compete with their popular recognition and appeal.

Is this international superstar status solely due to these men's talents and contributions? In no small part, of course, it is, but other leading athletes with equally commendable skills or who have performed attention-grabbing antics rarely reach the stratospheric level of stardom that basketball players enjoy. This special privilege is due to a concerted effort by the players behind the basketball players, that is, the basketball leagues' owners and sponsors.

Basketball has always been a distant third in sports rankings in the United States behind baseball and American football. Basketball league owners and managers wanted to change this traditional perception of the immutability of these statistics and in the 1960s began a concerted effort to make basketball the game of choice by hand-picking more colorful as well as professional players and by making alliances with the commercial sponsors of athletic equipment. By the 1970s, basketball team recognition in the U.S. had soared, with

dedicated fans in the millions. Teams like the Los Angeles Lakers, the Chicago Bulls, and the Boston Celtics had become household names. Players like Magic Johnson and Michael Jordan were worth millions of dollars in commercial advertising spots for athletic equipment manufacturers, a trend which continues to this day. Today, basketball is a billion-dollar business.

No amount of advertising, however, can account for the number of fans who not only double as spectators but as players themselves. Basketball courts, whether in schools, parks, or abandoned city lots, have sprouted throughout the urban landscape. A child is never far from a basketball ball and hoop. With land becoming more expensive in ever more crowded cities, city governments are far more likely to construct basketball courts than baseball diamonds or soccer fields. As basketball equipment is minimal and inexpensive, it is no wonder that the game has become more and more popular around the world.

What young boy doesn't dream of becoming as tall as a basketball player, or at least of having as much money or fame? Basketball's quick pace and dynamic plays are in contrast to the much slower moves in baseball or even in much of soccer and American football. This dynamism is part of the pulse of our times, and so long as we live in a fast-changing world, basketball and its players will continue to appeal to sports lovers around the world.

　　虽然足球和棒球拥有较多的球迷,但过去30年来,没有其他一项运动比得上篮球风行得这么快。这项毕竟还是由高得出奇的人才能打得最好的运动是如何迅速兴起的呢?篮球成功的秘诀在于它的三个特点:比赛中的明星球员、对这些球员和比赛本身的商业赞助,以及全球各地拥挤的都市环境的迅速发展。

　　所有的运动都有英雄人物。目前,棒球有马克·马奎尔和萨米·索萨两位全垒打王。网球有玛提娜·辛吉斯和彼特·桑普拉斯这两名球场宠儿。有些足球明星所到之处必定受到球迷的热情包围,特别是在欧洲和南美两地。然而,只有篮球明星独一无二地受到全球瞩目。迈克尔·乔丹太受欢迎了,所以即使在他正式宣布退休之后,还有人说他要竞选美国的公职人员。丹尼斯·罗德曼这个浑身肌肉、纹身且爱搞怪事的前芝加哥公牛队球员,每当他又出什么好玩的怪招打知名度时,就一定会成为头条新闻。像拉里·博德和魔术师约翰逊等已退役的球员,因为个人的高尚品格和无人能比的运动精神而依然受人尊敬。篮球鞋、T恤,甚至电影都用这些篮球超级巨星的肖像来制作。没有其他运动人物能和他们在知名度和吸引力方面一较高下。

　　这种国际超级巨星的地位完全是因为这些人的才能和贡献吗?乍看之下确实是如此,但其他才能同样出色或技艺震惊媒体的杰出运动员却很少有人达到和篮球球员平起平坐的巨星地位。这种特殊的礼遇来自于篮球球员背后运作者的共同努力,亦即篮球联盟的老板们和赞助商们。

　　篮球在美国的运动排名上始终一直位居第三,远远落在棒球和美式足球之后。篮球联盟的老板和经理们想要打破这些统计数字永远不会改变的传统印象,于是在60年代开始同心协力,精选较具特色且具职业水平的球员,并且和运动用品的赞助商结盟,努力要让篮球成为人人喜爱的比赛。到了 70 年代,篮球队在美国的知名度上升,并且拥有数百万的忠实球迷。诸如洛杉矶湖人队、芝加哥公牛队和波士顿凯尔特队等球队成了家喻户晓的名字。像魔术师约翰逊和迈克尔·乔丹这样的球员替运动用品商拍广告片,身价都有几百万美元,这种风潮一直持续到现在。今天,篮球是一个产值以亿万计的行业。

然而,广告量却不是球迷观众及球员人数倍增的原因。不管是在学校、公园或城市里废弃的地块,篮球场在城市的土地上遍布出现。小孩子到哪里都不难找到篮球和篮筐。在日益拥挤的城市中,土地越来越贵,比起棒球场和足球场,市政府当然比较可能兴建篮球场。由于打篮球需要的用具最少而且又便宜,难怪这种运动在世界各地越来越流行。

哪个年轻男孩不梦想长得像篮球队员那么高,或者至少像他们一样有钱或有名呢?打篮球时的速度感及冲劲和动作较为缓慢的棒球或甚至大部分时间动作都很慢的足球和美式足球恰好形成对比。这种冲劲正是我们时代脉博的一部分,只要我们活在快速变化的世界,篮球和它的球员们将继续吸引全世界的运动爱好者。

2 *Vocabulary & Idioms* 单词短语注解

1. **account for...** 说明 / 解释……
   There is no accounting for tastes.
   人的好恶是无法解释的 / 人各有所好。——谚语

2. **mushroom** [ˈmʌʃrum] *vi.* 急速增加或发展
   Growth in Internet users has mushroomed over the past five years.
   使用网络的人口在过去 5 年来急剧增加。

3. **be mobbed by...** 被……包围 / 围攻
   mob [mɑb] *vt.* 包围，围攻 & *n.* 一帮闹哄哄的人；暴民
   Michael Jackson is still mobbed by fans wherever he goes.
   迈克尔·杰克逊不管到哪里都依然受到歌迷的热情包围。

4. **catch the attention of...** 引起……的注意
   The baby's crying caught the attention of its mother.
   婴儿的哭声引起其母亲的注意。

5. **run for...** 竞选……
   Mr. Anderson wants to run for mayor again even though he has held the office for eight years.
   即使已经任职了 8 年,安德森先生还是想再出马竞选市长。

6. **ballyhooed** [ˈbælɪˌhud] *a.* 大肆宣传的，哗众取宠的

7. **command** [kəˈmænd] *vt.* 应得，博得(尊敬、同情等)；命令，下令
   command respect 博得尊敬
   The major commanded his troops to assemble at 6 o'clock.
   那位少校命令他的部队在早上 6 点整集合。

8. **unparalleled** [ʌnˈpærəˌlɛld] *a.* 无可比拟的，无比的

9. **compete with...** 和……竞争
   Today，every computer company must compete with hundreds of others.
   现今每一家计算机公司都必须和数百家的同行竞争。

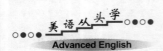

10. **commendable** [kə`mɛndəbḷ] *a.* 可称赞的，值得赞扬的

11. **stratospheric** [ˌstrætə`sfɛrɪk] *a.* 同温层的

12. **concerted** [kən`sɜtɪd] *a.* 协同的，一致的

13. **that is (to say)** 换句话说，也就是说
    It is winter now in England; that is, you should take warm clothing with you.
    英国现在是冬天；换句话说，你应该带些保暖的衣物。

14. **immutability** [ɪˌmjutə`bɪlətɪ] *n.* 不变(性)

15. **make alliances with...** 和……结盟
    Many airlines are now making alliances with one another to improve their business prospects.
    许多航空公司现在都彼此联盟以期改善商业前景。

16. **soar** [sɔr] *vi.* 升高；高涨
    During the "oil crisis" of the 1970s, the price of oil soared.
    在 70 年代的"石油危机"中，油价高涨。

17. **dedicated** [`dɛdəˌketɪd] *a.* 忠诚的，热忱的
    be dedicated to + N/V-ing 致力于……
    Doctors are dedicated to caring for their patients the best that they can.
    医生们都致力于尽他们最大的力量来照顾病人。

18. **sprout** [spraʊt] *vi.* 迅速地发展；萌芽
    Foreign fast-food stores are sprouting up in cities all around the world.
    外国的快餐店在世界各地迅速地发展起来。

19. **it is no wonder + that** 从句 难怪……，……不足为奇
    It is no wonder that Kevin passes all his exams; he's a very diligent student.
    难怪凯文每次考试都会过关，他是个很用功的学生。

20. **dynamic** [daɪ`næmɪk] *a.* 活跃的；有力的；动态的
    dynamism [`daɪnəˌmɪzəm] *n.* 精力；活力

21. **(be) in contrast to...** 和……成对比

In contrast to Tokyo, Sapporo is a very laid-back city.

和东京相比，札幌是个非常悠闲的城市。

22. **so long as...** 只要……（＝as long as...）

So long as Marcia is not late, we'll be able to see the first showing of the movie.

只要马莎不迟到，我们就看得到电影的开场。

23. **appeal to sb** 吸引某人；引起某人的兴趣

Cartoons appeal more to children than they do to adults.

卡通比较能吸引小孩，而不能引起大人的兴趣。

Lesson 10

Marlena Smalls and the Gullah: The Revival of a Unique Community

原音再现

Reading 阅读

Does the name Marlena Smalls ring a bell? Probably not. At least not yet. If this large woman with an even larger smile and sparkling eyes has her way, however, the language, customs, and songs of the Gullah will become happily familiar to millions of people outside of the Sea Islands. For it is Mrs. Smalls' dream that through her and her performing troupe's efforts their Gullah community will no longer be an isolated, anachronistic hangover from the days of slavery in the United States, but a vibrant cultural addition to the 21st century global village.

The Sea Islands comprise a group of islands just off the southeast U.S. Atlantic coast of South Carolina and Georgia. Descendants of slaves settled here tilling the fertile land of these islands and the adjacent coastline. A rich overlay of a mixture of West African languages onto 17th and 18th century colonial English has resulted in Gullah, a creole language featuring its unique blend of African tongues and pidgin English. Thousands of distinct African words coming from various West African languages have been identified by linguists. A few words have been added into contemporary mainstream American English. These include goober (peanut), gumbo (okra), and voodoo (witchcraft). The word Gullah itself also hails from West Africa. Many of this ethnic group's given names are taken directly from languages passed down for hundreds of years, such as Abiona and Pitipa. American English is the language used when dealing with outsiders, but Gullah is the language of the marketplace and the home.

As with most African cultures, the Gullah have a rich tradition of music. The banjo, a stringed musical instrument, was an African invention brought over with the slaves to the New World. It has been popularized in both North America and Europe over the past 200 years. A great variety of drums, too, accompanied African music to the colonies in North and South America. Singing both solo and a cappella with rich harmonies was also part of the slave heritage. Despite their demanding and depressing lives, the slaves held their original languages and music as well as their masters' Christianity close to their hearts. Much of the music today involves church music, also referred to as spirituals or gospel music.

An evening with Marlena Smalls and her Hallelujah Singers is nothing short of inspirational. They are dressed at times in traditional African clothing, and at other times in the simple and conservative rural dress of Southern U.S.

society. This unusual performance includes much singing, frequent samples of Gullah as used in the marketplace or between women gossiping. A great deal of emphatic body language, and even occasional tribal dance steps to thumping drums and enthusiastic shouting are also features of the performance. Mrs. Smalls introduces the background to individual songs or other performances to help the audience — often peppered with overseas tourists — have a clearer idea of how the Gullah communicate to each other. Even without the helpful introductions, however, music lovers will appreciate the peerless singing quality of the Hallelujah Singers as they render their traditional folk songs with obvious love and pride. Interspersed with Mrs. Smalls witty and classy narrative, the evening passes all too quickly.

It is refreshing to know that some ethnic groups are proudly clinging to their priceless legacies. Despite the tragedy of their origins in slavery, the Gullah have survived and revived to produce a viable, enviable folk culture even amidst the technological wonders of the 21st century. We can be thankful that in concert or on recorded media, Marlena Smalls and the Hallelujah Singers will touch all of us listeners with their heartfelt oral tradition through the magic of music.

马莉娜·史莫斯这个名字听来耳熟吗？也许不熟，至少到目前为止没听过。然而，如果这位笑容灿烂、眼睛闪亮的大块头女人如愿以偿的话，那么海洋群岛以外的许许多多人将会很乐意了解格勒人的语言、风俗和歌曲。因为史莫斯太太的梦想就是，通过她和她的歌舞表演团的努力，他们的格勒小区将不再是美国奴隶时代遗留下来的一个封闭而过时的产物，而是 21 世纪地球村的一支文化生力军。

海洋群岛由美国东南方大西洋沿岸的南卡罗来纳州和佐治亚州外海的一群岛屿所组成。奴隶后裔在此定居并耕种岛上和附近沿岸的肥沃土地。西非语系大量地混入 17、18 世纪殖民时期的英语后就产生了格勒语，一种结合非洲话和混杂英语为特色的独特克里欧耳语。语言学家们已经辨认出数千个来自各种西非语言的确定无误的非洲文字。其中有些文字已被加进现代主流美语中。这些字包括古柏（花生）、甘波（秋葵）和亚毒（巫术）等。格勒这个词本身也源自西非。许多这支少数民族出身的人都直接以几百年传下来的语言取名字，例如阿比欧娜和皮提巴。美语是用来和外来客打交道用的，但格勒语则是在市场上和家里说的。

和大部分非洲文化一样，格勒人也有着丰富的音乐传统。班戈原本是非洲人发明的一种弦乐器，后来和奴隶一起被带到新世界去。在过去两百年来则风行于北美和欧洲两地。许多各种不同的鼓也随着非洲音乐传入美洲殖民地。独唱和伴随着丰富和声的合唱也是奴隶传统的一部分。尽管生活艰辛苦闷，奴隶们心中仍紧紧拥抱着他们原本的语言、音乐以及主人的基督教。今天他们的音乐掺入了许多教堂音乐，教堂音乐也被称作心灵音乐或福音音乐。

观赏马莉娜·史莫斯以及她的哈利路亚合唱团的晚会表演绝

不会令人觉得枯燥无味。他们一会儿穿着传统非洲服装,一会儿穿着美国南方社会简单的传统乡村衣裳。这独特的表演节目大部分是歌唱,还不时穿插市集上以及妇女闲聊时所用的地道的格勒语。许多夸张的肢体语言,甚至偶尔来上一段和着隆隆鼓声和热烈叫喊的部落舞蹈也是表演的特色。史莫斯太太介绍每首歌曲或其他表演的背景,以帮助观众——时常夹杂国外观光客——更加了解格勒人如何彼此沟通。然而,即使没有这部分介绍的帮忙,当哈利路亚合唱团洋溢着爱和骄傲唱出他们传统的民谣时,音乐爱好者亦能欣赏他们如天籁一般的声音。在史莫斯太太机智而高明的叙述中,欢乐的夜晚时光一下就过去了。

得知有些少数民族正骄傲地固守着他们无价的遗产,真是令人振奋。尽管来自奴隶的不幸出身,格勒人仍在 21 世纪的科技奇迹中浴火重生,努力创造出一个成功在望、令人羡慕的民族文化。我们可以庆幸的是,在演唱会中或录制好的媒体上,马莉娜·史莫斯和哈利路亚合唱团将透过音乐的魔力,用他们真心的传统歌唱感动我们所有的听众。

2 Vocabulary & Idioms 单词短语注解

1. **ring a bell** 唤起记忆；听来耳熟

   When Marlene mentioned Jimmy, his name rang a bell, but I couldn't remember him clearly.

   玛兰妮提起吉米时，他的名字很耳熟，不过我无法清晰地回忆起他的长相。

2. 句型分析

   For it is Mrs. Smalls' dream that through her and her
       (1) (2)   (3)   (4)

   performing troupe's efforts their Gullah community will...
   global village.

   (1) 代词，作主语，于本句中为形式主语，代替其后 that 引导的名词从句。

   (2) 不完全不及物 be 动词。

   (3) 名词，作表语。

   (4) that 引导的名词从句，为真正的主语，但因主语太长，因此移至句尾；本句原为 "For that through her and her...global village is Mrs. Smalls' dream."。

3. **troupe** [trup] *n.* 歌舞团；剧团

4. **anachronistic** [ə,nækrə'nɪstɪk] *a.* 过时的；落伍的

5. **hangover** ['hæŋ,ovə] *n.* 残存物，残留物

6. **vibrant** ['vaɪbrənt] *a.* 生气蓬勃的

7. **The Sea Islands comprise a group of islands...**

   = The Sea Islands are made up of a group of islands...

   = The Sea Islands consist of a group of islands...

   = The Sea Islands are composed of a group of islands...

8. **descendant** [dɪ'sɛndənt] *n.* 后裔，后代

9. **identify** [aɪ'dɛntə,faɪ] *vt.* 辨识（身份）

   The police could not at first identify the body found in the burned

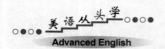

building.

警方起初无法辨识那具在该烧毁建筑物中发现的尸体的身份。

10. **contemporary** [kənˈtɛmpəˌrɛrɪ] *a.* 同时代的

11. **ethnic** [ˈɛθnɪk] *a.* 种族的

12. **popularize** [ˈpɑpjələˌraɪz] *vt.* 使流行 / 普及；推广
Sci-fi movies have popularized the idea of space travel in the public's mind.
科幻片推广了太空旅行在大众心中的想法。

13. **a cappella** [ˌɑkəˈpɛlə] *n.* （音乐）不用乐器伴奏；教堂音乐风格（指合唱）

14. **heritage** [ˈhɛrətɪdʒ] *n.* （文化）遗产

15. **involve** [ɪnˈvɑlv] *vt.* 牵涉；包括在内
Learning how to become a military officer today involves a lot of professional knowledge.
现在学习如何成为一名军官涵盖许多的专业知识。

16. **be nothing short of...** 不缺少……
be short of... 短缺……
The Beatles have remained nothing short of the best rock and roll band over.
"披头士" 绝对依然是有史以来最好的摇滚乐团。
We're short of bread, so please pick some up on your way home, honey.
亲爱的，我们没有面包了，所以麻烦你在回家途中买些面包回来。

17. **pepper** [ˈpɛpɚ] *vt.* 使夹杂，使混合
be peppered with... 夹杂……
Although rock concerts are mainly for the young, they are also peppered with some middle-aged people.
虽然摇滚演唱会的对象主要是年轻观众，不过也有中年观众夹杂其中。

18. **render** [ˈrɛndə] *vt.* 演奏，演出

19. **intersperse** [ˌɪntəˈspɜs] *vt.* 使点缀（通常与介词 with 连用）
    be interspersed with... 点缀 / 穿插……
    Much to the students' delight, the professor interspersed his lecture with jokes.
    令学生大为高兴的是，那位教授在讲课中穿插着笑话。

20. **cling** [klɪŋ] *vi.* 紧握不放（与介词 to 连用）
    动词三态为：cling, clung [klʌŋ], clung。
    The Amish have proudly clung to their agricultural and religious traditions for hundreds of years.
    亚米希人骄傲地固守着他们农业和宗教传统数百年 之久。

21. **legacy** [ˈlɛgəsɪ] *n.* 遗产；长久存在的结果

22. **viable** [ˈvaɪəbḷ] *a.* 可成功运作的

23. **enviable** [ˈɛnvɪəbḷ] *a.* 值得羡慕的

Lesson 11

English in the Caribbean
加勒比海英语

1   *Reading* 阅读

When we hear the word English, we naturally think of the language spoken by those living in the United Kingdom or of the people living in England. We also often think of their language as the international language, the one spoken as a native language in Ireland, the United States, Canada, Australia, and New Zealand, countries which have had a close association with England for centuries. However, English is spoken as a native or second language in a large number of other countries which were once colonies of the British Empire.

Latin America, including Mexico, Central America, the Caribbean, and South America, is often thought of as a linguistically homogenous area of Latinate languages (those languages like French, Italian, Portuguese, and Spanish which originated from Latin). This is generally true, as the vast majority of peoples there speak Spanish or Portuguese as their mother tongue. However, a number of small Caribbean island nations were also once part of the British Empire; accordingly, their citizens even after independence speak English. These nations include Antigua and Barbuda, the Bahamas, Dominica,

Grenada, Jamaica, Barbados, and the Republic of Trinidad and Tobago.

Do the Caribbean English speakers speak British English? Not exactly. All over the world where English has been spoken for hundreds of years by speakers of other languages, certain special accents or dialects have arisen. India is famous for "Indian English"; "Irish English" is unmistakable, too. Likewise, Caribbean English has its own special patterns, vocabulary, and even grammatical forms different from the standard RP (received pronunciation, also referred to as Received Standard) of British English. These special features include a lilt or "sing-song" sound to the language, and plenty of local slang.

As only a relatively few people live on these islands, how can we hear their special dialect or accent? One kind of pop music called reggae is the easiest way outside of befriending someone from these nations. Reggae music has been popular since the 1980s, when performers like Bob Marley of Jamaica pleasantly surprised the world with their own original reggae music as well as their interpretations of other well-known pop Anglo music. Reggae is famous for its strong, often syncopated beat, laid-back singing style, and, of course, the "island" dialect. Another perennial music favorite is calypso, which is also sung in the Caribbean island English dialect. The hit song "Yes, We Have No Bananas," is reminiscent of this drum-heavy musical style, especially from Trinidad and Tobago.

Given the islands' historic ties to both the United Kingdom and the United States, it is little wonder that today the peoples of these small nations continue to use English in government, academia, business, and trade. Local languages still exist alongside the Caribbean English dialect, too, but they are mostly the patois of the marketplace and home. Many of the residents of this area, also referred to as the West Indies or the Antilles, have emigrated to the U.K. or the U.S. and, because of their linguistic prowess, have done relatively well as so-called "third world" immigrants. A few writers of contemporary renown also hail from this area, as do some sports figures.

If you plan to visit any of the above-mentioned islands for any purpose, do not worry about your language skills. Caribbean peoples are well-known for their friendly, patient dispositions. After a few days, your ear will become attuned to the lilting cadence of the lovely Caribbean English dialects, and your stay in this tropical paradise will be all the more rewarding.

　　我们听到 English 这个词时,自然而然会想到那是住在英国的人或是那些居住在英格兰的人所讲的语言。我们也时常视他们的语言为国际语言,几世纪以来它在和英国有密切关联的国家如爱尔兰、美国、加拿大、澳大利亚和新西兰等国中被当作本国语使用。然而,英语在其他许多曾经是大英帝国殖民地的国家中也被当作本国语或第二语言使用。

　　包括墨西哥、中美洲、加勒比海和南美洲在内的拉丁美洲在语言上常被视为同属拉丁语系(法语、意大利语、葡萄牙语和西班牙语等语言皆源自于拉丁语)的地区。这种说法大致而言是对的,因为那些地区绝大多数的民族都使用西班牙语或葡萄牙语作为母语。然而,有一些加勒比海的小岛国也曾经是大英帝国的一部分;因此,它们的人民即使在独立后仍继续使用英语。这些国家包括安提瓜、巴哈马、多米尼加、格林那达、牙买加、巴巴多斯以及特立尼达和多巴哥共和国。

　　加勒比海人说的是英式英语吗? 不见得。英语在世界各地被其他语言的人使用几百年之后,产生了某些特别的腔调或方言。印度的"印度式英语"很出名,"爱尔兰式英语"也不会被搞错。同样地,加勒比海式英语有它自己特殊的句型、词汇,甚至还有和公认标准英语发音(或称公认标准英语)不同的语法结构。这些特色包括轻快的旋律或"歌唱般的"语言声调,以及丰富的当地俚语。

　　而因为居住在这些岛上的居民相当少,我们又如何听到他们特别的方言或腔调呢? 除了和来自这些国家的人交朋友之外,听一种叫雷鬼的流行音乐是最简单的方法。雷鬼音乐从 80 年代一直流行至今,当时诸如牙买加人鲍伯·马利等表演者以其独创的雷鬼音乐和诠释其他著名英国流行音乐让全世界的人大为赞叹称奇。雷鬼音乐以节奏强烈,且通常切分音拍的轻松演唱方式,当然还有"岛上"方言而闻名。另一种长久以来颇受喜爱的音乐是以加勒比海岛上的英语方言唱出的卡里普索(特立尼达岛上土人所演唱的歌曲)。畅销曲"是的,我们没有香蕉"令人想起这种特别是出自特立尼达和多巴哥鼓声沉重的音乐风格。

从这些岛屿与英国和美国的历史关系看来,也难怪这些小国中的各民族至今在政府机关、学术界、商业和贸易上仍继续使用英语。当地的语言也仍然和加勒比海式英语方言并存着,但它们大都是在市场和家里所用的土话。这地区有许多居民(又叫西印度群岛人或安的列斯人)已经移民到英国或美国,并且由于他们的语言天分,以所谓"第三世界"移民者的身份表现得相当不错。就像某些运动人物一样,当代一些著名的作家也来自这个地区。

如果你计划去拜访上面提到的任何国家,不必担心你的语言能力。加勒比海人友善和具耐心的天性是很出名的。几天之后,你的耳朵就会习惯美妙的加勒比海式英语方言那种抑扬顿挫的轻快节拍,而停留在这个热带天堂的你将获益良多。

2 *Vocabulary & Idioms* 单词短语注解

1. **think of A as B** 视 A 为 B，认为 A 是 B
   I always think of winter as an old, unfriendly man visiting my home.
   我总认为冬天是一位来我家造访的不友善的老人。

2. **association** [ə͵soʃɪˈeʃən] *n.* 关联；联合
   in association with... 与……有关联
   Although Australia is not part of Asia, it is in association with many Asian political organizations.
   虽然澳大利亚并非亚洲的一部分，但却和亚洲许多政治组织有联盟。

3. **homogeneous** [͵homəˈdʒinɪəs] *a.* 同类的；同质的

4. **originate from...** 发源 / 源自于……
   originate [əˈrɪdʒə͵net] *vi.* 起源；起因
   The word feminine originates from the Latin word "femina, " meaning "woman."
   "feminine" 一词源自拉丁语"femina"，就是"女人"的意思。

5. **accordingly** [əˈkɔrdɪŋlɪ] *adv.* 因此，所以
   = therefore
   The weather looks bad for this weekend; accordingly, we'll have to cancel our picnic.
   这个周末的天气好像很差的样子，因此我们必须取消野餐。

6. **independence** [͵ɪndɪˈpɛndəns] *n.* 独立；自立
   independent [͵ɪndɪˈpɛndənt] *a.* 独立的；自立的
   be independent of... 脱离……而独立；不依赖……
   Many American children try to become independent of their parents before they turn 20.
   许多美国小孩在他们满 20 岁之前就设法要脱离父母而独立。

7. **unmistakable** [͵ʌnməˈstekəbḷ] *a.* 显而易见的，不会弄错的

8. **lilt** [lɪlt] *n.* 轻快的旋律

85

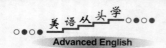

9. **reggae** [ˈrɛge] *n.* 雷鬼(西印度群岛一种节奏强烈的流行音乐)

10. **befriend** [bɪˈfrɛnd] *vt.* 和……交朋友;以朋友态度对待
    I have befriended several stray dogs in our city park; they come to me whenever I call them.
    我和城市公园里的几只流浪狗交上了朋友,所以每次我叫它们时,它们都会过来我身边。

11. **interpretation** [ɪnˌtɜprɪˈteʃən] *n.* 解释,说明
    interpret [ɪnˈtɜprɪt] *vt.* 解释,说明
    The Cubists interpreted the world around them in geometric shapes.
    立体主义以几何图形来诠释周围的世界。

12. **syncopate** [ˈsɪŋkəˌpet] *vt.* 切分(音乐的节拍)
    Latin and African music are highly syncopated; it is easy to dance to their music.
    拉丁和非洲音乐为高切分节拍的音乐,所以很容易随之起舞。

13. **be reminiscent of...** 使人想起……
    reminiscent [ˈrɛməˌnɪsnt] *a.* (引起)回忆的
    The antique furniture in the museum was reminiscent of my grandparents' house.
    博物馆里的古董家具使我想起祖父母的家。

14. **patois** [ˈpætwɑ] *n.* 方言,土话

15. **emigrate to...** (往外)移民到……(某地)
    Paul wants to emigrate to Canada to marry his sweetheart there and start a new life.
    保罗想移民到加拿大和爱人结婚,并在那里展开新生活。

16. **prowess** [ˈpraʊɪs] *n.* 杰出的才能,本领

17. **contemporary** [kənˈtɛmpəˌrɛrɪ] *a.* 同时代的
    Much contemporary music relies on electric musical instruments and strong percussion.
    当代许多音乐都依赖电子乐器和强烈的打击乐器。

18. **renown** [rɪ'naʊn] *n.* 声誉，名望

Our Physics professor at college is a man of great renown; he often travels overseas to give lectures.

我们大学的物理教授很有名；他经常到国外演讲。

19. **disposition** [ˌdɪspə'zɪʃən] *n.* 性情

20. **attune** [ə'tjun] *vt.* 使适应，使习惯于 (一般用于被动语态)

be attuned to... 适应 / 习惯于……

I'm quite attuned to her way of thinking. 我相当习惯她的思考方式。

21. **cadence** ['kedəns] *n.* (说话声调的) 抑扬顿挫

22. **rewarding** [rɪ'wɔrdɪŋ] *a.* 有益的；有报酬的

Lesson 12

The Louvre: The World's Best Museum?
卢浮宫——全世界最棒的博物馆？

1   *Reading* 阅读

Paris, City of Light, and of art. A playland for lovers and a painter's dream. What better place to situate the Louvre, considered by many to be the world's best museum of art? What makes this museum so worthy of that honor?

The museum building, or, more properly, the complex of buildings themselves is a good place to start. As with most Western and a few Asian and South American museums, large palaces or other traditional architecture are used to house museums of art and of natural science. In the case of the Louvre, officially known as Palais du Louvre (the Palace of the Louvre), the main building used today was formerly the fortress of King Philip Augustus in the 12th century. Not until 1546 did King Francis I begin to redesign and add onto the fortress. Subsequent kings did the same, especially during the 17th century with major additions by Louis XIII and Louis XIV. Not only did these kings and their ministers add to the buildings, they also stocked within their rooms the finest art that money could buy. After the French Revolution, the Palais du Louvre was opened to the public. In the early 19th century, both Napoleon and Napoleon III added to both the structures and the collections. A controversial see-through glass pyramid-shaped structure was added by the architect I. M. Pei in the 1980s. As a consequence of centuries of continuous construction and the amassing of art treasures, today the Louvre offers a world-class collection of both French and foreign art.

The outer shell of a museum, however, no matter how artistic or historic, cannot alone make a museum truly great. The inner collections are of course of paramount interest to both the art researcher and art lover alike. The Louvre does not disappoint them. Three of the West's premier works of art are here: the statues Victory of Samothrace and Venus de Milo accompany Leonardo da Vinci's most famous painting, the Mona Lisa. These alone attract art devotees from around the world, but far more awaits them. The French painting collection is, not surprisingly, unsurpassed. Other major painting collections include works from the middle ages and Renaissance. The treasures of the French royalty are on display here, too, such as their bronzes, miniatures, pottery, tapestries, jewelry, and furniture. Greek, Roman, Egyptian, and Mesopotamian antiquities as well as early Christian artifacts are also considered important collections. This clearly is not a museum to be seen in one morning!

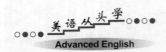

Finally, the site of the museum complex contributes to the mystique of the Louvre. Paris has long been considered one of the world's most charming cities, with its endless winding streets amidst spectacular royal and religious architecture. The fortress built by King Philip Augustus was situated on the right bank of the Seine, overlooking — at that time — splendid bucolic scenery. Today this prime location is within walking distance of many major Parisian tourist attractions, like the Cathedral of Notre Dame, the Royal Palace, and the National Library. One could easily spend a whole week touring the heart of Paris centered around the Louvre.

Taken altogether, then, the Louvre holds its own as one of the best museums — if not the best — among the dozens of major and internationally famous art museums around the world. Its many and varied buildings, the unparalleled collection of prestigious works of art, and the delightful site of the grounds overlooking France's most famous river all contribute to make the Palais du Louvre a must-see attraction for the serious art connoisseur and art museum-goer alike. Meet you at the Louvre!

巴黎:光和艺术之都,恋人们的游地和画家心中的梦想。还有什么更好的地方来安置这许多人心目中全世界最好的艺术博物馆卢浮宫呢?到底是什么使这座博物馆如此值得推崇呢?

这座博物馆的建筑,或者更确切地说,这座复合建筑物本身就是一个很好的开始。就像大部分西方和一些亚洲和南美洲的博物馆一样,大型宫殿或其他传统建筑被用来作为艺术和自然科学博物馆。以卢浮宫来说(正式名称为罗浮之宫殿),现今所用的主要建筑以前是 12 世纪时菲利浦·奥古斯都国王的堡垒。直到 1546 年国王弗朗西斯一世才开始重新设计和扩建该堡垒。接下来的国王们也如法炮制,尤其在 17 世纪期间,路易十三和路易十四更是大肆修建。这些国王及其大臣们不仅增盖建筑物,而且在其房间内典藏了所能买到的最好艺术品。法国大革命之后,卢浮宫对外开放。19 世纪初期,拿破仑和拿破仑三世两人都扩建了建筑物并增加其中的收藏品。20 世纪 80 年代,建筑家贝聿铭增建一座倍受争议的透明玻璃金字塔型建筑。由于几世纪来不停地增建和搜罗艺术珍品的结果,今天的卢浮宫提供了世界级法国艺术和国外艺术两方面的收藏。

然而,不管有多么具有艺术性或历史意义,光是博物馆的外壳并不能使一座博物馆真正伟大。对艺术研究及爱好者而言,最让他们感兴趣的当然还是里面的收藏品。这一点卢浮宫不会让他们失望。西方首要艺术珍品其中有三件便收藏于此处:"胜利女神雕像"、"爱神维纳斯雕像"以及列奥纳多·达·芬奇最有名的画作"蒙娜丽莎的微笑"。光是这些就吸引了世界各地的忠实艺术爱好者,但还有更多等着他们去欣赏的呢。法国画作收藏显然是无人可及的。其他重要的绘画收藏还包括中世纪和文艺复兴时期的作品。法国

王室的珍宝也在此地展出,例如他们的铜器、袖珍画、陶器、挂毯、珠宝和家具等等。希腊、罗马、埃及和美索不达米亚的古物以及早期基督教手工艺品也都被认为是重要的收藏品。这显然不是花一个早上时间就能逛完的博物馆!

最后,这座综合博物馆的位置增添了卢浮宫的神秘气息。巴黎长久以来一直被认为是世上最迷人的城市之一,无止尽的街道蜿蜒在雄伟的皇室和宗教建筑之间。菲利浦国王所建的堡垒就坐落在塞纳河的右岸,俯瞰着——在当时——秀丽的田园景色。今天这个主要位置距离巴黎许多重要的观光景点如圣母院大教堂、皇宫和国立图书馆都不远,走路过去即可到达。你很容易就可以花整个礼拜游览以卢浮宫为中心的巴黎市中心。

因此,整体看来,卢浮宫在全世界几十个闻名国际的主要艺术博物馆之中,就算不是最好的,也必定是最好的博物馆之一。它为数众多且多样的建筑,无可比拟的艺术名作收藏,以及俯瞰法国最著名河流的理想地理位置,使得卢浮宫成为艺术鉴赏行家和美术馆常客不容错过的观光点。咱们卢浮宫见吧!

2 *Vocabulary & Idioms* 单词短语注解

1. **playland** [`ple,lænd] *n.* 游乐场所

2. **situate** [`sɪtʃʊ,et] *vt.* 坐落于(常用被动式)
   Any house or building should be situated according to the needs of its dwellers.
   任何房屋或建筑都应依居住者的需要去建造。

3. **be worthy of...** 值得……
   Our teacher is worthy of our praise because he is diligent and caring.
   我们老师值得我们赞赏,因为他既勤勉又关心人。

4. **complex** [`kɑmplɛks] *n.* 综合物,复合体

5. **Not until** + 时间 / 从句 + 倒装句型 直到……才……
   Not until I had my own children did I realize how much my parents had sacrificed for me.
   直到有了自己的子女后,我才了解父母为我牺牲了多少。

6. **subsequent** [`sʌbsɪ,kwɛnt] *a.* 后来的;随后的

7. **not only...also...** 不仅……,而且……
   = not only...but (also)...
   = not only...but...as well
   注意
   "not only...but also..."可连接对等的名词、短语或句子,但连接句子时,not only 若放在句首时,之后的句子须采用倒装结构,but also(but 有时可省略,如本文)因为是连接词,因此之后的句子不须倒装,且 also 应置于句中,此时 also 亦可省略。
   Not only was Melvin late for class, but he had (also) forgotten to take his homework.
   梅尔文不仅上课迟到,他还忘了带作业。

8. **stock** [stɑk] *vt.* 贮存
   The local 7-Eleven is stocked with many daily necessities.
   本地的统一超市贮存了许多日常用品。

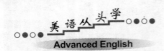

9. **controversial** [ˌkɑntrə'vɝʃəl] *a.* 争议性的；引起争议的
The dance was considered controversial because one of the dancers was nude.
那支舞蹈被视为有争议，因为其中有位舞者全身赤裸。

10. **pyramid-shaped** ['pɪrəmɪdˌʃept] *a.* 金字塔形状的

11. **as a consequence of...** 由于……
As a consequence of his tireless work, he eventually became rich.
由于努力不懈地工作，他终于成了有钱人。

12. **amassing** [ə'mæsɪŋ] *n.* 积聚，搜罗

13. **paramount** ['pærəˌmaʊnt] *a.* 最重要的
It is of paramount importance for all parents to provide a safe environment for their children to grow up in.
父母给子女提供一个安全的生长环境是非常重要的。

14. **unsurpassed** [ˌʌnsɚ'pæst] *a.* 无法超越的

15. **the Renaissance** ['rɛnəˌsɑns] *n.* 文艺复兴时期（欧洲 14 至 17 世纪时）

16. **(be) on display** 展出（中）
There are several paintings by Picasso on display in the museum this month.
本月在这座博物馆有几幅毕加索的画作展出。

17. **contribute** [kən'trɪbjut] *vi.* 有助于，造成（常与介词 to 连用）
The unusually dry weather contributed to the severity of the forest fire.
天气不寻常的干燥造成那场森林火灾更为严重。

18. **spectacular** [spɛk'tækjəlɚ] *a.* 雄伟的

19. **splendid** ['splɛndɪd] *a.* 壮观的

20. **bucolic** [bju'kɑlɪk] *a.* 乡村的

21. **within walking distance of...**
走路可及……的距离，离……不远

I need an apartment within walking distance of my job; I don't want to commute.

我需要一间离我上班地点不远的公寓，我不想乘车上下班。

22. **tourist attraction** 观光胜地

tourist [ˈtʊrɪst] *n.* 游客

attraction [əˈtrækʃən] *n.* 吸引人的事物

23. **unparalleled** [ʌnˈpærəˌlɛld] *a.* 无法匹敌的

24. **prestigious** [prɛsˈtɪdʒəs] *a.* 有名望的

Harvard Univeristy is the most prestigious institute of higher learning in the United States.

哈佛大学是美国高等学府中最有名望的。

25. **connoisseur** [ˌkɑnəˈsɜ] *n.* （美术品等的）鉴赏家

Lesson 13

The Ivy League Schools: Excellence in Education

常春藤盟校——教育界的佼佼者

Reading 阅读

The first permanent English settlement in the New World was at Plymouth Bay in what is now the state of Massachusetts in 1620. Merely 16 years later, a group of successful settlers in New Town (renamed Cambridge after their alma mater) started a college. They named it after the Puritan minister who willed half his estate and all his books to the college. This clergyman's name was John Harvard, and his namesake remains the most prestigious among the more than 2,000 institutes of higher education in the United States today.

Harvard is not the only great school in the U.S., of course. A small industry has grown up around the ranking of the best tertiary schools, and year after year, seven schools dominate most of these Top Twenty or Top Fifty lists. Harvard is nearly always at or close to the top, joined frequently by Yale (in Connecticut), Princeton (in New Jersey), Dartmouth (in New Hampshire), Cornell (in New York State), Columbia (in New York City), the University of Pennsylvania, and Brown (in Rhode Island). These eight private universities are collectively referred to as the Ivy League schools.

Why the name? Ivy is a vine; that is, a plant which grows up or along the surface of other plants such as trees, or, in the human landscape, along the sides of stone buildings. As these eight universities are old (the youngest among them, Cornell, was founded in 1853), ivy has had plenty of time to decorate the outsides of the more historic buildings on these campuses. The word league, however, is more an invention of imagination than a reality. Though there is an association called the Ivy League, it refers to the above schools' participation in an American football athletic conference rather than to any academic alliance. Further, despite the lengthy academic lineage of these schools, the footballing Ivy League was not formally formed until 1956, though highly competitive football and other athletic games have been hotly contested among the schools for many generations.

Since these institutes of higher learning had such an early start in the history of the United States, it is not surprising that they should individually and collectively have exerted a great influence on American society. Their status within national scholarly circles is unparalleled. Admission to these universities is highly demanding: many students apply for every one lucky enough to be accepted. As these universities are private, they are relatively expensive. Offsetting the extremely high tuition are many opportunities for scholarships. These scholarships are awarded to meritorious students regardless

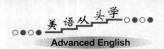

of their backgrounds.

Additionally, the roster of the faculties of these schools reads like a Who's Who list of important Americans (and quite a few foreigners, as well). Their intellectual integrity shows in the number of Nobel and other major prizes awarded which they have garnered over the years. Some of the country's most famous doctors, statesmen, engineers, scientists, and educationists have studied and taught within these ivy-covered walls. No fewer than 14 U.S. presidents have earned degrees here, including six at Harvard, six at Yale, and two at Princeton.

Though only a select few can join the ranks as Ivy Leaguers each year, Americans are endowed with a world-class tertiary educational system second to none. Not every graduate from an Ivy League school "makes the grade" in life; even a first-rate education is no guarantee of success. Still, those who do enter and leave the Ivy League universities in the northeastern United States have a much better than average chance to join the ranks of the movers and shakers of not only the U.S. society, but, once back in their home countries, of their native lands as well.

英国人于 1620 年在新大陆建立的第一个永久殖民地是在普利茅斯湾，即今天的马萨诸塞州境内。在仅仅 16 年后，一群功成名就的移民在新城（后来依其母校改名为剑桥）创办了一所大学。他们以一位在遗嘱中将半数产业和所有书籍都捐给这所大学的清教徒牧师来为学校命名。这位神父的名字就叫约翰·哈佛，一直到今天他的名声在美国两千多所高等教育学府当中仍是最有名望的。

当然，哈佛不是美国唯一的名校。多年来在这些出类拔萃的高等学府周围兴起了一群小小的教育团体，而年复一年，前 20 或 50 的排名大都由 7 所学校所囊括。哈佛几乎总是排名第一或接近第一，经常一起上榜的前 20 或 50 排名的学校还有耶鲁大学（在康涅狄格州）、普林斯顿大学（在新泽西州）、达特默思大学（在新罕布什尔州）、康奈尔大学（在纽约州）、哥伦比亚大学（在纽约市）、宾西法尼亚大学和布朗大学（在罗得岛）。这 8 所大学被总称为常春藤联盟学校。

为什么叫这个名字呢？常春藤是一种藤蔓，也就是一种往上或沿着树木等其他植物表面生长、或者在人工景观中沿着石造建筑物墙壁生长的植物。由于这 8 所大学都很古老（其中最年轻的康奈尔大学创立于 1853 年），常春藤有足够的时间装饰这些校园里历史较悠久的建筑物外观。然而，"联盟"这个词比较像是想象出来的产物而不是事实。虽然有一个叫做"常春藤联盟"的组织，但那指的是上列名校所参加的一项美式足球会，而非任何学术上的结盟。况且，尽管这些学校的学术历史悠久，而且竞争激烈的美式足球和其他运动比赛在各校之间也已热烈展开了好几个世代，但是美式足球的常春藤联盟却一直到 1956 年才正式成立。

因为这些高等学府在美国历史上起步非常早，它们能个别或共同对美国社会发挥巨大的影响也就不足为奇。在国际学术圈内它们的地位崇高无比。这些学校对入学标准的要求很严格：许多学生申请了常春藤盟校每一所大学，被一所接受就算幸运了。由于这些大学都是私立的，学费因此相当昂贵。而许多领取奖学金的机会可以对极高的学费作些补偿。这些奖学金颁给成绩优异的学生，不论他们的背景为何。

除此之外，这些学校的教职员名册读起来就像一份"美国名人录"（也有不少外国人）。他们丰富的学识表现在多年来所获得的诺贝尔奖和其他大奖的数量上。许多美国最有名的医生、政治人物、工程师、科学家和教育家都曾在这些墙上爬满常春藤的校园内学习和执教。有不下 14 位美国总统在常春藤盟校中取得学位，其中 6 位在哈佛，6 位在耶鲁，2 位在普林斯顿大学。

虽然每年只有少数雀屏中选的人可以加入常春藤盟校成为其中一员，美国人仍拥有无人能比的世界级高等教育体系。并不是每一个常春藤盟校的毕业生都能在人生中"出人头地"，即使一流的学府也不能保证功成名就。尽管如此，那些能够进出美国东北部常春藤盟校的人，比一般人更有机会晋升为美国社会的掌权人物，而且回到自己的祖国也更有机会成为呼风唤雨的人物。

2 *Vocabulary & Idioms* 单词短语注解 ✍

1. **name A after B** 用 B 为 A 命名

   I named my son after my father, so they both have the same name Richard.

   我用父亲的名字为我儿子取名,所以他们两个的名字都叫理查德。

2. **will** [wɪl] *vt.* 立遗嘱赠与(财产等)

   will sth to + 人/机构/组织等   立遗嘱把某物给某人/机构/组织等

   Before my father died, he willed his savings to my sister and his house to me.

   我父亲在死前立下遗嘱将他的积蓄留给我姐姐,而将房子留给我。

3. **namesake** [ˈnemˌsek] *n.* 依某人名字取名者

4. **tertiary** [ˈtɜʃɪˌrɪ] *a.* 第三(位)的;大学的

5. **dominate** [ˈdɑməˌnet] *vt.* 在……中拥有重要地位;支配,控制

   The taller basketball team was able to dominate the court and thus won the game.

   球员个子较高的篮球队能够称霸球场因而赢得比赛。

6. **participation** [pɑrˌtɪsəˈpeʃən] *n.* 参与

   participate [pəˈtɪsəˌpet] *vi.* 参与(与介词 in 连用)

   participate in... 参与……

   Most students participate in at least one extracurricular activity each semester.

   大部分学生每学期至少都会参加一种课外活动。

7. **lineage** [ˈlɪnɪɪdʒ] *n.* 血统;世系

8. **competitive** [kəmˈpɛtətɪv] *a.* (好)竞争的

   Shirley is very competitive; she always tries to outperform the other workers.

   雪莉很好强;她总是努力要在工作表现上胜过其他员工。

9. **contest** [kənˈtɛst] *vt.* 竞争,争夺,角逐

   The election was hotly contested, but the incumbent won again.

那场选举的竞争十分激烈,但执政者再度赢得了选战。

10. **exert** [ɪɡ`zɜt] *vt.* 施以(影响);发挥(力量);运用

Because her parents exerted such great pressure on Susan to become a doctor, she finally committed suicide.

因为苏珊的父母施加很多压力要她成为医生,所以她最后自杀了。

11. **unparalleled** [ʌn`pærəˌlɛld] *a.* 无比的;空前的

12. **admission** [əd`mɪʃən] *n.* 允许进入;入学/会/场许可

13. **offset** [ɔf`sɛt] *vt.* 补偿;抵销(动词三态均为 offset。)

The difficulty of being a teacher is offset by the high social status of teacher.

当老师的困难性因其崇高的社会地位而得到补偿。

14. **regardless of...** 不管/顾……

She said, "I'll always love you, regardless of how you feel about me!"

她说:"不管你对我的感觉如何,我都永远爱你!"

15. **garner** [`ɡɑrnə] *vt.* 收藏;收集

The politician traveled around her district trying to garner support for her election.

那个政治家四处走访她的选区,努力要获得选民对她的支持。

16. **be endowed with...** 天生具有……

endow [ɪn`dau] *vt.* 使具有某种特质(一般用被动语态)

Jack is endowed with great strength, so he can do difficult work for long hours.

杰克天生体力就很好,所以他可以长时间做费力的工作。

17. **(be) second to none** 无人能比,无人能出其右

When it comes to singing, Angela is second to none.

说到唱歌,没人比得上安吉拉。

18. **make the grade** 成功;达到水平

You need not only a high IQ but also a high EQ to really make the grade in life.

你不仅智商要高,情商也要高,才能出人头地。

Lesson 14

Alpine Treasures

乐在阿尔卑斯山

① Reading 阅读

From the Atlantic Ocean to the Ural Mountains stretches the continent of Europe. The most striking geographic feature within this densely-populated area is the Alps Mountain Range, commonly called the Alps. The Alps covers most of Austria and Switzerland as well as significant areas of Germany, France, and Italy. The picture-perfect land and lifestyle of the Alps contain many treasures for all the peoples of the world. Who hasn't dreamed of visiting the Alps for a vacation? If you are lucky enough to vacation in the Alps, what delights await you?

The ladies can look forward to dirndls and Alpine flowers. A dirndl is a special Alpine dress worn particularly by the German-speaking populations of the Alps (in most of the Swiss and all of the German and Austrian areas). This long, often colorful and simple-patterned dress includes a full skirt, gathered waist, and tightfitting bodice. Most women fall in love with a dirndl the moment they see one. Save up to buy one, though. Most dirndls are hand-made and rather pricey. Compared to the cost of the intercontinental voyage to the Alps, though, a dirndl is well worth the expense. The wearer will have a cool weather treasure to wear for many years.

If dirndls are really too expensive, though, the hundreds of species of Alpine flowers will also delight not only women, but all nature lovers, for free. Of course, to see these botanical wonders, one must visit the Alps during its relatively brief spring through fall, that is, between June and September for most blossoms. The hills are alive with tiny, multi-colored petals in sometimes bizarre shapes. Don't touch! Most plant species are protected by laws carrying stiff fines, even for unsuspecting tourists. Instead, these natural treasures are available on the many postcards or in the coffee table books available at the ubiquitous souvenir shops and bookstores throughout the region. Taking one's own pictures or movies is an even better idea. With luck, it is still possible to find the rare edelweiss growing on a mountain slope. Its yellow center with white star-like petals has become an Alpine symbol, present in many folk art handicrafts.

Speaking of handicrafts, in addition to the dirndl, there are other assorted wares which can be taken home as a fond remembrance of one's all-too-brief stay in this mountainous playground. Alpine women take pride in their embroidery. Scarves, shirts, blouses, wall hangings, and table coverings can still be bought in the smaller, more remote hamlets in tiny mountain valleys. Many modern imitations are also available, however, so be sure of any item's authenticity before buying. In the off-season from farming, some Alpine men enjoy woodcarving. Items from as large as grandfather (also called "cuckoo") clocks to palm-sized miniature animals, farm utensils or equipment, or creations from the imagination can be had at roadside stands or local markets.

It's a pity that so much local food does not carry well; otherwise, Alpine dairy products, sausages, and breads are well worth taking home. On the other hand, bottled wild honey with its extra-thick consistency and exotic wildflower tastes and scents is relatively easy to transport with care in one's carry-on baggage. Mountain wine and liquor may also be carefully taken home. In the meantime, enjoy the calorie-laden but delicious Alpine cuisine where it was meant to be eaten.

Some Alpine treasures cannot be taken home. World-class skiing, mountain climbing, mountain hiking, and white-water rafting are among them. The views of the permanent glaciers of Mount Blanc, the Alps's highest peak at just over 4,700 meters will last a lifetime. Jolly Alpine music and dancing quicken the heart and set the feet tapping. With so much to see and appreciate, perhaps the next priority vacation spot on the discriminating traveler's list should be the Alps.

　　欧洲大陆从大西洋一直绵延至乌拉尔山。这个人口稠密区最引人注目的地理特征就是阿尔卑斯山脉,俗称阿尔卑斯山。阿尔卑斯山横亘了奥地利和瑞士的大部分,以及德国、法国和意大利相当大的地区。阿尔卑斯山绝佳的风景及民情蕴含了许多可供世人挖掘的宝藏。谁没有梦想过到阿尔卑斯山度假呢? 如果你有幸到阿尔卑斯山度假的话,有什么乐事等着你呢?

　　女士们可以期盼紧腰宽裙和阿尔卑斯山上盛开的花朵。紧腰宽裙是阿尔卑斯山德语系族群(在瑞士大部分地区和德、奥全境)特有的一种阿尔卑斯连衣裙。这种样式通常很简单且色彩鲜艳的长连衣裙包括一条长裙、束腰和紧身上衣。大部分的女人一看到紧腰宽裙就会爱上它,但是想买的话就得先存钱了。大部分紧腰宽裙都是手工缝制的,价格相当昂贵。然而和横越欧陆的旅费比起来,买一件紧腰宽裙还是很划算的。穿的人往后多年就可以有一件天气凉爽时穿的宝贝衣服。

　　但是如果紧腰宽裙真的太贵的话,还有好几百种阿尔卑斯山的花朵可以取悦女性和所有自然爱好者,而这是不必花任何费用的。当然,为了观赏到这些神奇植物,游客必须在相当短暂的暮春到秋天之间,也就是 6 到 9 月间大部分花朵盛开的时候来阿尔卑斯山。这时候的山丘上开满了五颜六色,有些花瓣还是奇形怪状的小花。不要去碰喔! 大部分品种的花都有高额罚款的法律条文保护,甚至连不知情的观光客也照罚不误。然而,这些自然奇珍却可在许多明信片上,或是散布全区随处可见的纪念品商店和书店里茶几上的书本里找到。自己拍照或摄影则更理想。运气好的话,还可能发现生长在山坡上稀有的雪绒花呢。它黄色的花蕊和白色星状的花瓣已成为阿尔卑斯山的象征,在许多民俗工艺品中都可以看到。

说到手工艺品，除了紧腰宽裙之外，还有其他各式商品可以带回家当作此次山间乐土短暂停留的甜美纪念。阿尔卑斯山的妇女以其刺绣而自豪。围巾、衬衫、女短衫、挂毯和桌巾等东西在小山谷里较偏远的小村落中仍可买到。然而，当中也有许多现代的仿制品，所以购买前务必确定是真品。农闲季节，有些阿尔卑斯山的男子以木雕为乐。作品大至祖父级时钟(或称"咕咕钟")，小到手掌般大小的动物雕像、农器或耕具、或想象的创作等，在路边的摊子或当地市场都买得到。

很可惜的是许多当地食物都不易携带，否则，阿尔卑斯山的乳制品、香肠和面包都很值得带回家。话又说回来，浓度超高且具异国野花味道和香味的瓶装野蜂蜜若小心放在随身行李里运送是相当方便的。还有山上酿的酒也可以小心地带回家。在此同时，该享用时就尽情享用高卡路里但美味可口的阿尔卑斯山佳肴。

有些阿尔卑斯珍宝不能被带回家。世界级的滑雪、登山、山地远足和激流泛舟便是其中几样。恒久不变的冰河及海拔超过 4700 米的阿尔卑斯山第一高峰布朗峰的景象则令人永生难忘。快乐的阿尔卑斯山的音乐和舞蹈让人心跳加速，双脚不禁动了起来。有这么多可以看和欣赏的景物，喜欢挑三拣四的旅行者也许应该把阿尔卑斯山列入下次度假的首要地点吧。

2 *Vocabulary & Idioms* 单词短语注解

1. **From the Atlantic Ocean to the Ural Mountains stretches the continent of Europe.**

= The continent of Europe stretches from the Atlantic Ocean to the Ural Mountains.

2. **stretch** [strɛtʃ] *vi.* 伸展
China stretches from the frozen tundra in the north of Asia to the tropics in its south.
中国从亚洲北部的冰原地带一直延伸到亚洲南部的热带地区。

3. **geographic** [dʒɪə'græfɪk] *a.* 地理的；地理学上的

4. **densely-populated** [ˌdɛnslɪ'pɑpjəˌletɪd] *a.* 人口稠密的

5. **vacation** [ve'keʃən] *n. & vi.* 休假，度假
We vacationed last year in New Zealand, but this year we're thinking of vacationing in Mexico.
去年我们在新西兰度假，不过今年我们考虑到墨西哥度假。

6. **delight** [dɪ'laɪt] *vt. & n.* 使喜悦，使快乐
Uncle Perry delighted his nieces and nephews by taking food and presents to their home.
派瑞叔叔带着食物和礼物到他侄女、侄子家，让他们很开心。

7. **tightfitting** [ˌtaɪt'fɪtɪŋ] *a.* 紧身的

8. **bodice** ['bɑdɪs] *n.* 女人穿的紧身上衣

9. **compared to...** 和……比较起来
Compared to the 19th century, literacy is much more common nowadays.
与 19 世纪相比，现在会读写的人多多了。

10. **intercontinental** [ˌɪntɚˌkɑntə'nɛntl̩] *a.* 大陆间的，洲际的

11. **botanical** [bo'tænɪkl̩] *a.* 植物（学）的

12. **be alive with...** 充满……
Tropical rain forests are alive with many beautiful and unusual species

of both plants and animals.

热带雨林里有许多美丽又稀有的动植物品种。

13. **ubiquitous** [ju'bɪkwətəs] *a.* 到处都有的，无所不在的

14. **edelweiss** ['edl̩ˌvaɪs] *n.* 雪绒花

15. **assorted** [ə'sɔrtɪd] *a.* 分过类的；各式各样类别的

Every department store offers many assorted tools for its customers.

每家百货商店都提供许多分门别类的工具好让顾客选购。

16. **remembrance** [rɪ'mɛmbrəns] *n.* 回忆；纪念

He gave her his picture in a frame as a remembrance of their friendship.

他送给她一幅加相框的照片，纪念他们之间的友谊。

17. **take pride in...** 以……为傲

Chinese people can take pride in their contributions to technology，such as paper，gunpowder and silk.

中国人能够以他们在造纸、火药和丝绸等科技上的贡献为傲。

18. **embroidery** [ɪm'brɔɪdərɪ] *n.* 刺绣

19. **authenticity** [ˌɔθɛn'tɪsətɪ] *n.* 真迹；真实性

20. **off-season** ['ɔfˌsizn̩] *a.* 不合时节的

21. **It's a pity + that** 从句 可惜／遗憾……

It's a pity that it's raining；we'll have to cancel the backyard barbecue.

很可惜现在正下雨，我们将必须取消后院的烤肉会了。

22. **dairy product** 乳制品

dairy ['dɛrɪ] *a.* 乳制的

23. **be meant to V** 注定……

Jill and Thomas are deeply in love；I guess they were meant to be together.

吉尔和托马斯深爱着对方；我想他们注定要在一起。

24. **permanent** ['pɜmənənt] *a.* 永久的

25. **priority** [praɪ'ɔrətɪ] *n.* 优先事项

Lesson 15

Webcams: Electronics Tool or the End of Privacy?

网络摄影机：电子工具或隐私终结者？

1   *Reading* 阅读

What are webcams? The word webcam is a compound word formed from two abbreviations, "web" from the World Wide Web and "cam" from camera. Webcams are cameras which are situated at various places and linked to the World Wide Web. They allow 24-hour viewing of a wide array of places and activities around the world. They can be as educational as they are fascinating, entertaining as they are eye-opening. Not everyone raves about this new technology, however. Some cite sinister implications in a technology which can unobtrusively spy on our goings-on without our permission. Others note that with rapid increases in telephotography and the science of acoustics, the days of privacy are numbered. Anyone can mount a webcam with a telephoto lens and microphone, aim it at his neighbors' living room or bedroom, and then broadcast one's "private" life to the whole world. A script for the next scifi film, or a current reality? Are these doomsayers overreacting, or is their charge legitimate?

On one side of the debate are those who point out

that webcams offer more real advantages than supposed disadvantages. They cite numerous websites on which people can observe the world around them for educational or aesthetic purposes. Today one can watch urban scenes like city streets and squares or even haunted houses! Nature lovers can revel in the undetectable webcasting of bats, sharks, and penguins at various sites around the world. A huge collection of webcams can be found at www.earthcam.com. Another great collection can be viewed at www.discovery.com. Most educators, parents, and politicians would agree that these websites allow for a better understanding of both the human and natural environments in the world we all live in. Certainly, they would say, webcams provide an invaluable service and should not be restricted.

Others are not so sure. Every technology cuts both ways. Even fire can cook food as it can burn our flesh. Railroads gave us faster and more convenient transportation as they simultaneously signaled the death knell of many species of migratory animals as well as served up noise and air pollution. Nuclear energy gives millions heat, light, and power just as it creates unwanted radioactive side effects. Seemingly harmless technologies such as telecommunications also have their dark side.

Opponents of webcams note that the sleazy, commercial instinct of some people is unleashed with the offering of for-pay viewing of certain starlets or other celebrities' home

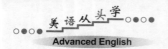

lives, which most people prefer to think of as their "private" life. Perhaps not much longer. In some controversial cases, webcams have been mounted in public installations such as washrooms so that voyeurs may watch the intimate goings-on of anonymous people. Even more sinister is the capacity for the new technology to be used in both economic espionage and "good old" state-to-state spying. Webcams mounted surreptitiously in business offices or factories can reveal on-screen "secrets" from those unaware that they are being bugged. With microelectronics technology reducing the size of telecommunications devices, this is no paranoid fantasy any longer.

The human mind is as devious as the many progressive devices it produces. No matter what technology mankind develops in the future, we can be sure that it will offer an opportunity to exercise the dark side of our potential. On balance, we must move forward and allow these new technologies. Only by practicing them — for good or bad — can we realize our human potential. On balance, too, despite the horrific deadly or sinister potential in technology, the world offers a more productive, comfortable, and progressive environment today than in our previous low-tech centuries. At the end of the day, it is not our technology that we must learn to control so much as ourselves.

　　什么是 webcams（网络摄影机）？webcam 这个词是由两个缩写词组成的复合词，"web" 是全球网络的缩写，"cam" 则是摄影机的缩写。网络摄影机就是位于各地和全球网络联机的摄影机。它们能够让人 24 小时观看全世界许多不同的地方和活动。它们既具教育性同时又吸引人，有娱乐性并能让人大开眼界。然而，并非每个人对这项新科技都赞不绝口。有些人视这项科技为洪水猛兽，认为它可以不经我们同意就悄悄监视我们的行动；其他人则指出随着远距离摄影术和音响效果的快速增长，拥有隐私的日子屈指可数。任何人都可利用电子摄影镜头和麦克风架设一台网络摄影机对准邻居的客厅或卧室，然后将某人的"隐秘"生活转播给全世界。这是下一部科幻电影的剧本，还是当今的现状呢？是这些杞人忧天的人反应过度，还是他们的指控确实有道理呢？

　　这项讨论的一方人马指出网络摄影机提供的实际益处多过假想的坏处。他们举出无数的网站，人们可上网去观察他们周围的世界以达到教育或美学的目的。今天人们可以观看城市的风景，像是都市街道广场甚至鬼屋！爱好自然的人可以在全球的网站上尽情欣赏悄悄从旁拍摄的蝙蝠、鲨鱼和企鹅等。在 www.earthcam.com 这个网站可以找到许多网络摄影机。另外在 www.discovery.com 网站上亦可看到不少网络摄影机。大部分的教育家、父母和政治人物都会同意，这些网站让我们更加了解我们大家所住的世界上的人类和自然环境。他们当然会说网络摄影机提供了珍贵的服务，所以不该受限制。

　　有些人可就不这么认为。每项科技都像一把双刃剑；即使是火能够烹煮食物，但它却也会烧伤我们的皮肉。铁路为我们带来更快速和便利的交通，却也敲响许多迁移性动物的丧钟以及产生噪音和空气污染。核能源带给无数人暖气、光和电力,却也制造有害的辐射作用。表面看似无害的科技,诸如电子传播媒体同样也有黑暗的一面。

反对网络摄影机的人指出,某些人龌龊的商业本能被释放开来,他们为了赚钱而提供一些付费的网站,让上网者观看小明星或其他名人的家居生活,这部分大多数人宁愿视为是"私人的"生活。或许不再是这样也说不定。有些备受争议的案例中,网络摄影机被架设在厕所等公共设施,以便让那些爱偷窥的人看到匿名人士的隐密举动。更可怕的是,这项新科技可以被用在经济间谍活动和"昔日盛行"的国对国间谍战。被偷偷安装在商业办公室或工厂的网络摄影机,可以把不知道自己被监控者的"秘密"显露在屏幕上。随着微电子科技不断把电子信息装置的体积缩小,上述情况已不再只是胡思乱想了。

人心和它所制造出来的许多进步装置一样诡诈。不管将来人类发展出什么样的科技,我们都可确定它必然会提供我们机会去运用我们潜力的黑暗面。就整体看来,我们必须前进并且容许这些新科技。唯有通过应用这些科技——不管是好是坏——我们才能了解人类的潜力。另外,尽管科技有可怕的致命或凶恶潜质,比起以前那些低科技的世纪,今日世界仍提供了一个生产力较高且较舒适和进步的环境。总归一句话,我们必须学习去控制的不是我们的科技,而是我们自己。

2 *Vocabulary & Idioms* 单词短语注解

1. **compound** [ˈkɑmpaʊnd] *a.* 混合的，合成的

2. **abbreviation** [əˌbrivɪˈeʃən] *n.* 缩写
   The abbreviation B.C. stands for "before Christ."
   B. C. 为"耶稣诞生前"的缩写。

3. **be linked to/with sth** 与某物连接
   Some islands like Victoria island in Hong Kong are linked to the mainland by tunnels rather than bridges.
   诸如香港维多利亚等的一些岛屿以隧道而非桥梁和大陆连接。

4. **a wide array of...** 一长列的……；各式各样的……
   array [əˈre] *n.* 排成一大排
   Department stores offer a wide array of goods for their customers to buy.
   百货商店提供各式各样排列整齐的商品供顾客购买。

5. **sinister** [ˈsɪnɪstɚ] *a.* 邪恶的

6. **implication** [ˌɪmpləˈkeʃən] *n.* 暗示

7. **unobtrusively** [ˌʌnəbˈtrusɪvlɪ] *adv.* 客气地，不引人注目地

8. **telephotography** [ˌtɛləfoˈtɑgrəfɪ] *n.* 远距离摄影（术）

9. **acoustics** [əˈkustɪks] *n.* 音响效果

10. **mount** [maʊnt] *vt.* 安装，架设
    He mounted a camera on his telescope.
    他在望远镜上架设了一台摄影机。

11. **legitimate** [lɪˈdʒɪtəmɪt] *a.* 合理的
    Students have legitimate concerns: they have too much homework and the class size is too large.
    学生的担心合情合理：他们功课太多，班级人数也太多。

12. **numerous** [ˈnjumərəs] *a.* 极多的
    There are numerous ways to show agreement in English; for example,

you can say "yes," "yeah," or "uh-huh."
在英语里有极多可以表达同意的说法；例如，你可以说"yes"、"yeah"或者"un-huh"等。

13. **invaluable** [ɪnˈvæljəbl̩] *a.* 无价的，非常珍贵的
valuable [ˈvæljəbl̩] *a.* 珍贵的，有价值的
Friendship is invaluable; no amount of money can buy it.
友情是无价的；多少钱都买不到它。

14. **restrict** [rɪˈstrɪkt] *vt.* 限制
The police restricted the number of protesters and the area they could demonstrate in.
警方限制了抗议者的人数和他们能够示威的区域。

15. **radioactive** [ˌredɪoˈæktɪv] *a.* 放射性的，有辐射能的

16. **sleazy** [ˈslizɪ] *a.* 堕落的；低级的

17. **instinct** [ˈɪnstɪŋkt] *n.* 本能；直觉
The evidence says he is telling the truth, but my instincts tell me he's lying.
证据指出他说的是实话，不过我的直觉告诉我他在说谎。

18. **installation** [ˌɪnstəˈleʃən] *n.* 安装，设置
install [ɪnˈstɔl] *vt.* 安装，架设
I had to call two workmen to help me install my new air conditioner.
我必须打电话叫两位工人来帮我安装新空调。

19. **voyeur** [ˌvwaˈɝ] *n.* 喜爱窥视别人隐私的人

20. **anonymous** [əˈnɑnəməs] *a.* 不具名的，匿名的

21. **capacity** [kəˈpæsətɪ] *n.* 容量

22. **espionage** [ˈɛspɪənɑʒ] *n.* 间谍活动

23. **surreptitiously** [ˌsɝəpˈtɪʃəslɪ] *adv.* 鬼鬼祟祟地，神不知鬼不觉地

24. **paranoid** [ˈpærəˌnɔɪd] *a.* 疑神疑鬼的，好猜疑的
Paranoid old Mr. Higgins thinks that everyone is watching him.

疑神疑鬼的希金斯老先生认为每个人都在监视他。

25. **devious** [ˈdivɪəs] *a.* 诡诈的，狡诈的
The devious little boy blamed another kid for stealing the candy.
那名狡诈的小男孩把偷糖果的事赖在另一个小孩身上。

26. **progressive** [prəˈgrɛsɪv] *a.* 进步的

Lesson 16

When Is the Best Time?
最佳时机为何?

 Reading 阅读

Some people go so far as to say that time does not really exist; it is all in the mind, they claim. Others note that according to astrophysicists, time really does exist; it is inseparable from space, coexisting in what these scientists call the "time-space continuum." No matter which view you may hold, time is of relative importance in different cultures. However, when traveling, doing business, or studying in a German — or English-speaking country, it is a good idea to consider time to be of the utmost importance.

Many people have noted that the Germans and English are both methodical and well-organized. Naturally, not everyone among them is, but these peoples do seem to share a penchant for orderliness and punctuality. Clocks and time have played a great part in defining the character of the Anglo-Saxons. The geographic use of time began during the British Empire with the world divided by latitude and longitude, with zero degrees longitude running through the observatory at Greenwich, in London. According to the British of that day, the world began its time-keeping from London — and it still does.

Time is of paramount importance to these Europeans and their overseas descendants. If you are visiting or staying in these countries, here are a few pieces of advice to help you make the transition to a time-centered civilization.

As you probably already know, being punctual — to the minute — is held in high esteem among them. Time is the most valuable commodity one can have, according to the doctrine of the time worshippers. We are not given very much of it whilst on this planet, and we should do our best to utilize it efficiently each and every day, they say. Wasting others' time by forcing them to wait is a sign of disorganized living, a sort of admission to being low-class. It is also seen as an insult to those kept waiting, as if to say, "Your time is not that important." To them, this attitude borders on sin itself! In business, being late even only a few times may make the difference between your getting a promotion and being kept "in your place." For social dates, it is a sign of slovenliness at best, rejection of those waiting at worst. In school, never burst open the door of the lecture hall to announce, "I'm sorry I'm late, sir" as is the custom in many countries. The double crime of being tardy and interrupting the proceedings which began on time occurs, with a likely prejudiced and unfavorable grade awaiting the hapless student.

Of course, being late can sometimes not be avoided, as in unexpected traffic jams, home emergencies, or having been given the wrong information of date or place. When these

all-too-human mishaps do occur, it is important to explain the reason for being late. It is also a good idea, of course, to apologize for the useless waiting and to assure the other or others that it will never happen again. In this age of cell phones, every effort should be made to call ahead if tardiness of more than ten minutes is unavoidable, especially for business or professional appointments or important dates. The last phrase anyone wants to hear is a frosty "You could have called." That is the prelude to a ruined evening.

Not everything begins exactly on time, even in Anglo-Saxon culture. Many casual parties are "open" concerning time; the party begins when you get there. The same is generally true of backyard barbecues and picnics. Dinner parties, on the other hand, are obviously planned around a meal time; one should make every effort to arrive on (not before) time. A friendly "Drop by this evening" invites common sense to interpret: too early during the evening may embarrass the host who is eating dinner, while too late may disturb those who prefer going to bed early. A call first to make sure is never out of line.

Remember that time is relative in importance to people within a culture just as it is between cultures. Nothing is more important than human relations. If you commit the "crime" of being late with Anglo-Germanic friends, simply apologize. Few people intentionally keep others waiting, after all. Remember, too, that, "When in Rome, do as the Romans do." In English-and German-speaking lands, this means "Time waits for no man!"

有些人竟然说时间根本不存在,他们宣称都是心理在作祟。其他人则表示根据天文物理学家的说法,时间的确存在,它和空间是密不可分的,共同存在于这些科学家所谓的"连续时空"中。不管你持哪一种看法,在各个不同的文化中时间都相当重要。然而,当你到说德语或英语的国家旅行、做生意或念书时,最好把时间视为最重要的事。

许多人指出德国人和英国人做事有条不紊且组织严谨。当然,他们之中不是每个人都这样,但秩序和守时却似乎是这两个民族的共同爱好。时钟和时间大大说明了盎格鲁 - 撒克逊人的性格。地理时间的使用始于大英帝国时期,当时用纬线和经线划分世界,零度经线通过伦敦的格林威治天文台。根据当时英国人的说法,全世界从伦敦开始计算时间——至今仍然如此。时间对这些欧洲人和他们的海外后裔来说是最最重要的。如果你到这些国家去玩或居留,以下的一些建议有助于你适应一个凡事以时间为中心的文明社会。

你或许已经知道,准时到一分不差的地步在他们之间极受推崇。根据这些时间崇拜者的信条,时间是一个人所能拥有最宝贵的资产。他们说我们在这世上的时间不多,所以每一天都应该尽全力有效运用它。强迫他人等待而浪费他们的时间是生活紊乱的表现,也是一种低水平的自白。这也被视为是对等待者的一种侮辱,仿佛在说:"你的时间没什么重要。"对他们而言,这种态度本身简直就是罪恶!在工作上,即使只迟到个几次也会对你造成升迁或继续留在"原位"的差别。在社交约会上,迟到的最好情况是被认为行事马虎,而最坏的情况则是被等待的人拒绝往来。在学校中,千万不要骤然推开课堂的门宣称说:"老师,对不起,我迟到了。"这在许多国家中是习以为常的事。犯下迟到又打断准时上课进行的双重罪行,很可能一个印象恶劣的低分成绩就等着这位不幸的学生。

当然,有时候迟到是无可避免的,就像突如其来的交通阻塞、家庭紧急事故或者被通知的日期和地点错误等。当这些人之常情的不幸意外真的发生时,务必要解释迟到的理由。当然,最好也必须为引起无谓的等候道歉,并向对方保证绝不再犯。在现今这个移动电话普及的时代,如果避免不了要迟到超过 10 分钟,要尽可能事先打电话通知,生意上或职业上的会面,或者是重要约会更是如此。绝没有任何人想听到一句冷冰冰的:"你可以先打电话啊。"那一晚的约会就在这前奏声中毁掉了。

即使在盎格鲁-撒克逊人的文化中,也不是每件事都准时开始。许多轻松的派对是随着时间"开始"的;人何时到,派对便何时开始。在后院举办的烤肉和野餐通常也是如此。另一方面,晚宴则显然是吃饭时间办的,客人应该尽量准时(而非提前)到达。一句友好的"晚上过来吧"得用常识解释:傍晚太早过去可能让正在吃晚餐的主人尴尬,而太晚又可能吵到喜欢早睡的人。先打电话确定总是妥当之计。

记住时间对同文化或不同文化的人来说都一样很重要。人与人之间的关系是任何事也比不上的。如果你犯了和英、德友人约会迟到的"罪",道歉就好了。毕竟,很少有人故意要让别人等候。同时记住:"入乡随俗。"在说英语和德语的国家中,这句谚语就表示"时间不等人!"

2 *Vocabulary & Idioms* 单词短语注解 ✍

1. **go so far as to V** 甚至……
   In order to please her boyfriend, Mary went so far as to go over to Eddie's house every morning to cook him breakfast.
   为了要讨男友欢心,玛丽甚至不惜每天早上到艾迪家做早餐给他吃。

2. **be inseparable from...** 和……密不可分 / 离不开
   inseparable [ɪnˈsɛpərəbḷ] *a.* 不可分的,不能分离的
   The twin brothers are inseparable from each other; you always see them together.
   那对双胞胎兄弟离不开彼此,看他们总是形影不离的。

3. **coexist** [ˌkoɪgˈzɪst] *vi.* 同时存在,共存
   Even when countries disagree on their national policies, they must learn to coexist peacefully rather than go to war.
   虽然国与国之间政策互不兼容,但彼此还是要设法和平共存而不要兵戎相见。

4. **continuum** [kəˈtɪnjuəm] *n.* 连续体

5. **penchant** [ˈpɛntʃənt] *n.* 倾向,爱好

6. **transition** [trænˈzɪʃən] *n.* 转变,变迁;过渡期
   In our office's transition to a new computer system, many workers felt confused.
   我们公司在更换新的计算机系统期间,有许多员工都感到很困惑。

7. **be held in high esteem** 受到尊重 / 推崇
   hold...in high esteem 非常尊敬……
   The citizens of Thailand hold their king in high esteem; you can see his pictures everywhere there.
   泰国人民都非常尊敬他们的国王,他的相片在那儿随处可见。

8. **commodity** [kəˈmɑdətɪ] *n.* 有用的东西;商品

9. **border on...** 接近……
   Your homework borders on failing, Mark, but I will let you pass this time.

马克,你的功课近乎不及格,但这次我姑且让你过关。

10. **at best** 据最好的估计;充其量,至多

    at worst 在最坏的情况下

    Although Richard loves Mandy more than anything else in the world, she only likes him at best.

    虽然理查德爱曼蒂胜过一切,但她顶多只能算喜欢他而已。

    Though it's cloudy, let's still go hiking; at worst, if it starts to rain, we can take the bus back home.

    虽然是阴天,咱们还是去远足;最坏的情况就是如果开始下雨的话,我们可以坐公交车回家。

11. **assure sb + that** 从句 向某人保证……

    The computer salesman assured us that if anything went wrong with the computer, he would repair it.

    那个计算机推销员向我们保证如果计算机有任何毛病的话,他一定会修理。

12. **make every effort to V** 尽全力……

    If we make every effort to do our best in life, we will live without regret.

    如果我们在人生中尽全力做到最好的话,那我们此生将无所遗憾。

13. **on the other hand** 另一方面

    With my free time tonight I could go out to see a movie; on the other hand, I could use the time to catch up on my reading.

    我今晚有空可以去看场电影,但另一方面来说,我也可以利用这段时间来赶上我的读书进度。

14. **embarrass** [ɪmˈbærəs] vt. 使困窘 / 难为情

    Betty felt embarrassed when she spilled the tea she was going to serve.

    贝蒂将她端上来的茶洒出来了,觉得很难为情。

15. **be out of line** 不妥当,不合适;行为不检

    Everyone felt that Andy was out of line when he began to tell off-color jokes at the party.

    当安迪在派对上讲起黄色笑话时,每个人都觉得他这种行为有失检点。

Lesson 17

Precious and Semi-Precious Stones
宝石和半宝石

1 *Reading* 阅读

"My! What a beautiful ring you're wearing!" This compliment never fails to flatter and honor the lucky wearer of the ring or other pieces of jewelry bedecked with precious or semi-precious stones. Most people know the names of only some of these natural treasures. Many people are surprised to learn that all semi-precious stones can be bought inexpensively, not to mention that the precious stones can also be had for far less than one imagined. However, as with everything else in life, you have to pay for the best quality. This lesson will give the reader both information and tips on gem stones and their purchase.

Just what are precious and semi-precious stones? The word semi refers to anything which is half or only partial; thus, semi-precious stones are not precious, by definition. Actually, some high-quality semi-precious stones are far more expensive than some low-grade precious stones, so the terms "precious" and "semi-precious" when applied to stones do not refer necessarily to their cost.

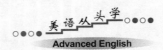

All authorities on gems agree that the diamond, ruby, sapphire, and emerald are precious stones. Some of these experts include the opal as a fifth precious stone while others consider the pearl in this class. The latter may surprise the reader, but on reflection, pearls are also a kind of stone, though organically produced by certain shellfish rather than by geologic forces.

Semi-precious stones include all other stones considered worthy of use in jewelry. The list of these stones is very long; suffice it to say that there are several hundred such stones, though most people are aware of only a couple of dozen of their names, and few people can readily recognize more than a couple of any type of stone at all.

Diamonds and the colored stones ruby, sapphire, and emerald are often considered the most expensive among all stones. This is generally true, though quality is more important than stone type on price. One can buy a "real sapphire" for US$10, but it would be considered not much better than junk to a jeweler. These professionals consider several features of stones before assessing their value. Carat size, or the weight of the stone (one carat = 200 milligrams) is one such feature. The cut of the stone is another. Some styles of cuts are considered more costly than others; besides, in the technical cutting of the gem from the rough stone, great care must be taken not to cut into or scratch the surface of the finished stone. The color is also important. Rubies, sapphires, and emeralds, for instance, in order to fetch the highest prices, must be solid colored throughout. Finally, clarity or translucence, with neither streaking nor a "cloudy" inner appearance, also determines the final price. Gems with these qualities are far and few between, commanding nearly astronomical prices. A good jeweler will advise you of these characteristics and how to look for and evaluate them yourself. Also remember that for a gem ring or pendant, roughly 70% of the value of the piece of jewelry is in the primary stone(s), with the rest in labor and metal.

Specific names of semi-precious stones are too numerous to mention, but jade is well known to Chinese. The finest jade (apple green in color) commands very high bids at auction. The trouble with semi-precious stones is that they are not so hard as precious stones so they far more easily scratch, crack, or chip. If this happens, the value of the semi-precious stones plummets. Diamonds, the hardest natural stone, and rubies and sapphires, the second hardest, are actually rather hard to deface.

Don't let anyone sell you a "good deal on a gem" on the street. Go to several professional jewelers before committing yourself — and your money — to a piece of jewelry with precious or semi-precious stones. Part of the value of that good piece of jewelry is the fact that it can be handed down generation after generation with increasing value. People in all cultures never seem to tire of the brilliance of gems.

　　"哇！你戴的戒指好漂亮！"这种赞美总是能够恭维并让佩戴镶着宝石或半宝石戒指或其他珠宝的幸运儿感到很有面子。大部分的人只知道一些这类天然珍宝的名字。许多人得知所有的半宝石都可用低价购得时都感到很惊讶，更别提拥有宝石的代价竟也低得出人意料之外。然而，就像生活中其他一切事物一样，最高质量必须多花钱才能得到。本课将提供读者有关宝石以及如何选购宝石的信息和秘诀。

　　究竟什么是宝石和半宝石呢？ semi 这个词指的是任何只有一半或是部分的东西；因此，就定义来说，半宝石并不算宝贵。但实际上，有些高质量的半宝石远比某些级数低的宝石要贵重许多，所以宝贵和半宝贵的名称用在石头上时，未必是指它们的价值而言。

　　所有的宝石权威都同意，钻石、红宝石、蓝宝石和绿宝石是宝石。其中有些专家把猫眼石列为第五种宝石，而有些专家则认为珍珠才是第五种宝石。后者也许会让读者觉得惊讶，但仔细想想，珍珠也是一种石头，尽管它是某些贝类而不是地质力产生的有机物体。

　　半宝石包括具有珠宝使用价值的其他所有石头在内。这些石头的名单非常长，可以说有好几百种这样的石头，虽然大部分的人只知道二十几个名称，而且仅有极少数人能够一眼就认出任何种类超过两种以上的石头。

　　钻石和红宝石、蓝宝石和绿宝石等有颜色的宝石常被认为是所有宝石中最名贵的。虽然质量对价格的影响比种类更为重要，但一般来说这是事实。虽然你可以用 10 美金买到一颗"真的蓝宝石"，但对珠宝商而言那颗蓝宝石比垃圾好不了多少。这些专家在评估宝石的价值之前会考虑几项要点。克拉大小，或宝石的重量（1 克拉＝200 毫克）即是其中一项。宝石的切割是另一项要点。有些切割方式被认为比其他方式价值高。此外，在把原石加工为宝石的专业切割过程中，必须非常小心，避免切到或刮伤宝石成品的表面。颜色也很重要。例如，红、蓝、绿宝石必须要整颗纯色才卖得到最好的价钱。最后，清澈度和透明度——没有细纹或内部色泽非呈"阴暗"——也决定了最终的价格。具有这些质量的宝石非常稀少，价格几乎都高达天文数字。好的珠宝商会告诉你这些特性以及你自己如何寻找并评估它们的价值。此外要记住，就宝石戒指或珠宝首饰而言，原石本身大约占珠宝价格的 70%，其他才是工钱和金属的钱。

半宝石的个别名称多得不胜枚举，但中国人对玉却一点也不陌生。最好的玉（颜色为苹果绿）在拍卖会上可以叫到非常高的价钱。半宝石的缺点是它们不如宝石坚硬，所以比较容易刮伤、龟裂或破成碎片。如果发生这种情形，半宝石的价值就一落千丈。钻石（最坚硬的天然石）和次硬的红、蓝宝石，要刮伤其表面其实相当困难。

别让任何人在街上卖你一颗"半买半相送"的宝石。在把自己——以及你的钱——投在一件镶宝石或半宝石的珠宝之前，多找几家专业的珠宝商。好珠宝的部分价值事实上来自于它可以代代相传而价值也越来越高。各种文化背景的人们对于耀眼的宝石似乎永远都不会厌倦。

2　*Vocabulary & Idioms* 单词短语注解　✍

1. **fail to V** 未能……
   We should never fail to help others when we can.
   当我们有能力时，我们应该努力帮助别人。

2. **flatter** [ˈflætɚ] *vt.* 谄媚，拍马屁
   Mrs. Anderson flattered the boss all day.
   安德森太太整天都在拍老板的马屁。

3. **...or other piece of jewelry bedecked with precious...**
   = ...or other piece of jewelry which is bedecked with precious...
   * be bedecked with... 装饰有／点缀着……
   The Christmas tree was bedecked with lights and cards from friends.
   那棵圣诞树上装饰了灯饰和来自朋友的卡片。

4. **semi-precious** [ˌsɛmɪˈprɛʃəs] *a.* 半珍贵的

5. **refer to...** 言及……；引用／参考……
   In the interview, I was asked to translate an English letter into Chinese without referring to a dictionary.
   在面试中，我被要求不查阅字典而将一封英文书信翻译成中文。

6. **reflection** [rɪˈflɛkʃən] *n.* 沉思
   on reflection 仔细考虑；熟思之后
   I had a big argument with my boyfriend; later, on reflection, I realized I was wrong.
   我和我男朋友大吵一架；后来，经过反思才明白我错了。

7. **geologic** [ˌdʒiəˈlɑdʒɪk] *a.* 地质学的，地质的

8. **suffice it to say + (that)** 从句 只要说……就够了
   A: How did Peter make out in the national lottery?
   B: Suffice it to say that he'll never have to work another day in his life.
   A：彼得买的国家彩票结果如何？
   B：可以说他这辈子都不需工作了。

9. **assess** [əˈsɛs] *vt.* 评估

After our car accident, the insurance company assessed the damage to our car and sent us a check.

在我们发生车祸后,保险公司评估我们车子的损害程度并把支票寄给我们。

10. **carat** [ˈkærət] *n.* 克拉(宝石的重量单位)

11. **clarity** [ˈklærətɪ] *n.* 清澈度

12. **translucence** [trænsˈlusn̩s] *n.* 半透明

13. **evaluate** [ɪˈvæljuˌet] *vt.* 评估

After her first three months of working for the company, Emily's performance was evaluated.

艾米莉在本公司工作三个月后,公司评估了她的工作表现。

14. **pendant** [ˈpɛndənt] *n.* (尤指项链、手镯等)垂饰

15. **command** [kəˈmænd] *vt.* 博得(赞赏、同情等)

The general is both so clever and compassionate that he commands great respect from his peers and the soldiers.

这位将军非常聪明又有同情心,所以他的同辈和部下都很尊敬他。

16. **auction** [ˈɔkʃən] *n.* 竞卖,拍卖 (at auction 拍卖)

When Prince Diana's clothes were sold at auction in New York, they sold for millions of U.S. dollars.

黛安娜王妃的衣物在纽约拍卖会中拍卖,售得了数百万美元。

17. **plummet** [ˈplʌmɪt] *vi.* 垂直或突然地坠下

After the two countries declared war on each other, their stock markets plummeted.

那两国彼此宣战后,他们的股市便大幅下跌。

18. **deface** [dɪˈfes] *vt.* 损毁……的外貌

Eric unintentionally defaced the paper currency when he spilled ink on it.

艾瑞克不小心把墨水洒在那张纸钞上而损毁了它。

19. **tire of...** 厌烦……; 讨厌……

I never tire of science-fiction movies. I could watch them all day and night.

我永远都看不厌科幻电影,我可以整日整夜地看。

Lesson ⑱

Hot Animals Around the World: The Koala

世界热门动物：树袋熊

① **Reading** 阅读

Why are all those people standing in line in the hot sun at the zoo? Maybe the zoo just opened a koala exhibit. With the survival rate of native Australian koalas on the rise, more and more zoos around the world are adding a "koala house" or "koala exhibit" to their roster of special animals. And the people keep coming, whether merely to catch a glimpse of one or, if really lucky at zoos which permit it, to hold and be photographed with one.

Why are koalas among the most beloved of all animals? At times referred to as "koala bear," this Australian marsupial is not a bear at all. It is one of the few tailless mammals besides the apes and man. Yet apes are not often considered cuddly; indeed, they are often feared for being either too large or too naughty. This Australian real-life teddy bear, instead, is the best of all worlds: it is quiet, soft, neither too large nor too small (adults are usually 65 to 80 cm. long), and really cuddly! With its soft fur, leathery nose, rounded ears, and big eyes, most people seem to melt when near one. Its disposition is perfect for children and adults alike; it rarely makes a fuss, even when being held. (Try that with a baby tiger!) No wonder the lines to see, hold, or just touch the koalas are always among the longest at zoos.

One reason zoos today are able to keep koalas is the rise in the koala population in its native habitat, the eucalyptus forests of southeastern Australia. This nation, famous for its unique fauna and flora, is now allowing applications for the professional export of its protected species to overseas zoological gardens. Once hunted for its fur, this arboreal leaf-eater is today protected by stringent laws and is making a slow but steady comeback. Indeed, everything about the koala seems slow. It sleeps more than 12 hours a day (often much more), eats only choice leaves from eucalyptus trees (which can now be grown in many zoos to provide the more than one kilogram of leaves that each adult koala needs per day), and rarely if at all descends to the ground because it is such a slow runner (from wild Australian dogs called dingoes or from human hunters). As koalas are such a great draw for visitors, many zoos are trying to include them among their species.

Mother koalas give birth to babies only every other year. These young ones, as with other marsupials, spend a period of time inside the mother's "pouch" before venturing out into the world. In the case of the koala, this pouch is located below and in back of the mother; the small koalas can climb out directly from the pouch and onto the mother's back before learning to

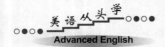

feed and fend for themselves. With all other marsupials, the pouch is located in the front, perhaps most famously with the kangaroo, where the "joey" can sometimes be seen popping its head out of its soft, warm pouch to survey the world about it safely.

Until the 1980s, zoologists feared that the koala might go the way of some other rare marsupials. Just as their eucalyptus habitat was being destroyed to make room for the ever-increasing suburban Australians, diseases peculiar to koalas began to take their toll. Combined with weak or non-existent laws against the hunting or poaching of this national treasure, the koala seemed doomed to extinction. Today, the koala has climbed back from the brink of extinction and is thriving again. Its main enemy today is forest fires. This slow-moving mammal cannot move quickly enough to escape the deadly fires which perennially ravage the land. With more land being set aside to protect this and other Australian species, however, the future of much of this special land's animal wealth seems secure.

All animals deserve man's protection, but some animals seem to attract the attention they need. The koala, one of the symbols of the great Down Under, is one of these. Holding a koala is fun, educational, and inspiring. If Australians could co-operate to save this special species, mankind should be able to prevent the extinction of all other animals, too.

　　那些人为什么顶着大太阳在动物园排队呢？也许是该动物园新推出树袋熊展吧。随着澳大利亚原产地树袋熊存活率的上升，世界各地有越来越多的动物园正在他们的珍奇动物名单上增加一项"树袋熊馆"或"树袋熊展"。而人潮不断涌入，不管是仅仅为了看一眼树袋熊也好，或者如果幸运的话，有些动物园还准许游客抱着树袋熊拍照。

　　为何树袋熊会在最受喜爱的动物名单中呢？虽然有时被称为"考拉熊"，这种澳大利亚有袋动物却根本不是熊。它是除了猿猴和人类以外，少数没有尾巴的哺乳动物之一。然而猿猴通常不被认为适合搂抱；的确，它们常因体型太大或太顽劣而令人害怕。反观这种澳大利亚活生生的玩具熊在各种动物世界中是最棒的：它安静、柔软、体型不大也不小(成年树袋熊身长通常为 65 到 80 厘米)而且非常适合搂抱！有着柔软的毛皮、皮革般的鼻子、圆圆的耳朵和大眼睛，大部分的人一靠近树袋熊心都软了起来。它的性情非常适合小孩以及大人，即使被抱住也很少会乱动。(你去抱一只小老虎试试看！)难怪动物园里要去看、抱或只是摸一下树袋熊的队伍总是大排长龙。

　　今天动物园能够豢养树袋熊的原因之一是原产地——亦即澳大利亚东南部的桉树林——的树袋熊数量增加了。该国以出产独特动物群和植物群闻名，如今开放专业申请将其保育类动物出口到海外的动物园去。这种以树为家的食叶族动物曾经因其毛皮而遭猎捕，如今因受到严格法令的保护，其数量成长正慢慢地回稳。的确，树袋熊的一切似乎都很慢。它一天要睡超过 12 小时(往往还更多)，只选择吃桉树的叶子(许多动物园现在可以在园内种植桉树，以供应成年树袋熊每天超过 1 公斤以上的叶子需要量)，而且它几乎很少下到地面上来,因为它跑得很慢(躲不过叫做"dingo"的澳大利亚野犬或猎人)。由于树袋熊对参观者有巨大的吸引力,许多动物园都设法要把它们列进他们的动物种类里面。

母树袋熊每两年才生产一次。小树袋熊就像其他有袋动物一样,在进入这世界冒险之前会先在母亲的"袋子"里待上一段时间。就树袋熊来说,袋子位于母亲的背后下方,在学会觅食和独立以前,小树袋熊可以从袋里出来直接爬到母亲的背上。其他有袋动物的袋子则位于前面——最有名的也许是袋鼠了——有时可以看见小家伙从它柔软而温暖的袋子里探出头来,安全地浏览周围的世界。

一直到20世纪80年代,动物学家们都还很担心树袋熊可能会步上其他一些稀少有袋动物的后尘。正当它们的桉树栖息地遭砍伐以容纳一直增加的澳大利亚郊区居民的同时,树袋熊特有的疾病也开始大量削减它们的数量。再加上禁止捕杀或偷猎这种国宝级动物的法令形同虚设,树袋熊在当时似乎是注定要灭绝了。今天,树袋熊从绝种边缘爬了回来并且再度繁衍。如今它的主要敌人是森林火灾,这种行动迟缓的哺乳动物跑得不够快,无法逃过那些不断破坏土地的致命火灾。然而,随着更多土地被预留下来保护诸如此类的澳大利亚动物,这块特殊土地上的大部分动物财富前景似乎很乐观。

所有的动物都应该受人类保护,但似乎只有一些动物能引起需要的关注。树袋熊,这澳大利亚大地的象征之一即为其中一例。抱着树袋熊很好玩、而且也具教育性和启发性。如果澳大利亚人可以通力合作拯救这种特别的动物,那么人类也应该能够避免所有其他动物的灭亡。

2 *Vocabulary & Idioms* 单词短语注解

1. **stand in line** 排成一列，排队
   The funs stand in line to buy tickets to the concerts.
   歌迷们排成一列购买演唱会门票。

2. **on the rise** 在增加；在上涨
   AIDS is on the rise in those countries which are not educating their people about this new disease.
   在那些没有教育其人民有关艾滋病的国家中，这种新疾病的病例一直在增加中。

3. **make a fuss** 紧张，急躁；大惊小怪
   Parents should not make a fuss when their kids make small mistakes.
   当小孩子犯了小错时，父母不应该大惊小怪。

4. **make a comeback** 卷土重来；东山再起
   Though the politician once lost an election, he made a comeback and became the provincial governor.
   那个政治家虽然曾落选过一次，但他卷土重来并当上了省长。

5. **if at all** 如果真有其事的话
   In deserts it rains very little, if at all, in the dry season.
   旱季时，沙漠上就算下雨，雨量也非常稀少。

6. **descend** [dɪˈsɛnd] *vi.* 下降；下来
   The airplane descended from 28,000 feet to 10,000 feet before beginning its final approach.
   那架飞机在开始降落前从 28000 英尺的高度下降到 10000 英尺。

7. **venture** [ˈvɛntʃɚ] *vi.* 冒险从事
   The winter is so long and brutal in Alaska that most people do not venture out of their home until spring.
   阿拉斯加的冬天非常漫长而且严寒，因此大部分人都不会冒险外出直到春天来临为止。

8. **fend for oneself** 自谋生计；独立生活

With both parents killed in a car crash and no other relatives, the teenage brothers had to fend for themselves.

由于双亲在一场车祸中身亡,而且又没有亲戚可以投靠,那几个少年兄弟只得自食其力。

9. **pop** [pɑp] *vt.* 突然伸出 & *vi.* 突然出现

If you look carefully, you sometimes see small heads popping out of the bird nest.

如果你仔细看,有时候可以瞧见几颗小脑袋从鸟巢里探出头来。

10. **make room for...** 让出地方给……

With the birth of their second child, the Williams had to make room for her in their son's room.

随着第二个小孩的出世,威廉夫妇必须在他们儿子的房中挪出地方来给他们的女儿。

11. **be peculiar to...** 是……特有的

peculiar [pɪ'kjuljə] *a.* 特殊的;特有的

Being blind is not peculiar to bats; some snakes are also sightless.

并非只有蝙蝠的眼睛看不到,有些蛇也同样眼盲。

12. **take its / their toll** (由于患病、事故等)造成伤亡 / 损失

Every year typhoons take their toll of human life, livestock, and property throughout the Asia-Pacific region.

每年台风都会横扫亚太地区造成人畜伤亡及财产损失。

13. **doomed** [dumd] *a.* 命运注定的

be doomed to... 注定……

Some animal species are doomed to extinction because their habitats are being destroyed by land development.

栖息地因土地开发而遭破坏,因此有些物种注定了要灭绝。

14. **ravage** ['rævɪdʒ] *vt.* 蹂躏;荼毒;破坏

The earthquake ravaged the land, even causing mountainsides to crumble and fall.

那场地震使大地遭到破坏,甚至还引起了泥石流和山崩。

Lesson 19

Asian Americans
亚裔美国人

1   *Reading* 阅读

    In the last census conducted by the U.S. government in 1990, one fact caught many people by surprise: the percentage of Asian Americans had grown faster than any other segment of the population. European Americans had, as expected, continued their slow decline in percentage of the total U.S. population, though they were still dominant at about 76%. Black Americans had stabilized at about 12% of the population. Hispanics had continued their fast growth and were, at 9%, aimed at toppling Black Americans as the country's largest minority group. The growth in Asian Americans, however, surged from only 2% of the total U.S. population in the 1980 census to 3% in 1990. By the year 2000 at least 4% of Americans will be of Asian ancestry. This relatively huge increase has caught many demographers by surprise. Clearly a new force is developing in U.S. demography, but few people seem to appreciate its implications. The Asian Americans are here and are here to stay, but exactly who are they, and what does their rapid increase mean for the country as a whole?

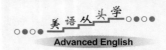
As a multi-ethnic nation, it should not be surprising that Asian Americans are becoming an increasingly large and important sector of the "rainbow nation" some Americans prefer to think of their country as. Indeed, the only surprise about this segment growing so fast is why it has not occurred sooner. After all, Asia is home to 60% of all the people in the world. However, Asia is also a vast land, encompassing East, Southeast, South, and West Asia, each region significantly different from its neighbors. Further, there is no sense of unity within Asia, as there is, say, among European or Latin American countries. Indeed, the term "Asian Americans" is more a fiction of the European mind, since people from this area unfailingly refer to themselves as Chinese, Japanese, Filipino, etc., rather than as Asian-Americans.

For more than 100 years, three primary groups of Asians emigrated to the United States: Japanese, Chinese, and Filipino. However, since the end of the Vietnam War, other groups from Asia have become increasingly prominent, especially those from Vietnam, Korea, and India. In addition, Iranians and Israelis from Southwestern Asia have also entered the U.S. in large numbers.

The patterns of Asian immigration have changed greatly over the past 30 years. In 1970, 96% of Asian Americans were Chinese, Japanese, or Filipino; as of 1997, this percentage had dropped to 55%! In that year, 24% of Asian Americans claimed Chinese ancestry, 21% Filipino, and 10% Japanese.

The "newcomers" among Asian Americans include the Indians at 13%, Vietnamese at 11%, and Koreans also at 11%.

What real numbers are we talking about? There were estimated to be nearly 9,600,000 Asian Americans in the U.S. in 1997. With such a high growth rate, there will be more than 10 million of them this year and perhaps 32 million in 2050 (about 8% of the total U.S. population at that time). Where do Asian Americans live? Currently, an astounding 40% of this regional group lives in California. Other states with relatively large Asian American populations include New York, Hawaii, Texas, New Jersey, Washington (the state), and Illinois (which contains Chicago). Overall, the West is home to 54% of all Asian Americans, the Northeast 19%, the South 16%, and the Midwest 11%.

What about future trends? As Asian nations continue to prosper, it is likely that they will contribute more to U.S. immigration, especially from Southeast Asia and India. All of these groups continue to have above-average birth rates. On the other hand, Chinese and Japanese Americans have very low birth rates; consequently, the percentage of these ethnic groups among the total will continue to fall. All in all, America can look forward to an increasingly large number of Asians enriching their new home with their diligence, investment, and diverse cultural contributions.

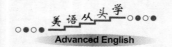
　　美国政府于 1990 年所做的人口普查中,有一项事实让许多人感到很惊讶:亚裔美国人的增长百分比要比其他任何一个人口组成部分都快。欧裔美国人一如所料在美国人口总数中所占的百分比继续缓慢下降,虽然他们还占大约 76% 的绝大多数。美国黑人继续维持约 12% 的人口比率。拉丁美洲人持续快速增长,约占 9% 的人口比率,目标是压倒黑人成为美国人数最多的少数民族团体。然而,亚裔美国人增长百分比从 1980 年普查时只占美国总人口的 2%,到 1990 年时冲到了 3%。到 2000 年,至少会有 4% 的美国人具有亚裔血统。这种颇为可观的增加量使得许多人口统计学家感到很惊讶。显然在美国的人口结构中有一股新的势力正在发展,但似乎很少有人了解到它的含义。亚裔美国人来了,并且定居下来,但他们究竟是谁? 他们的迅速增加对整个美国而言意味着什么?

　　作为一个多元民族的国家,亚裔美国人日益壮大成为这"彩虹国家"(有些美国人较喜欢这称呼)的重要一环应该是没什么好令人惊讶的。的确,这一部分人口快速成长唯一令人惊讶的是为何它没有早点发生。毕竟,全世界有 60% 的人口住在亚洲。而亚洲疆域亦很广大,包括了东亚、东南亚、南亚和西亚,各区域彼此之间差异相当大。再者,亚洲各国缺乏整体意识,不像好比说欧洲或拉丁美洲国家之间一样。的确,"亚裔美国人"的称呼大体上是欧洲人想出来的,因为来自亚洲地区的人们总是称自己为中国人、日本人、菲律宾人等等,而不是亚裔美国人。

　　过去 100 多年来,移民到美国的亚洲人主要有三个族群:日本人、中国人和菲律宾人。不过,自从越战结束后,其他亚洲族群亦不断激增,特别是来自越南、韩国和印度的人。此外,来自亚洲西南部的伊朗人和以色列人也大量涌入美国。

  过去 30 年来,亚洲移民的形态改变甚巨。1970 年时,96% 的亚裔美国人是中国人、日本人或菲律宾人;到了 1997 年,这个比率下降到 55%!同年有 24% 的亚裔美国人申报为中国血统、21% 为菲律宾血统,10% 是日本血统。"新来的亚裔美国人"则包括 13% 的印度人,11% 的越南人和同样是 11% 的韩国人。

  我们所说的实际数目为何?据估计美国的亚裔美国人于 1997 年时有将近 960 万人。以这么高的增长比率计算,今年他们的人数将超过 1000 万,2050 年时可能达到 3200 万(届时将约占美国总人口数的 8%)。亚裔美国人住在哪里?目前,该群体有高达 40% 居住在加州。其他拥有相当数量亚裔美国人口的州包括纽约州、夏威夷州、得州、新泽西州、华盛顿州和伊利诺伊州(包含芝加哥)等。整体来看,有 54% 的亚裔美国人住在西部,19% 在东北部,16% 在南部,11% 在中西部。

  未来趋势又是如何?由于亚洲国家持续繁荣,很可能会有更多亚洲人移民到美国,尤其是来自东南亚和印度。所有这些族群出生率将继续维持在平均以上。另一方面,华裔和日裔美国人出生率则非常低;因此,这些族群占总人数的比率将继续下降。总而言之,美国将可期待人数日益庞大的亚洲人以其勤奋、投资和多元的文化贡献来丰富他们的新家园。

2 *Vocabulary & Idioms* 单词短语注解

1. **catch sb by surprise** 令某人大吃一惊

   When our dinner guests arrived 15 minutes early, they caught us by surprise; we were not yet finished with our preparations.

   我们晚餐的客人早到 15 分钟让我们大吃一惊,因为我们尚未做好准备事宜。

2. **percentage** [pɚˈsɛntɪdʒ] *n.* 百分比

3. **segment** [ˈsɛgmənt] *n.* 部分(本文指人口组成部分)

4. **dominant** [ˈdɑmənənt] *a.* 占优势的,最具影响力的

   The Han people are the dominant ethnic group in China, not only in population but also in influence.

   汉族人是中国最占优势的民族,不仅指人口方面,在影响力方面也是。

5. **stabilize** [ˈstɛblˌaɪz] *vi.* 稳定

   The stock market stabilized after investors realized that the economy was not so bad after all.

   在投资人明白经济终究没有那么萧条后,股市便稳定下来了。

6. **Hispanic** [hɪsˈpænɪk] *n.* 西班牙裔美国人,拉丁裔美国人

7. **topple** [ˈtɑpḷ] *vt.* 使倒塌

   The earthquake toppled some large buildings, but many small ones remained intact.

   那次地震震垮了几栋大型建筑,但是许多小型建筑却安然无恙。

8. **minority** [maɪˈnɔrətɪ] *a.* 占少数的

9. **surge** [sɜdʒ] *vi.* 激增

   The price of oil surged in the 1970s; this was referred to as the "oil crunch."

   70 年代石油价格大幅上涨;这段时间被称为"石油危机"。

10. **demographer** [dɪˈmɑgrəfɚ] *n.* 人口统计学家

11. **as a whole** 就整体而言

There are old-fashioned women and feminists, but what do you think of women as a whole?

有旧式妇女和女权主义者两种界定,但就整体来看,你怎么看待女性的呢?

12. **multi-ethnic** [ˌmʌltɪˈɛθnɪk] *a.* 多种族的

13. **think of A as B** 视 A 为 B

= regard / look upon A as B

Most New Yorkers think of their home as the world's most exciting city.

大部分的纽约人把他们的家乡视为世界上最刺激的城市。

14. **be home to...** 是……的生长 / 聚集地

China is home to the panda, one of the world's most interesting animals.

中国是世界上最有趣动物之一熊猫的聚集地。

15. **encompass** [ɪnˈkʌmpəs] *vt.* 包括,包含

Antarctica encompasses more land than all of China, but that land is virtually all ice.

南极洲的面积大于中国的总面积,但南极洲几乎都是冰。

16. **refer to A as B** 把 A 称作 B

By referring to his female classmates as "chicks," Evan made them angry.

伊凡把他的女同学称作"马子",这让她们很生气。

17. **prominent** [ˈprɑmənənt] *a.* 突出的;重要的

18. **in large numbers** 大批地,大群地

Fish in large numbers gather off the coast of Peru every year.

每年有大批鱼群聚集在秘鲁外海。

19. **estimate** [ˈɛstəˌmet] *vt.* 估计

I estimate that we will arrive in Berlin after another two hours of driving.

我估计再开两个钟头,我们就到柏林了。

20. **astounding** [əˈstaʊndɪŋ] *a.* 令人大吃一惊的

Lesson 20

Scourge of the Plains: Tornadoes

平原之祸——龙卷风

1   *Reading* 阅读

Ellen Mae stepped out of her two-story home in central Illinois. "Fine morning," she said to herself after checking the weather, and then went back inside. The radio had mentioned a severe storm advisory, but the sky was clear, and it was rather calm. Still, she decided to be safe and kept her radio on.

About noon she felt a strange kind of pressure. Looking out her window, she noticed the sky had become overcast. Low, rounded, oddly colored clouds were forming. It was still and oppressive. "Maybe I'd better listen to the weather report again," she murmured to herself.

Again the radio forecast severe weather, warning citizens to listen for the siren and seek shelter should a twister, scourge of the plains, come down from the heavens like a "Devil's tail." "I doubt it'll happen over Crossville," she comforted herself. "It always happens in other towns."

By two o'clock it started to rain, and the wind picked up, too. The apple tree in front of Ellen Mae's house started to pitch back and forth violently. Her dogs started to bark and howl, and that was when she heard that awful sound.

At first she thought it was a locomotive, but she quickly remembered that there was no railroad within 20 miles of her home. She looked into the sky and then noticed it, a dark, swirling mass of black cloud sucking up everything it touched and hurling objects at horrific speeds straight up or straight to the side. Ellen Mae ran as fast as she could down into her storm cellar, a special room which had been prepared by her father when he was still alive. This room was located in the southwestern corner of the basement and had a door with a strong bolt. Ellen Mae ran in, locked the door behind her, and waited.

She didn't have long to wait. With shrieking and swooshing sounds right out of hell, the funnel cloud passed directly over her house. An enormous vacuum cleaner, the twister blew the house apart, scattering five generations of Ellen Mae's family belongings over half the rural county she lived in. Within minutes, the winds had stopped, and an eerie silence replaced the cacophony of moments earlier. Feeling it was now safe to venture out, Ellen Mae unbolted the door, peered out, and started to cry. She could look straight up into the sky. Even though she had lost her house and everything in it, she felt lucky. She knew that every year, hundreds of people could perish in tornadoes.

Just what are these "devil storms"? They go by many names across the Great Plains of the United States and Canada, not to mention many other countries around the world, but tornadoes are perennial plagues in central North America. The conditions there — flat land and proximity to cold air masses (from the Rocky Mountains to the west) and warm and humid air masses (from the Gulf of Mexico to the south) provide the optimum breeding ground for tornadoes. According to the U.S. National Weather Service, tornadoes form from thunderclouds and can reach swirling speeds in excess of 600 kilometers per hour. They last from minutes to an hour or more and can blast their way across as much as 150 kilometers of terrain at about 50 kilometers per hour. They vary in width from a few meters to 1,500 meters (average 200 meters). And they strike fear into the hearts of everyone.

The safest place to be when a tornado is in one's area is a basement, preferably the southwest corner (where the tornado normally comes from). If driving, track due north or south, as tornadoes usually move from west to east. Weather prediction and tracking these days is far superior to earlier years, but tornadoes can appear without any warning at all, as a large one did right in the heart of Salt Lake City in 1999, leaving a trail of shocked, wounded, and dead as well as pulverized property.

Though relatively few people have ever seen a tornado, those who have wish they hadn't. The "Finger of God" is nature's atmospheric fury at its worst.

　　梅艾伦走出她位于伊利诺伊州中部两层楼的家,察看过天气之后,她自言自语说:"美丽的早晨。"然后回到屋里。收音机提到一则有关强烈暴风雨的警讯,但天空晴朗无云,一切都相当平静。尽管如此,为了安全起见她还是决定让收音机开着。

　　大约中午时分,她感觉到一股奇怪的气压。从窗口望出去,她看到天空乌云密布,而且一团团颜色怪异的云正在低空形成,空气凝滞而且沉闷。"也许我最好再收听一下气象报告,"她喃喃自语着。

　　收音机里再度传来恶劣天气的预报,警告市民注意收听警报,万一龙卷风这平原祸害突然像"恶魔的尾巴"一样从天而降时要寻找掩护。"我想不会发生在克罗斯镇吧,"她自我安慰道,"因为每次都是发生在其他镇上。"

　　到了下午两点开始下起雨来,风也变强了。梅艾伦屋前的苹果树开始剧烈地左右摇晃,她的几只狗开始狂吠嚎叫。就在这时,她听到了那个可怕的声音。

　　起初她以为是火车头,但她很快就想到她家附近方圆 20 多公里内并没有铁路。她向天空一望,然后看到了一大团黑压压旋转的乌云将所有碰到的东西都吸了进去,并且以骇人的速度将各种物体直接甩到空中或旁边。梅艾伦飞快地跑进躲暴风雨的地窖,那是她父亲生前设置的一间特殊房间。这个房间位于地下室的西南角落,有一道门闩很坚固的门。梅艾伦跑进去锁上身后的门然后等待。

　　没等多久,那夹带着尖锐刺耳呼啸声的漏斗云就直接扫过她的房子。龙卷风就像支巨大的吸尘器一样把梅艾伦的房屋吹散,并将她家中传了五代的家产撒落在半个她所居住的乡村小镇上。几分钟之后风停了,一片诡异的宁静代替了片刻之前的喧嚣声。心想现在出去很安全了,梅艾伦打开门闩往外一瞧,然后就开始哭了起来,她抬头就可以直接看到天空。即使失去房子和里面所有的一切,她仍觉得很幸运。她知道每年都可能会有好几百人在龙卷风中丧生。

这些"魔鬼暴风"到底是什么呢?它们在美、加大平原中就有许多种名称,更不用说全世界其他许多国家了,只不过在北美中部龙卷风是长期性的祸害。那儿的情况——地势平坦而且又靠近冷气团(来自西边的落基山脉)和湿暖气团(来自南边的墨西哥湾)——提供了龙卷风绝佳的滋生地。根据美国国家气象局的资料,龙卷风是由雷雨云所形成,旋转速度每小时可高达 600 公里以上。它们持续的时间从几分钟到 1 小时或更久,并且能以 50 公里左右的时速横扫过 150 公里之地。它们的宽度从几米到 1500 米都有(平均 200 米),并将恐惧深植在每个人的心中。

龙卷风来袭时最安全的去处是地下室,最好位于西南角落(龙卷风通常从这个方向过来)。如果正在开车,就往正北或正南方向走,因为龙卷风通常由西向东移动。现今的气象预测和追踪远比早期先进,但龙卷风会毫无预警地出现,就像 1999 年出现在盐湖城市中心的大龙卷风一样,留下一路的惊魂者、伤者、死者以及支离破碎的房屋。

虽然曾经见过龙卷风的人相当少,但看过的人都希望他们从未看过。这只"上帝的手指"是自然界大气之怒的终极展现。

2 *Vocabulary & Idioms* 单词短语注解

1. **scourge** [skɜdʒ] *n.* 灾害, 祸患

2. **oppressive** [əˈprɛsɪv] *a.* (天气)沉闷的, 闷热的; 压迫的

3. **murmur** [ˈmɜmə] *vt. & vi.* 低语, 低声而言
   Grandpa was so old that he murmured nearly everything that he said,
   so we couldn't understand him.
   祖父年纪大到几乎什么话都喃喃自语,因此我们都没办法了解他
   的意思。

4. **forecast** [ˈfɔrkæst] *vt.* 预报, 预测
   动词三态: forecast, forecast / forecasted, forecast / forecasted。
   The sales manager forecast a boom year, so we ordered many products
   to sell.
   业务经理预测今年生意兴隆,所以我们订了许多货物来销售。

5. **...should a twister, scourge of the plains, come down from
   the heavens like a "Devil's tail."**
   = ...if a twister, scourge of the plains, should come down from the
   heavens like a "Devil's tail."

6. **comfort** [ˈkʌmfət] *vt.* 安慰; 鼓舞
   The school counselor comforted the boy after his cat died.
   学校的辅导老师安慰那个死了猫咪的男孩。

7. **By two o'clock it started to rain, and the wind <u>picked up</u>,
   too.**
   = By two o'clock it started to rain, and the wind <u>blew stronger</u>, too.

8. **pitch** [pɪtʃ] *vi.* 颠簸; 向下倾斜
   During the earthquake, our apartment pitched back and forth.
   地震发生时,我们的公寓前后摇晃。

9. **suck up...** 吸进……
   Bobby sucked up all the milk in his glass with a straw.
   巴比用吸管吸光了他玻璃杯里的牛奶。

10. **hurl** [hɜl] *vt.* 用力投掷

David was so angry that he hurled a few rocks at the young men who had scratched his car.

大卫气得拿几块石头扔向那些刮伤他车子的年轻人。

11. **bolt** [bolt] *n.* 门闩 & *vt.* 闩(门)

unbolt [ʌn'bolt] *vt.* 拔开(门闩)

The farmer herded his cattle inside the corral, closed the gate, and bolted it firmly.

那个农民将他的牛赶进畜栏后就关上大门并闩紧。

12. **scatter** ['skætə] *vt.* 撒布，散播 & *vi.* 四散，离散

As soon as Millie turned on the fan, her paperwork scattered around the room.

米莉一打开电风扇,她的文件就在房间中到处散了开来。

13. **cacophony** [kə'kɑfəni] *n.* 刺耳的声音

14. **perish** ['pɛrɪʃ] *vi.* 死亡；灭亡

In the big fire, at least four people perished before the firemen could come.

那场大火中,至少有四个人在消防队员赶去前就已命丧火场。

15. **proximity** [prɑk'sɪmətɪ] *n.* 接近

16. **optimum** ['ɑptəməm] *a.* 最适宜的；最佳条件的

17. **in excess of...** 超过……

The sports car is capable of speeds in excess of 200 m/h.

那辆跑车的时速最快可超过 200 英里。

18. **vary** ['vɛrɪ] *vi.* 改变；不同；有变化

These computers vary in price according to how many functions they can perform.

这些计算机的价格依功能多寡而有所不同。

19. **pulverized** ['pʌlvə,raɪzd] *a.* 毁坏的

pulverize ['pʌlvə,raɪz] *vt.* 粉碎；毁坏

The bulldozer pulverized the old building so that it could be cleared to prepare for a new one.

推土机破坏那栋旧建筑物，以便能清除后准备盖新的。

20. **at its worst** 在最恶劣的状况下

The typhoon dumped 8 centimeters of rain an hour at its worst.

那场台风刮得最厉害时，1小时就降了8厘米的雨。

Lesson 21

What's So Big about Moby Dick?

白鲸记

Reading 阅读

A pretty, young lady goes swimming alone off the coast of New England in twilight. She is an agile swimmer, full of grace and speed. Without warning, though, she disappears from sight, only to reappear a moment later, screaming in pain. A few shocking moments later, she is again dragged under the water, this time only to reappear the next morning in pieces on the shore.

Sound familiar? By now nearly everyone has seen or heard the story of a killer Great White Shark in Jaws, a hit novel turned into a blockbuster movie. Few people realize, however, that the story broadly follows the events depicted in what many people consider one of the best of American novels. Published in 1851, *Moby Dick* has been making waves ever since.

The author, Herman Melville, was born in New York on August 1, 1819. As a youth in a large family he suffered many insecurities due to the family's constantly changing fortunes. As a young man he worked as a farmer and seaman, the latter providing most of the material for several of his later novels and essays. In his 20s Melville found fame with two novels based on imaginary happenings in the South Pacific. *Moby Dick*, ironically, was not well received. Afterwards, Melville produced another masterpiece, *Billy Budd*. He continued writing until his death in 1891.

Why has *Moby Dick* since become such a classic despite its initial lukewarm reception? Melville had a keen eye for not only the human condition but for the tenor of his times: the United States was in his day a country of disadvantaged and mistreated immigrants (many of whom became sailors and laborers), with untrammeled capitalism crushing both nature and man underneath its new country exuberance. His stress on the individual and fate — often pessimistically, or at least realistically — were harbingers of the future of literature.

Why does the story of *Moby Dick* continue to enthrall generation after generation? The story line is simple enough: a mad sea captain vows revenge against a white whale which, on a previous expedition, bit off one of his legs. In his vain attempt at "justice" against nature, the captain meets the ultimate tragedy. This was no documentary, however; the characters and setting become vehicles for far larger and more universal themes of the setbacks and successes of the human spirit as well as its darker urges. So accurately does Melville depict the whaling scenes and sea voyages that the reader is taken on an exhilarating ride. Coupled with the absorbing, mad

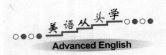

Captain Ahab, the book is "a good read" even by 20th century standards.

Earlier last century, the Nobel Prize winner Ernest Hemingway penned *The Old Man and the Sea*, another story of a man's struggle with nature on the open ocean. This theme strikes a chord in Americans, whose culture developed along the Atlantic coast of North America and whose seaward passage from the Old World took them to the colonies of the 18th century or the young country of the 19th century by the millions. This fascination with the maritime still holds today: over half the population of the United States lives in counties touching the Atlantic, Pacific, or Gulf coasts. Perhaps some future writer will once again use the metaphor of sailors and the sea to create yet another Great American Novel.

　　黄昏时刻，一位年轻貌美的小姐独自在新英格兰外海游泳。她是一名游泳健将，泳姿优雅而动作矫健。但毫无预警地，她从视线上消失，一会儿后再出现时只见她痛苦地尖叫着。经过几次惊险的场面后，她又被拖到水底下，只是这次在次日早晨再出现时却只剩下破碎的肢体散落在岸边。

　　听起来耳熟吗？到现在几乎每个人都看过或听过《大白鲨》这部由畅销小说改编的卖座电影中那头吃人大白鲨的故事。然而，却很少有人知道故事的大部分情节源自许多人公认的最佳美国小说之一中所描述的情节。《白鲸记》自 1851 年出版以来即不时引发争议。

　　作者赫尔曼·梅尔维尔 1819 年 8 月 1 日在纽约出生。他生长在一个大家庭中，少年时因家境不断变化而极没有安全感。年轻时他当过农民和船员，后者提供了他日后几部小说和文章所用的大部分题材。梅尔维尔 20 多岁时即以南太平洋虚构事件为根据的两本小说崭露头角。具有讽刺意味的是，《白鲸记》却未受好评。之后，梅尔维尔又写了另一本杰作《毕利·伯德》。他持续不断地写作直到 1891 年去世为止。

　　《白鲸记》最初并未造成轰动，但为何后来会成为经典之作呢？梅尔维尔对人情世故及当时的思想潮流皆具有独到的眼光：在他那个时代，美国是一个由受欺凌的弱势移民组成的国家（其中有很多移民成为船员和苦力），而无限制的资本主义将大自然和人类踩碎在这个新国家的繁荣之下。他对个人和命运的强调——通常是悲观的，或者至少是写实的——预告了文学未来之路。

　　为何《白鲸记》的故事不断吸引一代又一代的读者呢？故事的情节实在很简单：一个疯狂的船长誓言报复在之前远航途中咬掉他

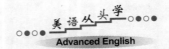
一条腿的一只白鲸。在他向大自然讨回"公道"的徒劳的尝试中，这位船长终究落得悲剧的下场。然而，故事并不像纪录片，它的人物和场景传达了更宽广、更具世界性的主题，反映出人类心灵的成败及黑暗的欲望。梅尔维尔对捕鲸情形和航海的描写是如此精确，读者仿佛踏上一段刺激的海上之旅。加上独具魅力的疯狂船长艾哈伯，这本书即使以20世纪的标准来看也是一本"好书"。

　　20世纪初时，诺贝尔奖得主海明威写了另一本人类和大海搏斗的故事《老人与海》。这个主题在美国人心中引起共鸣，美国人的文化沿着北美大西洋岸发展，他们的海上通道将数以百万计的人们从旧世界带到18世纪的殖民地或19世纪时的新兴国家。这种对海洋的迷恋到今天仍然存在：超过半数的美国人口住在大西洋、太平洋或墨西哥湾沿岸的市郡。或许将来会有某个作家再度使用水手和大海的暗喻，创造出另一本伟大的美国小说。

2 *Vocabulary & Idioms* 单词短语注解

1. **twilight** [ˈtwaɪˌlaɪt] *n.* 黄昏；曙光

2. **agile** [ˈædʒaɪl] *a.* 敏捷的

3. **scream** [skrim] *vi.* 尖叫
   Little Billy screamed when the doctor gave him a polio vaccinatin.
   小比利在医生为他注射小儿麻痹疫苗时大声尖叫。

4. **blockbuster** [ˈblɑkˌbʌstɚ] *n.* 轰动的人或事物
   The Star Wars movies have all been blockbusters; they attracted millions of people to theaters around the world.
   "星球大战"系列电影一直都很卖座；它们吸引了全世界数百万人到电影院观赏。

5. **depict** [dɪˈpɪkt] *vt.* 描述，描写
   The TV documentary depicted life in the Andean countries very realistically.
   那部电视纪录片非常真实地描述安第斯山脉各国的生活。

6. **Published in 1851, *Moby Dick* has been making waves ever since.**
   → Since *Moby Dick* was published in 1851, it has ever been making waves.
   1851 年《白鲸记》出版后，一直受到人们的关注。

7. **make waves** 兴风作浪；引起骚动
   Paula made waves at the school dance when she wore a very short mini-skirt.
   保拉穿了条超短迷你裙而在学校舞会上引起一阵骚动。

8. **constantly** [ˈkɑnstəntlɪ] *adv.* 不断地；时常地

9. **imaginary** [ɪˈmædʒəˌnɛrɪ] *a.* 想象中的，虚构的
   imaginative [ɪˈmædʒəˌnetɪv] *a.* 富于想象力的
   imaginable [ɪˈmædʒɪnəbl̩] *a.* 想象得到的
   * imaginable 常与最高级形容词连用，且常不译出。

Science fiction is an imaginary world based on science and technology.
科幻小说是一个以科学和技术为基础的虚构世界。

In order to be a good writer one must have an imaginatvie mind.
想成为好的作家，必须要有想象力。

That painting has the most beautiful combination of imaginable colors.
那幅画极尽色彩组合之美。

10. **masterpiece** [ˈmæstəˌpis] *n.* 杰作；极品

11. **lukewarm** [ˌlukˈwɔrm] *a.* 冷淡的

12. **have a keen eye for...** 对……有敏锐 / 独到的眼光
    Mom has a keen eye for good fruit; she always buys the freshest fruit
    at the best price.
    妈妈对挑选好水果有独到的眼光；她总是以最好的价格买到最新
    鲜的水果。

13. **tenor** [ˈtɛnə] *n.* （生活）进程；一般趋势

14. **untrammeled** [ʌnˈtræml̩d] *a.* 未受束缚的；不受限制的

15. **capitalism** [ˈkæpətl̩ˌɪzəm] *n.* 资本主义

16. **crush** [krʌʃ] *vt.* 镇压；征服
    Our baseball team crushed theirs; we beat them by 12 to 2.
    我们的棒球队大败他们那一队；我们以 12 比 2 赢了他们。

17. **exuberance** [ɪgˈzjubərəns] *n.* 丰富；繁荣

18. **harbinger** [ˈharbɪndʒə] *n.* 先驱者

19. **enthrall** [ɪnˈθrɔl] *vt.* 使……入迷
    The little boys were obviously enthralled by the story the sailor was
    telling them.
    那位水手讲的故事令小男孩们听得入迷。

20. **revenge** [rɪˈvɛndʒ] *n.* 报仇
    Some people say, "Revenge is sweet;" others realize that revenge only
    incites further violence.
    有人说："复仇甚为甜美"。有些人则明白复仇只会带来更多的暴力。

21. **vehicle** [ˈviːkl] *n.* （传播）媒介，跳板

The movie *Die Hard* became a vehicle for Bruce Willis's success; since then he has become a superstar.

《虎胆龙威》成为布鲁斯·威利斯成功的跳板；从这部电影后他就成了超级巨星。

22. **urge** [ɜdʒ] *n.* 冲动；驱策

During pregnancy, many women have the urge to eat unusual foods.

许多妇女在怀孕期间都有想吃平常不吃的食物的冲动。

23. **exhilarating** [ɪgˈzɪləˌreɪtɪŋ] *a.* 使人兴奋的

24. **Coupled with the absorbing, mad Captain Ahab, the book is...**

= The book is coupled with the absorbing, mad Captain Ahab; the book is...

* be coupled with... 加上……

His lack of education (which was) coupled with the region's poverty ensured that Mark would become a laborer.

没受多少教育再加上该地区很贫穷使马克注定成为一名苦力。

25. **pen** [pɛn] *vt.* 写

Shakespeare penned many of the world's best loved plays and sonnets.

莎士比亚写了许多世上最脍炙人口的戏剧和十四行诗。

Lesson 22

Boston: Hearth of American Culture

波士顿：美国文化重镇

1   *Reading* 阅读

When people think of "American culture and values," they are unconsciously referring to a set of principles, a world view, and a lifestyle which can best be found in Boston, capital of the state of Massachusetts and the major city in all of New England, those six relatively small states tucked away in the northeastern corner of the United States. Although Boston is perhaps the seventh or eighth largest city in the U.S., no other city in America can compare with the influence which Boston has had on the development of government, education, medicine, and the arts.

This influence is due in no small part to Boston's central role in the building of a new nation. Many people think that the United States was established in 1776; however, that was the year of the *Declaration of Independence*, a revolutionary document claiming self-rule from its mother country, England. Actual independence — the formation of a government with an acting president (George Washington) — did not begin until 1789. Boston was nearly middle-aged then, as it had had its beginnings a century and a half earlier, in 1630. It maintained its position as the colonies' pre-eminent center for politics, education, and commerce until the mid-18th century, when both New York and Philadelphia (the young nation's first and second capitals, respectively) overtook Boston in size.

Boston was settled by religious immigrants from the Church of England. It was with these early settlers that the first outlines of an American culture began: a strict adherence to religious dicta, diligence in work, educational aspirations, and a conservative lifestyle. Because Boston is closer to Europe than any other city in the U.S., it was the point of entry to the colonies until the 19th century, when New York became the new magnet for the "poor, tired, and huddled masses" who were to become the backbone of the new American economy. Boston remained, however, an important commercial center until the 20th century.

Today Boston caters to finance and banking, education, and medicine, with some of the top international mutual fund and insurance companies, world-renowned educational institutes, and state-of-the-art medical centers and schools. The city has also managed to preserve much of its earlier identity as the home of the American Revolution; thus, tourism is an important sector in the economy of Boston as well. Like San Francisco or New Orleans, Boston has a reputation for being a pleasant city to admire while walking around it.

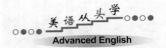
What can one do in Boston? Important historic sites, well-preserved examples of architecture from the 17th-20th centuries, and spacious parks invite the tourist or resident to "smell the roses" while in Boston. Its unhurried but sophisticated citizens boast not only high incomes but also high levels of education. Music flourishes here: the Boston Symphony Orchestra, the New England Conservatory of Music, and the Boston Pops Orchestra offer first-class musical entertainment in both public and private venues. The Museum of Fine Arts is a major world gallery. Science Park, situated midway between Boston and its major satellite city, Cambridge, offers the Museum of Science. Had enough of "high-brow culture"? Boston affords its citizens and visitors many first-class restaurants and shopping dockside in Faneuil Hall. Historic walking tours are a must for the tourist, especially Boston Commons, a city park, and Beacon Hill, with its roads still paved with the original stones from the 17th century. Admirers of university campuses steeped in tradition should see Harvard, the nation's oldest university (1636), as well as the Massachusetts Institute of Technology, Emerson College, Boston College, and Boston University, all in the metropolitan area.

In short, no matter one's interest, any visitor is sure to enjoy his stay in Boston, hearth of American culture and still a leader in education, medicine, and music.

当人们想到"美国文化和价值观"时，他们不自觉中指的是以波士顿最具代表性的一套准则、一种世界观以及一种生活方式；波士顿是麻省首府和新英格兰（位于美国东北角六个相当隐蔽的小州）全境的主要城市。尽管波士顿也许是全美第七或第八大城市，但没有其他一个美国城市能够在政府、教育、医学和艺术等各项发展的影响上与它媲美。

这种影响力大部分归因于波士顿在新国家建立时所扮演的中心角色。很多人以为美国是在 1776 年建立的；然而，该年是《独立宣言》（宣布脱离母国英国而自治的革命文件）发表的那一年，真正的独立要到 1789 年才开始——也就是代理总统乔治·华盛顿政府的成立。那时波士顿几乎已步入中年，因为它早在一个半世纪以前（即 1630 年）就已存在了。它继续保持殖民地政治、教育和商业的首要中心地位，直到 18 世纪中叶，纽约和费城（分别为新国家第一个和第二个首都）的规模超越过波士顿。

波士顿是由来自英国教会的宗教移民所开垦。这些早期拓荒者开创了美国文化的雏型：严守宗教训示、勤奋工作、热心教育和保守的生活方式。由于波士顿比任何其他美国城市更靠近欧洲，一直以来它都是殖民地的门户，直到 19 世纪纽约成为"贫穷、疲累和拥挤混乱的移民"心目中的新乐土，而这些人日后成了美国新经济的主干。然而，波士顿直到 20 世纪仍是一个重要的商业中心。

今天波士顿以财政、金融、教育和医学为重点，有一些首屈一指的国际共同基金和保险公司，世界知名的教育机构、最先进的医学中心和学校都在这里。该市也设法维持美国早期革命发源地的原貌；因此，旅游业也是波士顿经济重要的一环。如同旧金山和新奥尔良一样，波士顿是出名的宜人城市，很值得去走走。

　　在波士顿能做什么呢？重要的历史遗迹、保存完善的 17 到 20 世纪的建筑典范，以及宽广的公园都吸引游客或居民在停留波士顿期间去"好好享受人生"。波士顿悠闲但世故的市民不仅以高收入自豪，而且也以教育水平高而自豪。音乐在此很兴盛：波士顿交响乐团、新英格兰音乐学院和波士顿流行管弦乐团在公开和私人的场合都提供一流的音乐欣赏。这里的美术馆是世界主要的美术展览会场。位于波士顿和其主要卫星城剑桥中间的科学公园内则有科学博物馆。受够了"高格调文化"吗？波士顿提供市民和游客许多一流的餐厅和位于法纳尔大厅船坞的购物区。游览历史步道是观光客不可错过的一件事，特别是波士顿市民公园（一座市立公园）和道路仍铺着 17 世纪原始石头的比肯山。偏爱悠久传统校园的人应该去看看美国最早的哈佛大学（1636），以及麻省理工学院、埃默森学院、波士顿学院和波士顿大学，这些全都在都会区内。

　　总而言之，不论你的兴趣为何，任何访客到波士顿这个美国文化重镇以及依然居教育、医学和音乐领导地位的城市游玩，都一定会玩得非常尽兴。

2 *Vocabulary & Idioms* 单词短语注解

1. **unconsciously** [ʌnˈkɑnʃəslɪ] *adv.* 无意识地；不知不觉地

2. **tuck** [tʌk] *vt.* 使隐藏

   Some of the wildest natural scenery in the United States is tucked away in Maine, New England.

   美国有些最原始的自然景观都隐藏在新英格兰的缅因州而鲜为人知。

3. **compare with...** 和……相匹敌

   Though I sing well, my singing cannot compare with Peter's.

   虽然我歌唱得很好，但我的歌喉仍无法和彼得相媲美。

4. **Declaration of Independence**

   美国独立宣言（1776 年 7 月 4 日于国会通过）

5. **revolutionary** [ˌrɛvəˈluʃənˌɪərɪ] *a.* 革命（性）的

6. **pre-eminent** [prɪˈɛmɪnənt] *a.* 卓越的，超群的

7. **respectively** [rɪˈspɛktɪvlɪ] *adv.* 各自地；分别地

   James and Andy stand guard over the factory on Saturdays and Sundays, respectively.

   詹姆斯和安迪分别在星期六及星期日看守工厂。

8. **overtake** [ˌovəˈtek] *vt.* 赶上，超过

   Some economists think that in the future Shanghai will overtake other cities as the economic center of Asia.

   有些经济学家认为上海将来会超过其他城市，成为亚洲的经济中心。

9. **adherence** [ədˈhɪrəns] *n.* 坚持；固守（与介词 to 连用）

   adhere [ədˈhɪr] *vi.* 追随，依附；坚持（与介词 to 连用）

   adhere to... 追随 / 依附……；坚持……

   Those who adhere to society's laws will suffer the fewest problems.

   遵守社会法规的人所遭受的问题会最少。

10. **dicta** [ˈdɪktə] *n.* (专家的)意见；断言(为 dictum [ˈdɪktəm] 的复数形式)

11. **magnet** [ˈmægnɪt] *n.* 磁铁；有吸引力的人或物

12. **huddle** [ˈhʌdḷ] *vt. & vi.* (使)挤作一团,(使)聚成一堆
   * 在本文中为过去分词作形容词用。
   The stray dogs huddled around each other to keep warm during the cold winter night.
   那些流浪狗在寒冬的夜里互相挤在一起取暖。

13. **cater to...** 投合/迎合……
   Some cruise ships cater to young single people.
   有些游轮旅游主要是为迎合年轻的单身男女而办的。

14. **state-of-the-art** [ˈstetˌəvðɪˈɑrt] *a.* 使用最先进技术的

15. **preserve** [prɪˈzɜv] *vt.* 保存；维护；保持
   The Thai people have preserved their ancient culture very well.
   泰国人民将他们的古老文化保存得很好。

16. **sophisticated** [səˈfɪstɪˌketɪd] *a.* 老于世故的；有(高度)教养的

17. **boast** [bost] *vt.* 以拥有……自豪；自夸
   Sydney boasts one of the most beautiful harbors in the world.
   悉尼以其拥有世上最美丽的港口之一而自豪。

18. **flourish** [ˈflɝɪʃ] *vi.* 繁荣,兴隆
   During the 16th century, trade and commerce flourished in France and the Netherlands.
   16世纪时,贸易和商业在法国和荷兰两地蓬勃发展。

19. **venue** [ˈvɛnju] *n.* 举办地点,举行场所

20. **high-brow** [ˈhaɪˌbraʊ] *a. & n.* 被认为文化修养高的(人)

21. **be a must for...** 对……而言是必须的
   Seeing the Statue of Liberty is a must for every tourist who visits New York.
   每个到纽约的游客都非得去参观自由女神像不可。

22. **steep** [stip] *vt.* 使沉湎，沾染（多用被动式）

be steeped in... 沉湎于／埋首……

Nearly every school boy in Arabic countries is steeped in learning his religion and culture.

阿拉伯国家中几乎每个男学生都埋首于学习其宗教和文化。

23. **in short** 简而言之，简单地说

I spent 12 hours researching and four hours writing this report; in short, I think it's a good one.

我花了十二个小时做研究，又用四个小时写好了这份报告；简单说呢，我认为这是一份好报告。

Lesson (23)

Paper's Long March
纸张的演进

①   *Reading* 阅读   📖

Remember when the 1980s brought us the first wave of the modern computer and electronics revolution? At that time, heady young technocrats foresaw "the paperless office." It was claimed that paper would become a thing of the past as everyone would access all information needed from video screens.

The reality today is quite different. More paper than ever is being used in offices, schools, and residential homes. One's first possession in life is a birth certificate, made of paper. Childhood immunizations are recorded on paper and kept in the doctor's office and at home. What would school be like without paper? Paper follows most people throughout their education and into their working life. Wedding invitations and marriage certificates are printed on paper, as are virtually all major life passages and social occasions. Finally, a death certificate on paper will continue to be around long after the person named on it. Perhaps the one item which defines modern civilization more than any other is paper.

The word paper derives from papyrus, the name of a riverside plant similar to grass, from which an ancient form of paper was used in Egypt and Mesopotamia. It could be argued that these empires were made possible by the use of official records on papyrus. However, paper as we know it today has its origins in the Han dynasty of China. In about A.D. 105, an official in the imperial court produced the forebear of what has become today the world's most indispensable product. The art of paper making reached westwards to Baghdad, Iraq in the 8th century at the height of the Islamic culture. From there it entered Europe, where it was polished into its contemporary form during the 19th century.

Paper can be made from any plant, but trees are the best source of cellulose for paper production. In fact, earlier forms of paper were made from processed cotton waste and rags, but trees contain a better proportion and type of cellulose than any other plant. In countries with a deficiency of forest land, other natural fibers such as sugar cane pulp, bamboo, cereal straws, flax, and hemp are used. Today's paper and paper product mills rely on a steady inflow of wood logs or chips. In the United States alone, the paper and paper products industry is worth more than US$80 billion, with world production well over 100,000,000 tons annually.

Everyone knows what paper is, since most people use at least one sheet of it a day, but few people stop to consider the different kinds of paper available to us today. Office workers

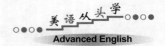
are well aware of the many kinds of paper they use, such as regular typing or computer printing or copier paper. They also come into contact with bond, a high-grade paper used for important documents. It is thicker and more durable than other forms of paper. Book paper comes in at least four different finishes. These may be seen in books, magazines, brochures, and calendars. Newsprint is used for newspapers and some magazines or books, while kraft paper is used for shopping bags. Paperboard is seen daily as box lunch containers, cardboard boxes, and even building materials. Finally, sanitary paper has been developed for use in tissue paper, paper toweling, and paper napkins. Carbon paper, postcards, and envelopes are also daily use items made of paper. Even a tea bag is made of paper!

Paper and its products seem endless, but conservation of even the abundant resource of trees is in everyone's interest. Recycling of paper and better designed pulp and paper factories have helped decrease waste. Many offices encourage the use of both sides of a piece of paper, for example, and students or private organizations sometimes collect old newsprint to send to reprocessing centers. By conserving paper, the average paper user in his lifetime can save at least one tree from being felled. As valuable as trees are, and as valuable as paper is, everyone should cooperate to use this essential commodity wisely.

　　还记得上世纪 80 年代带给我们的第一波现代计算机和电子革命吗？当时，一群不可一世的年轻科技主义者预知了"无纸张的办公室"，他们宣称由于每个人都将从电视屏幕上获取一切所需的信息，纸张将因此成为历史名词。

　　如今实际情况却大不相同。在办公室、学校和家庭中，纸张的使用比以往都要多。人一生中拥有的第一项财产便是一张纸做的出生证明。儿童的预防注射被记录在纸上，存放在医生办公室和家里。学校中没有纸的话又会变成什么样子？纸张跟着大部分的人走过他们的教育阶段，并进入他们的工作生涯。结婚喜帖和结婚证书是纸印的，而且所有重要的人生过程或社交场合也几乎都是印在纸张上。最后，死亡证明文件在注明死者之后仍将继续存在很久。或许纸张比任何其他事物更能诠释现代文明吧。

　　paper 这个词源自于 papyrus（纸草），这是一种在古埃及和美索不达米亚被用来制作纸张而形状像草的河边植物。我们可以推论这两个地区的王国可能是因为用纸草来作官方纪录才得以建立的。然而，就我们今天所知，纸张源于中国的汉朝。在公元 105 年左右，朝廷的一位官员制造出今日世上最不可或缺产品的前身。伊斯兰教文化在 8 世纪时达到全盛时期，造纸技术在此时向西传到伊拉克的巴格达。它从那儿进入欧洲，19 世纪期间纸张在欧洲被改进成如今的样子。

　　任何植物都可以用来造纸，但树木才是造纸用纤维的最佳来源。事实上，早期的纸是用加工处理过的棉花屑和破布制成的，但树木所含的纤维比例和形态比其他任何植物都要好。在森林地缺乏的国家，则用其他如甘蔗渣、竹子、谷类的茎杆、亚麻和大麻等天然纤维来造纸。今日的纸张和造纸厂依靠固定的圆木或木片供应。

光是美国一地,纸张和造纸工业年产值就超过 800 亿美元,而全世界每年产量则远超过 1 亿吨。

每个人都知道纸张是什么东西,因为大多数的人一天都至少会用上一张,但很少有人会去思考我们现在所用的纸张有哪些不同的种类。办公室人员很清楚他们所用的许多种类的纸张,例如一般的打字或计算机打印或复印纸张。他们也会接触到铜版纸,一种高级的重要文件用纸。它比其他种类的纸更厚且较耐久。书本用的纸张至少有四种不同的质地。你也许可以在书籍、杂志、小册子和月历中看到。新闻纸被用来制作报纸和一些杂志或书籍,而牛皮纸则被用来制作购物袋。纸板可见于日常的午餐盒、硬纸箱甚至建筑材料。最后,清洁纸张被发展成卫生纸、纸毛巾和餐巾纸。复写纸、明信片和信封也是日常使用的纸制品,甚至连茶包都是纸做的!

纸张和纸制品似乎无穷无尽,但即使森林资源丰富,每个人对它的保存仍表关切。纸张的回收再用以及设计较佳的纸浆和造纸厂都有助于减少浪费。例如,许多公司鼓励纸张的两面都使用,而学生或私人机构有时也会收集旧报纸送到资源回收中心。通过节省纸张,平均每位纸张使用者在一生中至少可以拯救一棵树免于被砍伐。树木很珍贵,纸张也很珍贵,大家应该通力合作好好使用这项基本的消费品。

2 *Vocabulary & Idioms* 单词短语注解

1. **revolution** [ˌrɛvəˈluʃən] *n.* 革命

2. **heady** [ˈhɛdɪ] *a.* 不可一世的

3. **technocrat** [ˈtɛknəˌkræt] *n.* 科技主义者；担任行政官职的技术专家

4. **foresee** [fɔrˈsi] *vt.* 预知
   动词三态：foresee, foresaw [fɔrˈsɔ], foreseen [fɔrˈsin]。
   The 19th century Frenchman Jules Verne foresaw inventions such as
   the submarine and the space rocket.
   19 世纪时法国人儒勒·凡尔纳预知了诸如潜水艇和太空火箭等发
   明。

5. **It is claimed + that** 从句 据称……
   It is claimed that by the year 2050, India will have more people than
   China.
   据称到了公元 2050 年时，印度的人口会超过中国。

6. **access** [ˈæksɛs] *vt.* 取得
   You can access a lot of information through the Internet.
   透过互联网你可以获取许多信息。

7. **residential** [ˌrɛzəˈdɛnʃəl] *a.* 居住的，与居住有关的

8. **possession** [pəˈzɛʃən] *n.* 拥有；财产

9. **birth certificate** 出生证明（文件）
   death certificate 死亡证明（文件）
   marriage certificate 结婚证书
   certificate [səˈtɪfəkɪt] *n.* 证明（文件）

10. **immunization** [ˌɪmjunəˈzeʃən] *n.* 免疫作用

11. **define** [dɪˈfaɪn] *vt.* 下定义；详细说明
    The quality of a nation's infrastructure defines whether or not it is a
    developed country.
    一个国家的基础设施的质量说明了它是否为发达国家。

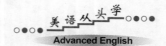

12. **derive from...** 源自于……

The English word "house" derives from the German word "Haus."

house 这个英文字源自于德文的 Haus。

13. **papyrus** [pə'paɪrəs] *n.* 纸草

14. **forebear** ['fɔr,bɛr] *n.* 祖先；前身

The Chinese or Roman chariot is the forebear of the modern automobile.

中国或罗马的两轮战车是现代汽车的前身。

15. **indispensable** [,ɪndɪs'pɛnsəbl̩] *a.* 不可或缺的

Tom loves music so much that his CD player is an indispensable part of his daily life.

汤姆非常喜欢音乐，因此他的 CD 随身听是他日常生活中不可或缺的一部分。

16. **at the height of...** 处在……的巅峰

Men are usually at the height of their physical strength while in their 30s.

男人通常在 30 岁时达到体能的巅峰。

17. **cellulose** ['sɛljə,los] *n.* 纤维质；细胞膜质

18. **deficiency** [dɪ'fɪʃənsɪ] *n.* 欠缺；不足

19. **come into contact with...** 接触……

If you come into contact with someone who has a cold, you are likely to catch it from him.

如果你和某个感冒的人接触就很有可能会被他传染。

20. **conservation** [,kɑnsə'veʃən] *n.* 保存；保护

conserve [kən'sɝv] *vt.* 保护

We must conserve trees because they're so valuable to both the ecology and humans.

我们必须保护树木，因为它们对生态及人类而言都非常珍贵。

21. **abundant** [ə'bʌndənt] *a.* 富裕的；充足的

The fish in the sea are not so abundant as they used to be.

海里的鱼儿已不再像从前那么多了。

22. **decrease** [dɪˈkriːs] *vi.* 减少

The number of new babies born in Western Europe is decreasing; those nations are aging quickly.

西欧的新生婴儿数目正逐渐减少；那些国家正迅速老龄化。

23. **fell** [fɛl] *vt.* 砍伐

If we fell all the forests, where will the wildlife live?

如果我们把所有的森林都砍光的话，野生动物要住哪里呢？

Lesson 24

Coffee or Tea Break?

喝咖啡或喝茶？

1   *Reading* 阅读

Do you prefer a coffee break or a tea break? Are you getting off the lift at the ground floor, or are you going to get off the elevator on the first floor? Travelers to English-speaking countries have to adjust to differences between British and American English. There are also cultural traditions to understand, ways of life which differ between London and New York, Auckland and Toronto, and Sydney and San Francisco. Learning these differences is fun, and, when you travel to different English-speaking countries, it's very useful.

So, what is a coffee or a tea break? Americans and Canadians prefer coffee drinking to tea drinking. Tea lovers need not worry, though; millions of North Americans drink tea and only tea every day. Though teahouses are rare there, every supermarket has a wide variety of Far Eastern, South Asian, and herbal teas to choose from. Still, coffee is the preferred drink in the Americas; after all, South America is one of the world's greatest coffee-producing areas. One social custom in the U.S. and Canada is the mid-morning and mid-afternoon coffee break. This is very informal; it may be spontaneous

(Hey! Let's break for coffee) or institutionalized (The coffee break in our office is from 3:30-3:50 daily). Coffee (or tea) may be drunk only, or, more likely, a selection of baked goods such as doughnuts, cookies, slices of cake, or crackers will be available, too. These breaks are not only for eating and drinking but also for chatting.

In Great Britain, New Zealand, and Australia, people prefer a spot of tea during their tea break in the mid-morning or mid-afternoon, and later on at home, they have high tea in the early evening. High tea consists of a light, cold meal or baked goods, followed by a more substantial meal later in the evening. Tea breaks may be formal in homes, with a silver tray filled with tea cups on saucers, a silver bowl with sugar, and a silver pitcher with cream brought into a living room, dining room, or drawing room. Baked goods are also served at tea breaks. In both the U.K. and the U.S. as well as in other English-speaking countries, most people eat three full meals daily, but stopping for coffee or tea breaks has also become customary.

Another useful difference to understand between the British and American ways of life concerns traffic, which is of the utmost importance to travelers or visitors. In London, one takes the underground, whereas in New York it's the subway (whether or not traveling below the ground). Streetcars are taken in American cities, but trams are found in Britain. Make sure you fill up with gas at the gas station in Miami, but in Manchester you should top up the tank with petrol at the

petrol station. Not sure whether you need oil? Check under the bonnet in Bristol but the hood in Houston. Check your wing mirror in Wales but your side mirror in Rochester. And watch out for those traffic circles in Tampa but those roundabouts in Reading.

It should not surprise anyone that British and American English are a little different grammatically (Americans say, "I don't have" and "I have a lot" but the British say "I haven't" and "I have much"). Their pronunciation and vocabulary also differ. These should not be sources of consternation when you visit different Anglo countries; instead, they should be occasions for adventure and enjoyment. Just as Mandarin-speaking foreigners can manage their way through the various dialects of Mandarin spoken in mainland China, so, too, should anyone versed in conversational English — of any stripe — succeed in having fun with the different worlds of English.

你比较喜欢喝咖啡时间还是喝茶时间？你要在地面那层楼（ground floor）出电梯（lift）还是在一楼（first floor）下电梯（elevator）？到英语系国家旅行的人必须适应英式英语和美式英语之间的差异。此外也要了解他们的文化传统，也就是要了解伦敦和纽约、奥克兰和多伦多以及悉尼和旧金山之间不同的生活方式。学习这些差异很有趣，而且当你到不同的英语系国家旅行时也会非常有用。

那么，什么是喝咖啡时间或喝茶时间呢？美国人和加拿大人喜欢喝咖啡胜过喝茶。但爱喝茶的人不必担心，有数以百万计的北美洲人每天只喝茶。虽然那儿的茶馆很少，但每家超市都有很多种远东和南亚出产的茶以及天然植物茶可供选择。然而，咖啡仍是美洲地区较受欢迎的饮料；毕竟，南美洲是世上最大的咖啡产区之一。在美国和加拿大早上约9到10点，下午约3到4点钟左右习惯上为喝咖啡时间。这并不是很正式的；它也许是随兴而起的(嘿！咱们喝杯咖啡休息一下)，也有可能是制度化的(本公司的喝咖啡时间为每天下午3点半到3点50分)。这段时间也许只喝咖啡(或茶)而已，更有可能的情况是，同时也享用了一系列如甜甜圈、饼干、切片蛋糕或酥饼等烘焙食品。这些休息时段不只是吃吃喝喝而已，也是用来闲聊的。

在英国、新西兰和澳大利亚，那里的人喜欢在早上9点到10点或下午3点到4点的喝茶时间来上一杯茶，而稍后在黄昏时则在家中享用"茶餐"。"茶餐"包含清淡的冷食或烘焙食品，之后晚上再接着吃一顿较为丰盛的餐食。在家庭中喝茶时间可以是很正式的——一个盛满碟子上放着茶杯的银盘、一个装糖的银碗和一个装奶精的银壶被端进起居室、饭厅或客厅里。喝茶时间也享用烘焙食品。在英、美及其他英语系国家,大部分的人 1 天吃 3 次正餐,但其间的喝咖啡时间或喝茶时间也已经成为习惯。

　　另一个英式和美式生活之间值得了解的实用差别则和交通有关,这对旅行者或游客而言是最重要不过了。在伦敦人们乘坐的地铁叫作"underground",然而在纽约它叫"subway"(不管是不是在地底下行走)。美国城市里有街车(streetcar)可搭乘,但在英国则是电车(tram)。在迈阿密的加油站(gas station)时务必说把油加满(fill up with gas),但到曼彻斯特的汽油站(petrol station)时则应该说把油箱加满汽油(top up the tank with petrol)。不确定你是否需要加机油吗?在布里斯托说打开车前盖(bonnet)看看,但在休斯顿则说引擎盖(hood)。在威尔士说看侧翼镜(wing mirror),但在罗彻斯特说侧视镜(side mirror)。此外,在坦帕市要当心注意的圆环叫"traffic circle",但在里丁市则叫"roundabout"。

　　任何人都应该不会惊讶英式英语和美式英语之间语法会有一点不同(美国人说"I don't have"和"I have a lot",但英国人说"I haven't"和"I have much"),还有它们的发音及字词也有差异。当你造访不同英语系国家时,这些差异不但不应该是恐惧惊慌的来源,反而应该是探险和享受的时刻。就像说汉语的外国人能够设法通行于中国大陆各种汉语方言之间,同样地,任何精通英语会话——任何一种都行——的人也应该能成功地悠游在不同的英语世界中。

2 *Vocabulary & Idioms* 单词短语注解

1. **get off/on +** 电梯 / 大型交通工具 下 / 上电梯 / 大型交通工具
   When Linda got off the bus, the bus driver reminded her to pay the fare.
   琳达下公交车时,公交车司机提醒她要付车费。

2. **adjust (oneself) to + N / V-ing** (使自己)适应……
   After living in Singapore for two months, Philip finally adjusted himself to his new way of life there.
   在新加坡住了两个月后,菲利浦终于适应了那里的新生活方式。

3. **prefer A to B** 喜欢 A 胜过 B;宁愿……而不愿……
   I prefer salads and sandwiches to Chinese food in the summer because they are lighter.
   夏天时我比较喜欢吃色拉和三明治而不喜欢吃中国菜,因为那两样东西比较清淡。

4. **spontaneous** [spɑnˈtenɪəs] *a.* 自然发生的;自发 / 动的
   Spontaneous laughter erupted from the students when the professor spelled his own name wrong on the blackboard.
   当教授在黑板上拼错自己的名字时,学生们不由自主地爆发一阵笑声。

5. **institutionalized** [ˌɪnstəˈtjuʃənlˌaɪzd] *a.* 成惯例的
   institutionalize [ˌɪnstəˈtjuʃənlˌaɪz] *vt.* 使成惯例;把……送进(收容所、养老院等)
   People who can no longer function on their own are often institutionalized.
   生活不能自理的人通常都被送进赡养机构。

6. **not only...but also...** 不仅……而且……
   Now that Mom is in the hospital, not only will we children have to cook for ourselves, but we will also have to wash our own clothes.
   因为妈妈住院了,所以我们小孩子不仅得要自己煮饭,而且还要自

已洗衣服。

7. **substantial** [səb'stænʃəl] *a.* 丰富的，多的；可观的

   substantial meal 丰富的餐食

   Mr. Stone makes a substantial income; he can afford a new car every other year.

   斯通先生的收入相当可观；他负担得起每两年就换一部新车。

8. **serve** [sɜv] *vt.* 提供（食物）；端上（饭菜等）

   Jane served her guests tea and muffins on her silver tray.

   简用银盘端来了茶和松饼招待她的客人。

9. **customary** ['kʌstə,mɛrɪ] *a.* 习惯上的，惯例的

10. **make sure + (that)** 从句 务必 / 确定……

    Make sure you keep an eye on the oven while baking, or your baked goods will burn.

    烘烤东西时务必要注意烤箱，否则你烤的东西会烧焦。

11. **watch out for...** 密切注意……；当心 / 提防……

    When walking barefoot at night, watch out for snakes in the fields.

    晚上赤脚走路时，要当心空旷地是否有蛇出没。

12. **grammatically** [grə'mætɪkl̩ɪ] *adv.* 就语法而言

13. **consternation** [,kɑnstə'neʃən] *n.* 惊慌 / 愕；惊惶失措

    We were filled with consternation when we learned that our supplies had not yet arrived.

    得知我们的补给品尚未到达时，我们感到非常惊愕。

14. **versed** [vɜst] *a.* 擅长的，精通的

    be versed in... 擅长 / 精通……

    My uncle is well versed in computer languages; he knows at least 15 different ones.

    我的叔叔精通计算机语言，他所知道的至少有 15 种之多。

15. **stripe** [straɪp] *n.* 种类；型

16. **succeed in...** 在……（方面）成功；成功做到……

Only hard work and a good plan will allow you to succeed in business.
只有努力和完善的计划才能让你事业成功。

17. **have fun +** $\begin{vmatrix} \textbf{with N} \\ \textbf{V + ing} \end{vmatrix}$ （从事）……很开心，……（玩得）很愉快

类似用法：

have difficulty+ $\begin{vmatrix} \text{with N} \\ \text{V + ing} \end{vmatrix}$ 做……有困难

Sandy had a lot of fun chatting with her boyfriend on the phone.
珊蒂和她的男友在电话中聊天聊得很愉快。

Theresa had great difficulty learning to swim until she lost her fear of water.
特雷莎在克服怕水的心理之前学游泳学得非常辛苦。

Lesson 25

Earthquake Precautions
地震防范措施

Bam! The bathroom door slamming against the wall woke me out of a sound sleep. Groggily wending my way in the dark to the bathroom, I secured the door latch to make sure I would have no further interruptions of much-needed sleep. I then lumbered back into bed and started to drift off.

Not for long. My body, the bed and the whole bedroom began shaking. After a few confused and frightening seconds, I realized "Earthquake!" "Big one," I added, noting that the neighborhood dogs had joined in the weird sounds the hills around my house were making. Within moments I was out of bed and on my feet, contemplating leaving the house. "I'll wait," I comforted myself. "Even these big ones pass in a few seconds."

This one wouldn't. It kept coming; everything was shaking and trembling, rattling. I heard a pane of glass crash onto the floor. The walls of the house and the things attached to them seemed to heave, not just shudder. I then noticed that the street lights had failed and my heart was pounding harder than when I used to lift weights. I acknowledged my fear.

Realizing that there was no time to flee the house, I simply waited and waited. The nearly one-minute long temblor finally subsided, and my reasoning came back to me. All was well, or well enough. I walked unsteadily to another room and looked outside. A neighbor with a flashlight was checking on his and others' homes for damage.

I knew it had been a major quake, though not centered where I lived. The next day I learned that a 7.6 Richter-scale earthquake had devastated the lovely rural communities of central Taiwan. For the next few weeks, everyone's life was centered around the quake due to the constant media coverage and electricity rationing.

Taiwan is but one of many places situated along the "Ring of Fire" encircling nearly half the globe around the Pacific Ocean. Constant volcanic and earthquake action occurs here, sometimes with cataclysmic results. In this century alone, major earthquakes have taken more than one million lives. Many more have been injured and made homeless. The economic, social, and personal costs are immeasurable.

Over the past quarter century, many countries in earthquake-prone areas have begun to educate their citizens on how to take appropriate precautions for earthquakes. The following list has been compiled from experience.

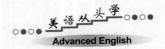

Before the earthquake:

Prepare an "earthquake kit" near everyone's bed; these kits should include drinking water, a flashlight with fresh batteries, and dry food.

Place an extra pillow, blanket, or quilt near the bed to be placed over the head during the earthquake and for warmth if trapped afterwards.

During the earthquake:

If possible, get out of the building you are inside of and into a clear area.

If escape from a building is impossible, get away from windows and doors; try to find shelter under structural beams or under any heavy piece of furniture, like a large table or bed.

After the major earthquake (remember that aftershocks will occur):

When shaking ends or subsides, turn off gas lines.

Leave the building (never use elevators) quickly but not in a panic.

If uninjured, be ready to assist rescue workers with information or labor.

When a Big One happens, there is little anyone can do. The above contingency preparations, however, could make the difference between life and death.

砰！浴室门重重关上的声响惊醒了熟睡中的我。我摸黑一路摇摇晃晃地走到浴室将门栓闩好，免得再次打断我宝贵的睡眠，然后又蹒跚地回到被窝进入梦乡。

不一会儿，我的身体、床和整个卧室开始摇晃。在搞不清状况下害怕了几秒钟后，才明白过来是"地震"。"而且是个大地震！"我接着又想到，注意到附近的狗狂吠着加入房子四周山丘所发出的怪声。我很快地下床站起来，考虑要不要往屋外走。"等一下吧！"我安慰自己。"就算大地震也不过几秒钟就结束了。"

但这次不一样。它不停地摇晃；每样东西都在摇动而且震得嘎嘎作响。我听见一片玻璃掉到地板上摔碎的声音。房子的墙壁及附在墙上的东西似乎不只是颤动，而是上下猛烈晃动。然后我注意到路灯都已熄灭，而我的心跳得比我过去举重时还剧烈。我承认自己很害怕。

我了解到已经来不及逃到室外，便乖乖地等着。将近一分钟的地震终于平息，我的理智也逐渐恢复。一切平安，或者说还好吧。我步履不稳地走到另一个房间往外一瞧。一位邻居拿着手电筒正在检查他家及邻舍有否损坏。

虽然我住的地方并非震中，但我知道这是个大地震。第二天我得知台湾中部许多偏远美丽的乡间都遭到里氏 7.6 级大地震的蹂躏。接下来的几个礼拜，因为媒体报道及限电措施，每个人的生活重心都围绕在地震这件事上。

　　台湾是诸多太平洋边缘环绕近半个地球的"火环"地区之一。这地区频繁的火山活动及地震时而造成惨重的后果。光是在 20 世纪就有 100 多万人在大地震中丧命；有更多人因地震受伤或无家可归；对经济、社会及个人更造成难以估计的损失。

　　过去 25 年来许多位于地震频繁地区的国家已开始教育其人民如何采取适当的防震措施。以下是从经验中得出来的防震措施。

　　地震前：

　　在每人床边准备一个"地震包"，内有饮水、备有新电池的手电筒及干粮。

　　在床边额外准备一只枕头、毛毯或棉被；地震发生时可用来保护头部，震后若遭困亦可用来保暖。

　　地震时：

　　若可能，立即离开室内到空旷处。

　　来不及逃离建筑物时，应远离门窗；并在主梁或较重的家具下寻找掩护（例如大型桌子或床）。

　　主震过后（别忘了余震）：

　　地震停止或平息后，关闭煤气管道。

　　尽快镇静地离开建筑物（不可搭乘电梯）。

　　若未受伤，随时准备协助救难人员提供信息或出力援救。

　　当特大地震发生时，任何人都无能为力，但上述防范措施却能决定一个人的生与死。

② *Vocabulary & Idioms* 单词短语注解

1. **slam against...** 猛力撞上……
   Martin's car slammed against a tree because his brakes didn't work.
   马丁的车子因刹车失灵而撞上了一棵树。

2. **groggily** [ˈɡrɑɡɪlɪ] *adv.* 酒醉地；东倒西歪地

3. **wend one's way** 前进，行走
   wend [wɛnd] *vt.* 向……而进；行(路)

4. **interruption** [ˌɪntəˈrʌpʃən] *n.* 中断；妨碍
   interrupt [ˌɪntəˈrʌpt] *vt.* 打断
   The ringing of the telephone interrupted Tom from his reading.
   电话铃声打断了汤姆的阅读。

5. **lumber** [ˈlʌmbɚ] *vi.* 笨拙地向前走

6. **drift off** 睡着，渐入梦乡
   = fall asleep
   It was 4 o'clock before I finally drifted off.
   我终于在 4 点时睡着了。

7. **contemplate** [ˈkɑntɛmˌplet] *vt.* 考虑(= consider，以动名词作宾语)
   We are contemplating taking a trip to Paris.
   我们正考虑到巴黎旅行。

8. **rattle** [ˈrætl̩] *vi.* 嘎嘎作响，发出嘎嘎声

9. **pane** [pen] *n.* 玻璃窗

10. **The walls of the house and the things attached to them seemed to heave, not only shudder.**
    = ...the things which were attached to seemed...
    * be attached to... 附着于……
    Mr. Milton's business card was attached to his letter, so I knew how to reach him.
    弥尔顿先生的名片就附在他的信上，所以我知道如何和他联络。

11. **heave** [hiv] *vi.* 上下晃动

12. **shudder** [ˈʃʌdə] *vi.* 颤动
Ned couldn't help but shudder as he walked the long way home during the cold winter night.
奈德在寒冬夜里走一大段路回家时不由自主地颤抖了起来。

13. **pound** [paʊnd] *vi.* 强烈打击

14. **acknowledge** [əkˈnɑlɪdʒ] *vt.* 承认
Rhonda acknowledged Simon's victory in the debate by shaking his hand.
朗达和西蒙握手承认他赢了辩论比赛。

15. **temblor** [tɛmˈblɔr] *n.* 地震

16. **subside** [səbˈsaɪd] *vi.* (地震、暴风雨等)平息,减弱
The best time to exercise is in the late afternoon after the heat of the day subsides.
运动最好的时间为午后太阳的热度减弱时。

17. **reasoning** [ˈriznɪŋ] *n.* 理智

18. **devastate** [ˈdɛvəsˌtet] *vt.* 摧毁;破坏
The Gulf War devastated Kuwait. 科威特饱受海湾战争的摧残。

19. **coverage** [ˈkʌvərɪdʒ] *n.* 报道(不可数)
There isn't much coverage of the plane crash in today's newspapers.
在今天的各报中并没有太多有关该起坠机事件的报道。

20. **encircle** [ɪnˈsɜkl̩] *vt.* 环绕

21. **cataclysmic** [ˌkætəˈklɪzmɪk] *a.* 剧变／烈的

22. **compile** [kəmˈpaɪl] *vt.* 编纂,编汇,编制
It takes years of hard work to compile a good dictionary.
编纂一本好字典需要花上多年的工夫。

23. **assist** [əˈsɪst] *vt.* 帮助
Ann's tutor assisted her in math until she passed her test.

安的家庭教师辅导她数学，直到她通过考试为止。

24. **make the difference between A and B**
造成 A 与 B 之间的差异
Previewing and then reviewing lessons can make the difference between passing and failing.
课前预习及课后复习会造成考试及格和不及格的差别。

Lesson 26

Berries: Nature's Natural Desserts

浆果——大自然的天然点心

1 ***Reading*** 阅读

The last child has left the house for school. The table is clean and neatly set, and the coffee is brewing. The cool orange juice stands like a sentry over the tableware. Mother sits down, pours cereal into a bowl, and sprinkles it lightly with sugar. She is then ready for the final masterpiece. She carefully spoons pre-cut ruby red strawberries onto the mound of golden corn flakes. Pouring ivory-white milk over the concoction, Mother smiles to herself. An attractive, nutritious breakfast fit for a queen.

Most people around the world are now familiar with and can enjoy strawberries, but few are familiar with other, more exotic berries, such as the gooseberry, blackberry, and raspberry. Indeed, even fewer people realize what the word berry technically refers to. The berry of the botanist and the berry of the public are often two quite different fruits.

Those whose specialty is plants define a berry as a simple, fleshy fruit with a thin wall and many seeds. Under this classification are several surprises. One would expect that cranberries are berries, of course, but less obvious members of this class are dates, grapes, tomatoes, and even potatoes, bananas, and asparagus! Indeed, according to botanists, some popular "berries" are not true berries at all. Experts in plant life consider the blueberry an "inferior berry" and the strawberry, raspberry, and blackberry an "aggregate fleshy fruit." However,no matter how scientists call them, most people think of berries as small, round, sweet, and delicious fruits.

Berries such as strawberries, blackberries, raspberries, and blueberries prefer cool and moist growing conditions. Though they rarely thrive in tropical conditions, they can be grown on the sides of taller hills and mountains there. Several species of wildlife forage for berries, the largest of these being the bear. Some smaller mammals and birds, too, enjoy berries, not to mention people. Wild berries are noticeably smaller than their domesticated cousins, but many people prefer the full, rich taste of freshly picked forest berries.

Besides being a condiment on breakfast cereals, are there any other uses for berries? Westerners make good use of their local fruits. Jellies, jams, and preserves can be easily made with berries, gelatin, and sugar. These three sweetened foods differ only in the process used to make them. Jellies are made from the juice of a fruit, jams from the thoroughly crushed fruit, and preserves from the partially crushed or cut fruit. They are all equally delicious!

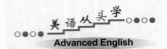

Berries are also used in baked goods. Pies and tarts often contain berries as do many other pastries. These small fruits are also added into cakes and even breads, especially after drying. In addition, the concentrated juice of berries can be used to make cool summer drinks. Concentrated further, various syrups can be added to foods as diverse as pancakes and ice cream. As flavorings, they are often added to candies and chocolates. In Western cuisine, life would be less sweet and interesting without the humble berry.

For some people, though, berries are best eaten fresh. They say that after washing and refrigerating, simply place a generous portion of berries into a cereal bowl, add chilled milk, and top with sugar. Enjoy! As the season for berries is usually in the summer and fall, this snack or dessert really hits the spot. For those who do not live where berries grow naturally and plentifully, these natural dessert fruits can be enjoyed while visiting those areas lucky enough to have them.

最后一个孩子也上学去了。餐桌已收拾干净且摆放整齐,咖啡正煮着,而清凉的橙汁好像站岗似的守卫着餐具。母亲坐下来倒了些早餐麦片在碗中,然后稍微撒了些糖。这时她已准备好要完成她的杰作。她小心地舀了些已切好如红宝石般的草莓,放在金黄的玉米脆片堆上,再浇上象牙白的牛奶以后,母亲自己笑了出来。好一份适合女王享用而诱人的营养早餐。

世界上大多数人现在都熟悉草莓,而且吃得到草莓,但却很少有人知道其他较具异国风味的浆果,例如醋栗、黑莓及树莓等。事实上,了解浆果其学理意义的人就更少了。植物学家所指的浆果和一般大众口中的浆果通常是两种颇为不同的果类。

专门研究植物的人将浆果定义为皮薄多籽而果肉丰富的单一果类。以此分类会产生一些令人料想不到的事。任何人都理所当然会认为蔓越莓是浆果类,但在上述定义中较不明显的同类还包含了枣、葡萄、蕃茄,甚至还有马铃薯、香蕉及芦笋!一点儿也没错,根据植物学家的说法,部分常见的"浆果"根本名实不符。这些植物专家视蓝莓为"较低等的浆果",而草莓、树莓及黑莓则为"聚集多果肉的果类"。然而不论科学家如何称呼,大多数人仍认定浆果就是小小圆圆又甜甜的美味水果。

像草莓、黑莓、树莓及蓝莓之类的浆果都喜好湿冷的生长环境。虽然它们在热带环境中极少长得很茂盛,但在热带地方较高的山坡和高山旁还是能够生长。有些种类的野生动物以采食浆果为生,其中以熊的体积最大。有些小型哺乳动物或鸟类亦喜食浆果,更别说人类了。野浆果明显比人工培育的浆果小,但许多人还是比较喜欢刚摘下的森林浆果那种浓郁的味道。

除了作为早餐麦片的佐料以外,浆果还有其他用途吗? 西方人

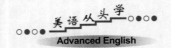
很会利用他们当地所产的水果。用浆果、明胶和糖很容易就制作出果冻、果酱以及蜜饯。这三种甜食唯一的差别仅在于制造过程。果冻是由水果榨汁而成,果酱来自于完全压碎的水果,而蜜饯则以半压碎或切过的水果制成。三种都一样好吃极了!

浆果亦用于烘烤食品中。派和馅饼常以浆果为馅,而许多糕饼类亦然。这些小果实也常被加在蛋糕或甚至面包中,尤其是在风干以后。此外,浓缩的浆果果汁亦可调制出夏日冷饮圣品。若再进一步浓缩便可制成各种糖浆,从薄煎饼到冰淇淋都可添加使用。作为调味品,则可加在糖果或巧克力中。在西方的烹调料理中,若没有这不起眼的浆果,生活便不会那么甜美有趣了。

不过对有些人而言,浆果还是新鲜的最好吃。他们说在清洗、冰镇后,将一大把浆果放入早餐麦片的碗中,加入冰牛奶,再撒上糖,那真是好吃的不得了! 由于浆果通常盛产于夏秋两季,而这样的点心或甜点在这两个季节里真是再恰当不过了! 对那些不住在浆果盛产地的人来说,当他们拜访这些幸运拥有它们的地方时,还是可以享用这些天然的水果点心。

② *Vocabulary & Idioms* 单词短语注解

1. **brew** [bru] *vi.* (茶或咖啡)冲好;泡开 & *vt.* 泡(茶);冲(咖啡)
    Old Mr. Chen brewed the tea a long time before serving it to his guests.
    陈老先生先让茶泡了很久后才端给客人喝。

2. **sentry** [ˈsɛntrɪ] *n.* 哨兵,岗哨

3. **sprinkle** [ˈsprɪŋkl] *vt.* 撒;洒
    If you add salt to your food, sprinkle it; don't pour it on.
    如果你要在食物中加盐,要撒,不能倒。

4. **spoon** [spun] *vt.* 用汤匙舀 & *n.* 汤匙
    Dad spooned the instant coffee into the cup and then poured the hot water.
    爸爸将速溶咖啡舀进杯子里然后倒入开水。

5. **mound** [maʊnd] *n.* 堆;小山,土丘

6. **concoction** [kənˈkakʃən] *n.* 混合调制的饮料;调制品

7. **botanist** [ˈbɑtənɪst] *n.* 植物学家

8. **specialty** [ˈspɛʃəltɪ] *n.* 专门,专长
    On the track team, Barry's specialty is the high jump while Paul's is the long jump.
    在田径队中,贝瑞的专长是跳高,而保罗的专长则是跳远。

9. **classification** [ˌklæsəfəˈkeʃən] *n.* 分类;类别

10. **asparagus** [əˈspærəgəs] *n.* 芦笋

11. **aggregate** [ˈægrɪgɪt] *a.* 聚合的 & [ˈægrɪˌget] *vt.* 聚集
    If we aggregate our savings, we'll be able to buy a house in ten years.
    如果我们将积蓄积攒起来,那么 10 年内我们就能买栋房子了。

12. **thrive** [θraɪv] *vi.* 茁壮成长;繁盛,欣欣向荣
    Most plants thrive in warm, sunny climates with plentiful rainfall.
    大部分植物在雨量充沛而阳光充足的温暖气候中都长得很茂盛。

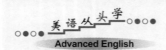

13. **forage** [ˈfɔrɪdʒ] *vi.* 搜寻(粮食)

While camping, we saw a bear foraging for food in the woods.

露营时我们看到一只熊在树林中觅食。

14. **domesticated** [dəˈmɛstəˌketɪd] *a.* 驯服的;驯养的

Domesticated pigs are much larger than wild boars.

驯养的家猪比野猪要大多了。

15. **condiment** [ˈkɑndəmənt] *n.* 调味品;佐料

16. **preserve** [prɪˈzɜv] *n.* 蜜饯(常用复数)

17. **gelatin** [ˈdʒɛlətn̩] *n.* 明胶

18. **in the process (of...)** 在(……)过程 / 进行中

Currently, I'm in the proccess of applying to Harvard.

目前我正在申请进入哈佛大学就读。

19. **be made from...** 由……制成(用于成品的性质和原料不同)

be made of... 由……制成(用于成品仍保有材料原来的性质)

Grandfather's homemade wine was made from plums.

祖父自制的酒是用梅子酿的。

This chair is made of pine while that table is made of oak.

这张椅子是松木制的,而那张桌子则是橡木制的。

20. **crushed** [krʌʃt] *a.* 压碎的,捣碎的

crush [krʌʃ] *vt.* 压碎,压坏

Without realizing it, Mom crushed Timmy's bicycle as she backed out of the driveway.

妈妈从车道上倒车出来时没注意而把蒂米的自行车轧坏了。

21. **concentrated** [ˈkɑnsn̩ˌtretɪd] *a.* 浓缩的

concentrated juice 浓缩果汁

22. **syrup** [ˈsɪrəp] *n.* 糖浆

23. **diverse** [daɪˈvɜs] *a.* 不同的;多样的

Africa has diverse habitats so that we can find many species of animals living there.

非洲境内有各种不同的栖息地，所以我们可以发现许多种动物在那里生长。

24. **hit the spot** （食物、饮料）令人满意，恰到好处

A cold beer on a hot summer day really hits the spot!

在炎热的夏天里来杯冰镇啤酒真是一大享受！

Lesson 27

The Global Proliferation of English

英语的全球化扩张

Everyone knows that there are more speakers of Mandarin than any other language in the world. Just over one billion people speak Mandarin as their native tongue. Compared to the nearly four hundred million native speakers of English, there would appear to be "no contest." Yet, it is just as well-known that English, not Mandarin, is the international language. Given these statistics, how can this be? Looking more closely at these and other facts reveals how English has become the world's most widespread language.

The history of written Chinese goes back at least 4,000 years, that of English little more than 1,000 years. The language called English is actually a hybrid of Scandinavian and German tongues created by immigrants to England in the 5th century A.D. Over the next 500 years, English developed into several major dialects spoken principally on most of the island of England. With continuous invasions by more Scandinavians and the French over the next few centuries, the English language received a fresh stimulus of foreign words, including Latin and Greek, the preferred classical languages in educational and political circles at that time in Europe. English as a principal language of literature did not evolve until the 14th century (Chaucer). By the 16th century, English was in full bloom, both in literature as well as in science.

England, referred to as Great Britain by this time, was amassing political, economic, and military power at breathtaking speed. The Industrial Revolution of the next century required foreign resources; imperialism gave the go-ahead for Britain and other European powers to not only take what they wanted from foreign lands but to lay conquest to those lands as well. Additionally, the rapid social changes engendered by the change from agriculture to manufacturing meant a surplus of farm workers, resulting in a waiting army of the dispossessed to emigrate to Britain's newfound colonies. In the 17th and 18th centuries, millions of Englishmen left their mother country for North America. In the 18th century, hundreds of thousands more set sail for Australia and New Zealand, as well as South Asia (the British Raj) and Africa (primarily South Africa). At the height of the British Empire, one-fourth of the world's people and lands were living under the Union Jack. Thus, by the close of the 19th century English rule had extended to the six principal continents (including British Guyana in South America).

This first-ever domination of the globe by one language is the primary reason for the international use of English today. A second reason lies in the rise of the United States of America

as a leading world power just as Britain's power began to fade. At the close of the 19th century, the U.S. fought with Spain (in 1898). After the U.S. victory, Spain ceded the Philippines, Guam, and Puerto Rico, resulting in the further introduction of English into Asia and the Caribbean. After U.S. involvement in both World Wars, despite Britain's continued decline, English became more commonly used around the world, especially in continental Europe and Japan. Since 1950, the rapidly growing U.S. economy as well as its academic and scientific excellence has insured that English remains the language of commerce and intellectual intercourse. The world of entertainment, most notably Hollywood, has also contributed to the popularization of English.

It is estimated that at least 300 million people around the world are now studying or using English as a second language, for purposes of education, employment, or personal interest. Some 75% of all international communications are in English, and with the rise of the Internet, it is doubtful that this figure will decrease any time soon. At the dawn of the new millennium, the world has one international language, English.

每个人都知道，全世界说中文的人口比说任何其他语言的人口都要多。大约有 10 亿以上的人口以中文为母语。相比之下，以英语为母语的人口只近 4 亿，显然是"没得比"。然而，众所周知，英语而非中文才是国际性的语言。看着这些统计数据，不禁要问怎么会这样？仔细看看这些统计数字和其他事实，便可得知英语是如何变成世界上最被广泛使用的语言。

中国书写文字的历史至少可追溯到 4000 年前，而英语的文字历史只有 1000 多年。英语其实是北欧语和德语的混合，由公元 5 世纪迁移至英国的移民所创。之后的 500 年间，英语发展成英格兰岛上绝大部分地区所说的数种主要方言。接下来的几个世纪，由于更多的北欧人及法国人不断入侵，英语接受了更多新奇外来语的刺激，其中包括当时在欧洲的教育及政治圈人士所偏爱的古典语言——拉丁语和希腊语。英语一直到 14 世纪(英国大诗人乔叟)时才发展成文学上的主要语言。到了 16 世纪时，英语在文学与科学上的使用均达到了巅峰。

当时被称为大不列颠的英格兰正以惊人的速度积聚政治、经济与军事力量。由于下一个世纪发生的工业革命需要外国的资源，再加上帝国主义兴盛，使得英国与其他欧洲国家的势力不断对外扩张，不仅竭尽所能地搜刮外国资源，更进一步征服了这些地方。除此之外，由于农业社会快速变迁至工业社会所造成的剩余农业劳动力，导致一群被迫失去一切的农民往外移民，在不列颠王国新建立的各个殖民地上生根。在 17 至 18 世纪时，有好几百万的英国人离开祖国移民至北美洲。18 世纪时，成千上万的英国人扬帆至澳大利亚和新西兰，甚至远达南亚(英属拉吉)和非洲(主要在南非)。在不列颠王国全盛时期，全球有近四分之一的人口与土地是在英国的控制之下。大约在 19 世纪末时,英国的势力遍及全球主要的六大洲(包括位于南美洲的英属圭亚那)。

这种空前第一次由单一语言统治全球的情况便是今日英语为何会成为国际语言的主要原因。第二个原因在于英国势力逐渐减弱而美国崛起成为最重要的世界强国。19 世纪末叶,美西交战(公元 1898 年)。美国胜利之后,西班牙放弃菲律宾、关岛以及波多黎各,促使英语势力延伸至亚洲及加勒比海一带。美国加入两次世界大战之后,尽管不列颠王国持续没落,英语在全世界却被更广泛地使用,特别是在欧洲大陆与日本。自 1950 年以来,美国的经济快速成长,而且在学术以及科学方面也表现优异,因此更确保英语继续成为商业与学术交流的主要语言。而像世界知名的娱乐王国好莱坞等娱乐圈对于英语的普及也功不可没。

据估计,全球至少有 3 亿人口为了教育、工作或个人兴趣等目的正在学习或使用英语为其第二语言。大约有 75% 左右的国际性交流以英语进行,而且随着互联网的兴起,这个数据恐怕短时间内是不会降低的。在新的千禧年开始之初,这个世界通用一种国际语言就是英语。

2 *Vocabulary & Idioms* 单词短语注解

1. **proliferation** [prə͵lɪfə'reʃən] *n.* 扩散；激增

2. **Compared to...,** 主语 + 动词 相较于……，……
   Compared to Florida, New York is very cold in winter.
   相较于佛罗里达，纽约的冬天非常寒冷。

3. **statistic** [stə'tɪstɪk] *n.* 统计数字（可数名词，常用复数形式）
   statistics [stə'tɪstɪks] *n.* 统计学（不可数名词）

4. **widespread** ['waɪd͵sprɛd] *a.* 广布的
   Evergreen trees are widespread around the globe.
   常青树广布于全球各地。

5. **go back** 追溯，回顾
   William claimed that his family could go back to 17th century.
   威廉宣称他的家族可追溯至 17 世纪。

6. **hybrid** ['haɪbrɪd] *n.* 杂种；混合物

7. **invasion** [ɪn'veʒən] *n.* 侵入；侵犯
   invade [ɪn'ved] *vt.* 侵犯
   In the popular movie *ID4*, space aliens invade Earth, but humans repel them.
   在卖座电影《独立日》中，外星人入侵地球却被人类击退。

8. **stimulus** ['stɪmjələs] *n.* 刺激；鼓励
   By lowering interest rates, the government gave business a stimulus for growth.
   政府通过降低存款利率刺激商业成长。

9. **be in full bloom** （花朵）盛开
   Tulips are in full bloom in April in the Netherlands.
   在荷兰郁金香于 4 月时盛开。

10. **evolve** [ɪ'vɑlv] *vi.* 发展，进化
    Darwin stated that man evolved from ape-like ancestors.

达尔文认为人类是由类似猿猴的祖先进化而来。

11. **imperialism** [ɪmˈpɪrɪəlˌɪzəm] *n.* 帝国主义

12. **go-ahead** [ˈgoəˌhɛd] *n.* 允许，同意（须与定冠词 the 连用）
As soon as we get the go-ahead from the manager, we'll start the new project.
我们一得到经理的同意便会立刻着手这个新计划。

13. **conquest** [ˈkɑŋkwɛst] *n.* 征服
The conquest of Mt. Everest finally occurred in 1953 by Sir Edmund Hillary.
珠穆朗玛峰最后终于在 1953 年被埃德蒙·希拉里爵士征服。

14. **engender** [ɪnˈdʒɛndə] *vt.* 酿成，产生
The strict policies of the new principal engendered dissatisfaction among the students.
新校长的严厉政策引发学生强烈的不满。

15. **surplus** [ˈsɝpləs] *n.* 剩余，过剩

16. **result in...** 导致……
The student's plagiarism resulted in his expulsion from college.
那名学生因剽窃而被大学退学了。

17. **the dispossessed** [ˌdɪspəˈzɛst]
= dispossessed people
被迫失去一切的人；无依无靠的人

18. **domination** [ˌdɑməˈneʃən] *n.* 支配；统治
dominate [ˈdɑməˌnet] *vt.* 支配；占主要地位
Due to its huge supply of oil, Saudi Arabia has dominated OPEC's decisions for many years.
沙特阿拉伯因供应大量石油，已经主导石油输出国组织的决策有多年之久。

19. **leading** [ˈlidɪŋ] *a.* 领导的；卓越的

20. **cede** [si:d] *vt.* 让给；放弃

Denmark ceded political rights to the inhabitants of Greenland.

丹麦放弃了对格陵兰岛上居民的政治权利。

21. **contribute to...** 导致 / 促使……；有助于……

Doing exercise regularly contributes to good health.

定期运动有助于身体健康。

22. **It's estimated + that** 从句 据估计……

It is estimated that millions of animal species have not yet been discovered.

据估计有好几百万种动物尚未被发现。

23. **doubtful** [ˈdaʊtfəl] *a.* 怀疑的，有疑问的

It's doubtful that man will ever live on the surface of Venus; the temperature there is about 500℃！

人类将来是否会住在金星表面令人怀疑；那里的气温大约为 500 摄氏度！

Lesson 28

Tips on English Body Language

使用英语肢体语言要诀

Reading 阅读

Mr. Garcia, a businessman from Madrid, Spain, is speaking English to one of his customers, Mr. Patton, from Vancouver, Canada. As they speak, a bystander notices that as Mr. Garcia slowly steps closer to Mr. Patton, the latter slowly steps away. This slow dance continues throughout the conversation until Mr. Patton is literally against the wall. He now crosses his arms in front of him. Mr. Patton appears nervous and a little annoyed; Mr. Garcia, aware of this, thinks he is not explaining himself well enough in English, even though Mr. Patton fully understands him. Thinking the business deal has gone sour, Mr. Garcia excuses himself and leaves.

What is going on here? If Mr. Garcia or any other non-native English speaking businessman, student, immigrant, or tourist had been aware of English body language, this unfortunate incident could have been avoided. Among English speakers, personal space is very important; indeed, personal space is important in all languages, but the distance considered critical to trigger discomfort differs. Spanish speakers tolerate a much closer speaking distance, a distance of some 30 centimeters, which is about half that which English speakers prefer. Thus, a Spanish speaker will instinctively move in closer to talk with an English speaker, who instinctively moves away, closer to his preferred speaking distance.

Body language is one kind of nonverbal communication, such as winking (to indicate "I'm kidding" or a sexual advance), or arms held akimbo (in some cultures, merely resting; in others, a threatening or defiant stance). This communication can, on occasion, be even more important than the actual words spoken.

Take winking for example. In most cases, English speakers will wink (the closing of only one eye) at each other to show that they are not serious about what they are saying. They may also cross their middle finger over their index finger to indicate the same thing. These gestures are extremely important as they virtually negate what the speaker says.

Another example is eye contact. In many American Indian and East Asian cultures, respect is shown by not looking directly into the eyes of a person considered of a higher social class than oneself. For Western Europeans, the opposite is true. For them, anything less than full eye contact is considered disrespectful or even devious. Problems have arisen when Chinese or Korean school children enter American or European schools. Western teachers assume that these children are

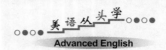
"up to something" or that they are showing disrespect, when, in actuality, they are behaving correctly for their own culture. One Chinese child was denied entry into a gifted students' school because he was considered "lacking leadership qualities" despite his overall excellence in his academic and interpersonal relations. When it was pointed out that Chinese children are taught not to be aggressive (show leadership qualities), the school reconsidered and admitted the lad.

Sometimes gestures used in different languages have contrary meanings. This can produce a humorous effect. In Vietnam and China, the gesture for "come here" is quite similar to that of waving "good-bye" in English. Thus, when speakers of these two cultures are leaving each other, if the English speaker gestures "good-bye," the Far Eastern speaker may misinterpret the signal as meaning, "come back here."

Learning body gestures is rather difficult from textbooks. The best way to learn gestures — for any language or culture — is to stay a while in a foreign country to learn not only what people say but how they say it. For most people, the learning of body language is an exciting and charming aspect of learning a foreign language.

　　加西亚先生是来自西班牙马德里的一位生意人,他正以英语和一位来自加拿大温哥华的客户帕顿先生交谈。当他们交谈时,一位旁观者注意到当加西亚先生慢慢向帕顿先生靠近时,帕顿先生就慢慢往后退。整个对话过程就像在跳慢舞似的一进一退,直到帕顿先生几乎要靠到墙壁了。这时候他把双臂交叉在胸前。帕顿先生显得紧张并有些恼怒。加西亚先生注意到这个现象,以为他的英语表达能力不够好,但其实帕顿先生完全了解他所说的话。加西亚先生认为这笔交易已经告吹,于是便找个借口离开了。

　　这到底是怎么一回事?假如加西亚先生或任何一位非英语系国家的生意人、学生、移民或游客曾经留意过英语肢体语言的话,上述的不幸事件就可以避免。个人空间对英语系人士而言非常重要;的确,个人空间对所有语言而言都很重要,但是被视为事关交谈时舒适与否的距离在各种语言中均有差异。西班牙语系人士与人所保持的距离比较近,大约为 30 厘米,这样的距离是英语系人士所能接受距离的二分之一。因此,西班牙语系的人在和英语系人士交谈时,会很自然地靠近对方,而后者会很自然地因为想保持他喜欢的交谈距离而后退。

　　肢体语言是一种非言辞的沟通方式,例如眨眼(以表示"只是在开玩笑"或者有性方面的暗示)或者两手叉腰(在某些文化里,它纯粹表示放轻松;而在某些文化里,它是一种威胁或挑衅的姿势)。这种沟通方式有时甚至比实际言语的沟通更为重要。

　　就拿眨眼来说,在大部分的情况下,英语系人士彼此眨眼(只闭一只眼)表示对正在交谈的内容不是很认真。他们也可能以中指交叉于食指之上的方式传达同样的意思。这些肢体动作极其重要,因为它们几乎否定掉说话者所说的话。

另一个例子是眼睛的接触。在许多美洲印地安文化与东亚文化里，不直视社会地位高于自己的人表示尊敬对方。对于西欧人士而言则恰好相反。对他们来说，如果不正视对方就会被视为不敬，甚至是不够坦诚。中国学生或是韩国学生进入美国或欧洲学校就读时，就曾经发生过问题。西方教师以为，这些孩童"在搞什么鬼"或者他们对老师不屑一顾，殊不知这些孩子是以自己的文化来表示对老师的尊敬。曾经有一位中国小孩被拒绝进入一所资优生学校就读，理由是该学生"缺乏领导才能"，尽管他学业成绩优异并且人际关系良好。后来经指出中国小孩被教导不可以太出风头（展现领导才能），校方才重新考虑同意该童入学。

有些动作出现在不同的语系里便有完全相反的意义。这时候会产生很有趣的效果。在越南和中国，"过来"的手势与英语系人士表示"再见"的手势很类似。因此，当这两种文化的人互相告别时，万一英语系人士以手势表示"再见"，那位远东人士很可能误解这个手势为"过来"之意。

从教科书上是很难学习到肢体语言的。最佳的学习方法是，不论学习任何一种语言或文化，最好是到当地待一段时间，而且不只学习"说"该语言，更要知道他们是"如何表达"的。对大多数的人而言，学习肢体语言是外语学习中令人感到刺激且充满吸引力的部分。

2 **_Vocabulary & Idioms_ 单词短语注解**

1. **bystander** [ˈbaɪˌstændə] *n.* 看热闹的人；旁观者

2. **go sour** 变坏；出差错
   sour [saʊr] *a.* 有酸味的
   It looks like all my plans are going sour.
   看来我所有的计划全部出问题了。

3. **unfortunate** [ʌnˈfɔrtʃənɪt] *a.* 不幸的，运气不好的
   An unfortunate incident occurred to Melvin today; his bicycle was stolen.
   梅尔文今天发生了一件不幸的小插曲；他的自行车被偷了。

4. **incident** [ˈɪnsədənt] *n.* 插曲；附带事件

5. **critical** [ˈkrɪtɪkḷ] *a.* 事关重大 / 重要的
   It's critical that we finish this project tonight, or the boss may fire us tomorrow.
   我们今晚完成这份计划事关重大，要不然老板明天可能会开除我们。

6. **trigger** [ˈtrɪgə] *vt.* 引起；触发
   His biased remarks triggered an argument.
   他偏颇的言论引发了一场争议。

7. **tolerate** [ˈtɑləˌret] *vt.* 容忍
   Our composition teacher tolerates no errors; we must rewrite until perfection.
   我们作文老师无法忍受错误；我们必须重写作文直到毫无瑕疵为止。

8. **instinctively** [ɪnˈstɪŋktɪvlɪ] *adv.* 本能地，直觉地
   When the little boy saw the candle, he instinctively moved closer towards it.
   那名小男孩看到蜡烛时便本能地靠近它。

9. **nonverbal** [nɑnˈvɝbḷ] *a.* 非言辞 / 口语的

10. **indicate** ['ɪndə,ket] *vt.* 表示，显示

Mr. Pinkerton indicated his displeasure with our work by ordering us to redo it.

平克顿先生命令我们重做来表示他对我们工作表现的不满。

11. **akimbo** [ə'kɪmbo] *adv.* 两手叉腰地

12. **threatening** ['θrɛtn̩ɪŋ] *a.* 恐吓的，有威胁性的

threaten ['θrɛtn̩] *vt.* 威胁

The movie star received several threatening phone calls.

该影星接到数通恐吓电话。

Many species of animal around the world are threatened.

世界上许多动物种类都受到威胁。

13. **defiant** [dɪ'faɪənt] *a.* 挑衅的，违抗的

Little Billy was defiant to his mother; he would go to bed right away rather than be forced to eat his broccoli.

小比利违抗他妈妈的要求；宁可立刻上床去也不愿被迫吃西兰花。

14. **stance** [stæns] *n.* (站立时的) 姿势；态度

15. **Take...for example.** 举……为例。

= Take...for instance.

Many large cities have serious traffic problems. Take Paris and Bangkok for example.

许多大城市都有严重的交通问题，巴黎和曼谷便是例子。

16. **middle finger** ['mɪdl̩ ,fɪŋgɚ] *n.* 中指

index finger ['ɪndɛks ,fɪŋgɚ] *n.* 食指

17. **negate** [nɪ'get] *vt.* 否定

18. **The opposite is true.** 实际上相反；反之为真。

Computers were supposed to reduce paperwork，but the opposite is true.

计算机本该减少文书处理工作的，但实际上刚好相反。

19. **devious** ['divɪəs] *a.* 不坦诚的；不率直的

20. **assume** [əˈsum] *vt.* 假设

It's January in Berlin, so you can assume that the weather there will be very cold.

柏林现在正值一月，所以你可以假定那里的天气会很冷。

21. **interpersonal relations** 人际关系

interpersonal [ˌɪntəˈpɜːsənl] *a.* 人与人之间的，人际的

22. **aggressive** [əˈgrɛsɪv] *a.* 具侵略性的

Tony's dog is very aggressive; don't play too rough with it.

托尼的狗极具侵略性；不要跟它玩得太凶。

23. **misinterpret** [ˌmɪsɪnˈtɜprɪt] *vt.* 曲解；误解

Sally winked at Joe to tell him she was kidding; Joe, however, misinterpreted the wink as an invitation.

萨莉跟乔眨眼表示她在开玩笑；然而乔却将之误解为是一种邀请。

Lesson 29

The Fundamentals of Public Speaking

演讲的基本要素

1   *Reading* 阅读

What is the most terrifying experience for most people? Is it drowning? Is it falling from a high place to their death? Is it being attacked by wild dogs? Though these experiences would certainly frighten most people, according to a recent poll, most people fear standing on a stage in front of a group of people to deliver a speech more than anything else, including the above life-threatening scenarios! What is going on here? Why is public speaking so menacing to most people?

Coaches of public speaking are fond of noting that public speaking "is an unnatural act." This is a tongue-in-cheek definition. Though people usually think of kinky sex as an "unnatural act," public speaking is in one important way unnatural. Human communication is inseparable from the human condition; that is, we actually spend more time in communicating with others (including listening to prerecorded spoken information) than we do anything else except breathing. There is, in other words, nothing unnatural in communicating. Standing on a stage in front of a group of people to deliver a speech, however, is certainly unnatural. In no other situation do so many humans have to keep quiet, watch the speaker attentively, and keep their minds on the message without an opportunity to respond. In no other situation can one speaker command the silence of an entire group of people. The responsibility on both sides is taxing; hence, the very act of speaking in public breaks the natural rules of human discourse and is thus unnatural.

The result of this unnatural act is to make both the speaker and the audience somewhat nervous in their new roles as dominant speaker and submissive audience. Most people do not understand the mechanics of crowd control or public speaking and are terrified by even the notion of appearing alone in front of what many perceive as a hostile group of people. Actually, the audience should be pitied, not the speaker. Who wants to sit through a long, boring speech? Who wants to sit and have to listen, without the chance to respond to the speaker? Accomplished public speakers learn to accept the tension between the audience and the stage and work with it. These savvy speakers have some tips for novice speakers.

An obvious suggestion is to be well prepared. Though it is not a good idea to write out a speech and memorize it (this is a recitation, not a speech), preparing an outline of the main ideas of the topic in logical order is. Further, practicing the speech out loud will help the speaker identify the strong and

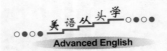
Advanced English

weak parts of the speech.

Another good idea is to face the audience. The audience, after all, is the object of the endeavor. By noting their expressions, a speaker can often monitor whether he is speaking loudly enough, too quickly or slowly, at too difficult a level, etc. "Sweeping" the audience with one's attention — looking at all sections of the audience at one time or another and regularly — helps the audience keep its attention focused on the speaker.

The most important of these suggestions, however, is simply to be sincere. The 16th president of the United States, Abraham Lincoln, said, "You can fool some of the people all of the time. You can fool all of the people some of the time. But you can't fool all of the people all of the time." These profound words are applicable to speakers in public. Since the audience is observing and listening to the speaker closely, it is virtually impossible for a speaker to fake sounding confident if he is not, nor is it possible for the speaker to convince an audience of his conviction if he himself is not convinced.

Following the simple tips listed above will improve a speaker's performance in public. Like any other skill or art, the more one practices, the better he is likely to become. Public speaking is not only for speech contests; all professionals must present themselves in public sooner or later. Rather than shirking the opportunity to speak, seize it and make the most of it the next time fortune knocks.

对大多数人来说,什么是最可怕的经历呢?是溺水吗?还是从高处掉下来摔死呢?或者是被野狗攻击呢?虽然这些经历的确会吓着很多人,然而,根据最近的一项调查指出,大多数人最害怕的一件事莫过于站在台上面对大众发表演说,害怕的程度甚至比上述要人命的情况还要高。到底是怎么一回事呢?为什么演讲会这么令人害怕呢?

教授演讲的人喜欢把演讲说成"是一种不自然的行为"。这种定义有嘲讽的意味。虽然大家通常会把怪异的性行为才当作是"不自然的行为",但严格地来说,演讲也是不自然的。人际沟通与人类的生活情况是密不可分的;也就是说,除了呼吸之外,我们花在与他人沟通的时间(包括收听事先录好的讯息)实际上比花在任何事情上的时间都还多。换言之,沟通根本就是一件很自然的事。不过,站在台上面对一群人做演讲确实是一件很不自然的事。只有在演讲的场合,才有那么多人得静下来全神贯注地看着演讲人,专心聆听演讲内容,而且还没有机会发问。也只有在这样的场合,演讲人才能掌控整个听众的肃静气氛。演讲人与听众双方的责任都很艰巨。因此,在公众前演讲这个行为已经违反了人际交谈的自然法则,因而是不自然的行为。

这种不自然的行为结果使得演讲者和听众皆对于他们的新角色——即演讲人很强势,而听众则处于从属地位——变得有些紧张起来。大部分的人都不懂得如何掌握群众和演说的技巧,因此一想到要单独站在这群他们认为具有敌意的群众面前,便感到害怕。事实上,该受到同情的是观众而不是演讲人。谁愿意从头到尾坐着听冗长又无聊的演讲呢?谁又愿意必须坐着听讲却没有机会向演讲人发问呢?经验老道的演讲人就会学习去接受他与听众之间的紧张关系,进而寻求应对之道。这些演讲老手有一些秘诀可供新手参考。

众人皆知的一个建议就是准备要充分。虽然把全部的演讲内容写下来并背下来不是一个好方法(这是背书,而非演讲),但是按逻辑顺序写下演讲大纲却不失为一个好点子。再者,大声演练讲稿也可以帮助演讲人知道演讲内容的强弱之处。

另一个好主意就是要面对听众。毕竟,听众是你得努力面对的对象。即由观察听众的表情,演讲人就可以知道他的音量是否够大,说得太快还是太慢,程度是否过难等等。用心扫瞄听众——不时并经常看着各角落的听众——可以帮助听众把注意力集中在演讲人身上。

不过最重要的建议就是要诚恳。美国第 16 任总统亚伯拉罕·林肯曾说:"你可以永远欺骗某些人,你也可以欺骗所有人于一时,但是你却无法永远欺骗所有人。"这些意义深奥的话也适用于在公众面前演讲的人。由于听众会仔细观察演讲人并聆听他的演讲,所以如果演讲人不够自信,要装成有自信的样子几乎是不可能的。同样地,如果演说者对自己的论点都无法信服,也就不可能让听众信服了。

听从上述简单的建议将可以改善演讲者在大众面前的表现。就像学习其他的技术和艺术一样,一个人越勤练就越棒。演讲不光是为了演讲比赛而已,各行各业的人迟早都得面对大众。与其逃避演讲的机会,倒不如在下次幸运之神降临身上时,抓住机会好好发挥一下吧。

2 *Vocabulary & Idioms* 单词短语注解

1. **fundamentals** [ˌfʌndəˈmɛntḷz] *n.*（常用复数）基本原理
The fundamentals of language learning include pronunciation, vocabulary, and grammar.
语言学习的基本要素包括发音、词汇和语法。

2. **deliver a speech** 发表演讲
= make a speech
When our English teacher asked us to deliver a speech, many students groaned out loud.
当我们英文老师要求我们发表演讲时，很多同学大声表示不满。

3. **scenario** [sɪˈnɛrɪˌo] *n.* 脚本；可能出现的情节
Mr. Johnson described the scenario of increased production and higher market share to enlist our support for his proposal.
约翰逊先生描述产量及市场占有率会增加等可能出现的情况，借以获得我们对他企划案的支持。

4. **menace** [ˈmɛnɪs] *vt.* 威胁，威吓
The chained dog menaced the children with snarling, but they merely laughed at him.
这只被链条锁住的狗不断吠叫想威吓这些小孩子，但他们只是嘲笑它。

5. **tongue-in-cheek** 以玩笑看待的
Though she knew he had failed the test, Maria taunted Erik with the tongue-in-cheek comment, "I suppose you aced the test, huh, Erik?"
虽然玛丽亚已经知道艾瑞克考试不及格，但她还是以嘲讽的口气对他说："我想你考得很不错吧，艾瑞克？"

6. **kinky** [ˈkɪŋkɪ] *a.* 古怪的，怪异的
Kinky sex acts shouldn't be encouraged. 怪异的性行为不应提倡。

7. **attentively** [əˈtɛntɪvlɪ] *adv.* 专心地
The students listened attentively to their teacher's telling of a ghost story.

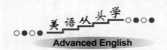

学生们专心地在听他们老师讲鬼故事。

8. **respond** [rɪ`spɑnd] *vi.* 回应(与介词 to 连用)

I would have responded to your letter earlier but I've really been quite busy.

我本该早一点回你的信,但我实在一直都没空。

9. **taxing** [`tæksɪŋ] *a.* 辛苦的, 吃力的

As far as I'm concerned, teaching is taxing but fun.

就我而言,教书很辛苦但蛮有趣的。

10. **discourse** [`dɪskɔrs] *n.* 交谈

Many sounds which are not considered words are nonetheless important in human discourse; in English these include "Hmm, " "Uh-oh, " and "Oops!"

许多声音虽然不被认为是具有意义的字,但在交谈里却非常重要;在英文里这些声音包括 Hmm、Uh-oh 及 Oops。

11. **submissive** [səb`mɪsɪv] *a.* 服从的;恭顺的

The students talked loudly and were very active until their teacher returned; then they were very submissive.

这些学生高谈阔论而且很活跃,直到老师回来后他们才变得很顺从。

12. **accomplished** [ə`kɑmplɪʃt] *a.* 有才艺的;有造诣的

By practicing the cello for many years with all his heart and concentration, Yo-yo Ma has become an accomplished musician.

经过多年全身心地练习大提琴,马友友先生终于成为一位很有造诣的音乐家。

13. **savvy** [`sævɪ] *a.* 有专业知识的

The savvy stock broker correctly predicted the success of many new companies and earned a fortune for his clients.

这名专业的股市经纪人正确地预测出许多新公司的成功,因此为他的客户赚了很多钱。

14. **novice** [`nɑvɪs] *a.* 初学的, 无经验的

The novice cowboy was so awkward that he even fell off his own horse once.

这位刚出道的牛仔笨拙到曾经从自己的马上摔下来。

15. **recitation** [ˌrɛsəˈteʃən] *n.* 背诵

Each second-grade pupil was responsible for the recitation of one nursery rhyme in the class performance.

每个二年级的小学生都要在班级的表演中，负责背诵一首童谣。

16. **endeavor** [ɪnˈdɛvɚ] *n.* 努力，尽力(= effort)

Only after many endeavors did Thomas Edison find the right metal to produce the first light bulb.

经过很多次努力后，爱迪生才找到正确的金属来制造第一只灯泡。

17. **profound** [prəˈfaʊnd] *a.* 深奥的；高深的

Many profound ideas were written down in the *Analects*.

《论语》记载了许多深奥的思想。

18. **convince** [kənˈvɪns] *vt.* 使相信

注意

a. 本动词多用于下列两句句型：

convince + sb + of + sth 使某人相信……

= convince + sb +that 从句

David convinced me of the feasibility of his idea.

= David convinced me that his idea was feasible.

大卫使我相信他的想法是可行的。

b. convinced [kənˈvɪnst] *a.* 相信的

I am convinced that Peter will offer me help.

= I am sure that Peter will offer me help. 我确信彼得会帮助我。

c. convincing [kənˈvɪnsɪŋ] *a.* 令人信服的

The swindler's story is definitely not convincing.

那个骗子的话当然不能信。

19. **conviction** [kənˈvɪkʃən] *n.* 坚信，信念

Only with diligence and conviction can young people reach their goals.

年轻人唯有靠努力不懈和坚定不移的信念才能达成他们的目标。

Lesson 30

New Orleans: Birthplace of Jazz
新奥尔良——爵士乐的发祥地

1   *Reading* 阅读

Welcome to Crescent City, birthplace of jazz! "Crescent City"? Yes, the nickname for New Orleans is Crescent City, due to its downtown location along a particularly deep bend of the Mississippi River. No matter what this unique American city is called, New Orleans has something for everyone.

To understand why this southern city is so different from any other city of the United States, and perhaps also how it evolved the musical form of Dixieland jazz, it is necessary to give a brief description of its history. Founded in 1718 by French developers, New Orleans grew rather slowly. Although ideal for shipping (New Orleans is only 180 kilometers from the mouth of the Mississippi, the world's fourth-longest river), the land around New Orleans is extremely low-lying (The city is actually below sea level!) and was at that time nothing more than a swamp. Despite this, the city attracted a wide range of peoples, including Canadian and European French, slaves, American Indians, and a few white British settlers. The area's continued slow growth, however, convinced France that it should sell all of its extensive land holdings in North America to Spain in 1763. Spain ruled this large area including New Orleans until 1800, when the whole area was again returned to France, only to be sold to the United States in 1803. The early French and Spanish cultures have remained with the city, even with the approach of 200 years of American rule.

The fortunes of New Orleans have always depended on its riparian location. The city gained importance in the War of 1812 and later as the terminus for shipping along the Mississippi through the Civil War. As shipping declined in importance due to the building of the railroads near the end of the 19th century, however, the Golden Age of New Orleans wound down. At this time, however, an artistic creation particular to New Orleans would resuscitate the city's fortunes.

Music has always played an important part in the daily lives of most Americans, and New Orleans happened to be home to some of the best musicians in the country. From 1880 to World War I, New Orleans with its cafe and night club society became host to a new form of music based mostly on the blues, but also on marches and ragtime music. In this style of music, the trumpet, clarinet, and trombone form the basis of instrumentation. As the trumpet is the loudest, it normally carries the melody, with the clarinet and trombone improvising above and below the trumpet, respectively. Sidney Bechet, Buddy Bolden, King Oliver, and most famously Louis Armstrong became symbols of the new music, playing to packed houses

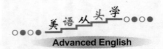

at first in the New Orleans red light district, and later to fans in music halls all around the world.

Though Dixieland jazz is today a preserved form of music like classical music, it later spawned Big Band music popular until the end of World War II, and urban jazz, still popular in the United States as well as in other countries. To hear the original Dixieland jazz one has only to book a hotel room in the Vieux Carre district of New Orleans anytime of the year. The French and Spanish architecture and laid-back lifestyle there is the perfect place to enjoy the upbeat but relaxing sounds of Dixieland jazz. Devotees of jazz pack Preservation Hall, Dixieland Hall, and the night clubs along Bourbon Street to hear their favorite songs. The New Orleans Jazz Club stages many jazz events, as does the city government, such as the International Jazz and Heritage Festival. If you can visit New Orleans only once in your life, though, save it for the world-famous Mardi Gras. You can then enjoy the best of New Orleans's night life with as many as one million other party revelers!

The city of New Orleans has so much to offer. Its history, unique cultural blend including world-acclaimed cuisines, and, of course, its musical gift to the world, Dixieland jazz, are reasons enough to place New Orleans high on everyone's "must list" of places to visit. Whether you want to travel to relax or join in spirited partying, New Orleans offers the tourist the best of both worlds.

欢迎莅临新月市,爵士乐的发祥地! "新月市"? 没错,新月市也就是新奥尔良的别名,因为它的市中心是沿着密西西比河上一段特别弯曲的河岸而得名。不管人们怎么称呼这个独特的城市,新奥尔良对每个人而言都有看头。

我们有必要简略说明这座南部城市的历史,才能了解该市与其他美国城市的不同,以及南方爵士乐风的演进史。新奥尔良是在1718年由法国人开发建立的,发展相当缓慢。新奥尔良因距离世界第四大河——密西西比河河口仅180公里,所以非常适合航运,不过新奥尔良四周属低洼地区(该市事实上低于海平面!),在开发初期它根本就是个沼泽区。虽然如此,新奥尔良却吸引了各类的移民包括法裔加拿大人、来自欧洲的法国人及奴隶、北美印第安人及少数英国白种殖民者。不过该区发展一直迟缓,这使得法国将它在北美洲所占有的广大土地于1763年卖给西班牙。西班牙便统治了这块包括新奥尔良在内的广大土地,一直到1800年,西班牙才又把整个区域归还给法国,不过在1803年却又卖给了美国。早期的法国和西班牙文化依然为该城所保有,即使美国统治了两百年,这种情形仍然未变。

新奥尔良的财富一直与其河岸的位置息息相关。1812年的美英战争突显其重要性,之后在南北战争整个期间,它又成了密西西比河的航运站。不过19世纪末期由于铁路的发展使得航运逐渐衰退,造成新奥尔良的盛况不再。但就在此时,新奥尔良独有的一项艺术创造再度造就这个城市的繁荣。

音乐在大多数美国人的日常生活中一直是很重要的一部分,而新奥尔良正巧是美国一些杰出音乐家的故乡。从公元1880年到第一次世界大战期间,新奥尔良的社会充斥着餐厅和夜总会,成了一

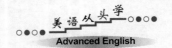

种新音乐风格的大本营,这种乐风大体上以布鲁斯为基础,也融合了进行曲和散拍乐曲。这种新乐风演奏的基本乐器包括小号、黑管和长号。因小号的声音最大,就由它吹奏主旋律,黑管和长号则配合小号分别作即兴高低音搭配。希尼·贝彻特、巴第·勃尔顿、金·奥利弗以及最有名气的刘易斯·阿姆斯特朗,就成了这种乐风的代表人物,早期在新奥尔良红灯区为满场的观众演奏,后来在全球各地音乐厅为乐迷表演。

　　虽然今天南方爵士乐像古典音乐般是一种刻意保留下来的音乐,但从中却发展出大乐团曲风,这种曲风一直流行至第二次世界大战结束,由此演绎出的都市爵士乐至今仍流行于美国及其他国家。如果想要听纯正的南方爵士乐,一年中任何时间,您只要向新奥尔良市福克区的旅馆订房间就可以了。那儿法式和西班牙式的建筑以及悠哉的生活方式正是享受南方爵士乐欢乐、轻松的旋律最理想的环境了。爵士乐的爱好者常常挤满了文化保护厅、南方爵士音乐厅以及波本街上的夜总会,以欣赏他们最喜爱的乐曲。新奥尔良爵士乐俱乐部和市政府也经常举办爵士乐演奏会,国际爵士乐和传统文化节就是其中的盛会之一。不过,如果一生中您只有一次造访新奥尔良的机会,建议你不妨就选在闻名世界的玛蒂歌节吧!(译注:玛蒂歌节为新奥尔良地区特有的天主教节庆,为时约一个半月。在这期间新奥尔良地区每日均轮流有花车游行。花车经过时,车上人员会投掷项链、面具、铜币给在两旁观看之路人以增加欢乐的气氛。在节庆的最后一天午夜时分前达到最高潮。午夜后教徒们则必须开始斋戒,禁酒、禁肉甚至禁欲以赎罪。)届时您就可以与多达百万的狂欢者一起分享新奥尔良夜生活的精华了。

　　新奥尔良大有看头。它的历史、独特的文化融合,包括享誉全球的美食,当然也包括它赐给全世界的大礼——南方爵士乐,这些都足以构成让每个人将新奥尔良列为旅游胜地的理由,不管你是要闲情逸致的旅游或者是参加派对狂欢,新奥尔良都能满足您的需求。

2 *Vocabulary & Idioms* 单词短语注解

1. **crescent** [ˈkrɛsṇt] *n.* 新月,弦月
   比较 : full moon 满月

2. **evolve** [ɪˈvɑlv] *vt. & vi.* 演进
   The automobile has evolved into a fast but safe driving machine today.
   汽车已经演变成一种快速而又安全的驾驶机器。

3. **description** [dɪˈskrɪpʃən] *n.* 描述
   give a brief description of 对……作简要的描述
   The salesman gave us a brief description of each computer in the store.
   这位售货员为我们简述店里的每部计算机。

4. **a wide range of** 各式各样的……
   range [rendʒ] *n.* 范畴
   Department stores offer us a wide range of goods to choose from.
   百货商店提供我们各式各样的货品让我们选购。

5. **convince** [kənˈvɪns] *vt.* 说服
   = persuade [pɚˈswed]
   Arnold is so stubborn that I don't think you'll be able to convince him to change his mind.
   阿诺德很固执,所以我认为你无法说服他改变他的心意。

6. **extensive** [ɪkˈstɛnsɪv] *a.* 广泛的
   The typhoon caused extensive damage in the area where it came ashore.
   台风在它登陆的地区造成广泛的灾害。

7. **only to + V** 却……，竟然……

本短语用以表示意想不到的结果使用时，之前多置逗号。

John studied very hard, <u>only to flunk</u> the test.

约翰读书很用功，可是竟然没考及格。

8. **with the approach of** 随着……接近

approach [ə'protʃ] *n.* 接近

With the approach of Chinese lunar New Year, all the Lin children became more excited.

随着农历新年的接近，林家的孩子个个都变得更兴奋了。

9. **riparian** [raɪ'pɛrɪən] *a.* 河滨上的；河岸上的

Some trees and bushes grow only along riparian banks; they are not found in any other environment.

有些树木和矮树丛只长在河滨上；在其他的环境里是看不到它们的。

10. **wind down** 平静下来

wind 的发音为 [waɪnd]，三态为：wind, wound [waʊnd]、wound。

It took the baseball players two hours to wind down from the excitement of their championship party.

这些棒球员花了两个小时才从冠军庆功宴的兴奋中平静下来。

11. be 　**particular**　 **to +** 地方名词　为某地所独有，原产于某地
　　　 unique
　　　 peculiar
　　　 native
　　　 indigenous

It is not too much to say that jazz is a kind of music particular to the U.S.

爵士乐是原产于美国的音乐，这样的说法并不为过。

12. **resuscitate** [rɪ'sʌsə,tet] *vt.* 使复苏

The government hopes that the building of a new Disneyland there will resuscitate its economy.

政府希望新迪斯尼乐园的兴建会带来经济的复苏。

13. **improvise** ['ɪmprə,vaɪz] *vi.* 即兴演出

Good musicians can not only play according to traditionally prepared scores, but they can also improvise at will with other musicians.

优秀的音乐家不但能够依据传统准备好的乐谱演出,而且能够随意与其他音乐家作即兴演出。

14. **respectively** [rɪˈspɛktɪvlɪ] *adv.* 个别地,分别地

My two favorite cities are New York and Berlin, in America and Germany, respectively.

我最喜欢的两个都市是纽约和柏林,它们分别位于美国和德国。

15. **spawn** [spɔn] *vt.* 大量出现,酿成

In the 1960s the Beatles helped spawn a whole youth revolution in music and fashion.

60 年代,披头士乐团在音乐及时装方面引发全面的青年革命。

16. **stage** [stedʒ] *vi.* 举办(一场演出)

Our school drama club will stage a short play for the Christmas program.

我们学校的戏剧社将会为圣诞节表演一出短剧。

17. **as does / do / is / are + 主语** ……亦是如此

此为倒装结构,变化如下:

a. 前一句有 be 动词时, as 引导的句子亦用该 be 动词。

Peter is handsome, as his brother is. 彼得很英俊,跟他哥哥一样。

= Peter is handsome, as is his brother.

b. 前一句有助动词(如 can, will, may), as 引导的句子亦用该助动词。

Peter can sing, as Mary can. 彼得会唱歌,跟玛丽一样。

= Peter can sing, as can Mary.

c. 前一句有动词时, as 引导的句子则用人称及时态使用助动词 do、does 或 did。

Peter studies hard, as Mary does. 彼得很用功,跟玛丽一样。

= Peter studies hard, as does Mary.

Lesson ③1

The Fine Art of Giving
给予的艺术

❶   *Reading* 阅读   📖

Ralph is all excited. When his poor wife Lisa comes home after a hard day's work in the office, he enters the living room beaming. "Happy birthday, darling!" he exclaims while thrusting the neatly packed gift at her. Momentarily delighted as she quickly unwraps the package, Lisa murmurs, "Oh, Ralph, I thought you'd forget my birthday again this year. Gee, thanks, sweet..." Her voice trails off as she lifts the cover of the box to disclose its contents: steak knives. Ralph, still beaming, then pulls the trigger of the rifle aimed at his own foot: "I bought some steaks, so you can use your new birthday gift to get us dinner ready!"

Most women, of course, would use the new knives on Ralph, not the steaks. What did poor Ralph do wrong? He certainly meant well. He noted his wife's birthday carefully, sacrificed time and money to buy a gift on time, and even had the box gift-wrapped. Where did he go wrong? Long before Ralph bought the knives, he should have paid more attention to those things Lisa expressed or showed an interest in. While walking or shopping, many people notice things that obviously

234

interest them; this is the time to make a mental note of what those items are for future purchase. While talking, too, many people reveal "wish list" items they dream of having. Noting these items and turning them into gifts at a later time, whether for Christmas, birthday, anniversary, graduation, or any other important occasion, distinguishes just another item on a shelf in a department store or in a catalogue from "the perfect gift."

Gifts do not have to be objects. Doing house chores for parents or spouses which normally are "theirs," taking someone out on the town or wheeling an invalid around the block, or taking the time and effort to create one's own personalized handicraft can bring smiles as wide as those aroused by the giving of expensive presents. Many a child would prefer to have an afternoon at the cinema and an evening in their favorite restaurant with Dad than another of his expensive gifts, some with the price tag still on them! Many parents would rather happily settle for a full day with their children at home or on a picnic than with a mailed check or "Happy Birthday" greeting on their answering machine. Perhaps the expression "Time is money" really is true: time spent with those whom we do not often see is indeed precious. Sacrificing time from one's busy schedule to give to another is often more meaningful than a pricy gift from an upscale department store.

Of course, there is nothing wrong with buying gifts. Everyone has needs, including material needs. Close friends or family members often know what their loved ones need even

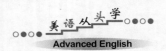

before they do! Few compliments can make us happier than "You always know what to give me." For those who never seem to know what to prepare for others but who would like to learn, observing the successful giving of gifts to others is as good a place to start as any. In any class, family, or crowd, someone always seems to know the right gift to give at the right time. Making mental notes of these occasions and then writing them down in a special notebook can make the difference between a future present well-received and one politely accepted.

Still, only a social incompetent would criticize or refuse a gift from another. Being gracious even in disappointment is a sign of good manners. Besides, a gift is an expression of thoughtfulness and a token of love. We should never question the judgment of the donor; instead, as we say in English, "It's the thought that counts." Learning to appreciate whatever little surprises life prepares for us is a sure sign of maturity and poise. When the giving of symbols of our appreciation and love to others becomes an art form to the giver, these profound words can be understood: "It is more blessed to give than to receive."

拉尔夫兴奋极了。他可怜的妻子莉莎在公司辛苦了一天回到家时，拉尔夫就脸上带着微笑走进了客厅。他忙不迭地把包得漂漂亮亮的礼物递给爱妻，同时高兴地说道："亲爱的，祝你生日快乐！"她匆匆拆开礼物，刹那间高兴起来，喃喃地说道："哦，拉尔夫，我还以为今年你又会把我的生日给忘了呢。哦，谢谢你，亲……"她把盒盖打开来看看到底里面装的是什么礼物：居然是一组切牛排的刀子，这时她的话也静止了下来。拉尔夫脸上仍然带着微笑，自讨没趣地说道："我买了一些牛排，所以你可以用你这次新的生日礼物为我们准备一顿晚餐。"

当然，大多数女人会把刀子用在拉尔夫身上而不是用在切牛排上。可怜的拉尔夫到底做错了什么呢？他原本当然是好意的。他仔细地记住了太太的生日，花费时间和金钱准时买了礼物，甚至还把刀组盒包成礼品。他哪里出了差错呢？早在拉尔夫买下这组牛排刀前，就应多留意一下莉莎曾表示过中意的东西。许多人逛街购物时，会注意到自己明显感兴趣的东西；也就是在这个时候，我们心中就要记下这些东西，将来再买下来。同样地，很多人在谈话时也会透露自己梦寐以求的东西。把这些东西记下来，以后在圣诞节、生日、结婚周年纪念、毕业典礼，或者是其他重要场合买下来当礼物送给对方，这样的做法将使原本只不过是百货商店货架上或目录上的一件商品变成"完美的礼物"。

礼物不一定是实物。帮父母或配偶做通常是属于"他们干的"家务、带某人上街、帮残疾者推轮椅到街区转一转，或者是花点时间和心思做一些具有个人特色的手工艺品送人也可以带给对方欢笑，这种欢笑跟对方收到名贵礼物时所发出的欢笑是一样灿烂的。不少小孩宁可在下午跟爸爸看场电影或是晚上跟爸爸在餐厅用餐而不愿接到一份他送的贵重礼物,有些礼物甚至还有价格标签在上面呢! 很多父母宁可整天与孩子在家欢聚一天或者出外野餐也不愿收到儿女寄来的支票或是电话录音机上的一句"生日快乐"的问候话。或许"时间就是金钱"这句话是千真万确的:花点时间陪陪我们难得见面的亲友,确实是每一刻都很珍贵。从繁忙的日程表中牺牲一些时间来陪陪别人要比在高级百货商店中买贵重礼物送人有意义多了。

当然,买礼物并没错。每个人都有需求,包括物质上的需求。好友与家人要比他们挚爱的人更清楚了解他们的所需! 所有的赞美言词没有几句话要比这句更令我们开心了:"你总是知道要送什么东西给我。"对那些似乎永远不知道该准备什么礼物给别人但是却愿学习的人来说,观察别人如何成功地送礼给对方是最好的学习起点。在任何班级、家庭或者群体中,似乎总有人懂得在适当的时机送适当的礼物。心中暗记这些场合并用特别的笔记本记下来,这关系着你未来送礼时,对方是否会很乐意接受或只是礼貌性的收下来而已。

当然,只有不懂社交的人才会批评或拒绝对方的礼物。在失望中仍流露出落落大方的风范是有风度的表现。何况,礼物是一种体贴和爱的象征。我们千万不可质疑送礼者的判断力;相反地,诚如英文的一句话:"心意才是最重要的"。学会感激生活所带给我们的小惊奇是一种成熟和稳健的表现。我们若愿将那些代表我们的感激及爱的东西赠与对方,而这种赠与也成为一种艺术时,就能深深体会到这句深奥的话:"给予比收受更有福"。

2 *Vocabulary & Idioms* 单词短语注解 ✍

1. **beam** [bim] *vi.* 微笑（与 at 连用）
   I almost passed out when I spotted that stunning beauty beaming at me.
   我发现那位美女对着我微笑时，几乎快昏了过去。

2. **thrust** [θrʌst] *vt.* 攻击；刺入（本文则表 "快速递上" 之意）
   thrust 三态均为 thrust。
   The courageous soldiers thrust themselves into danger without hesitation.
   勇敢的士兵毫不犹豫地冲入险境。

3. **unwrap** [ʌnˈræp] *vt.* （将包裹）打开（为 wrap "包扎" 的反义词）
   Little John unwrapped the box and, much to his delight, found a toy car in it.
   小约翰打开盒子，发现里面有一部玩具车，他高兴极了。

4. **disclose** [dɪsˈkloz] *vt.* 透露，揭发
   The suspect's parents didn't disclose their son's whereabouts to the police.
   嫌犯的父母未对警方透露他们儿子的去向。

5. **gift-wrap** [ˈɡɪftˌræp] *vt.* 将（某物）包装成礼物
   "Have this watch gift-wrapped and send it to my son, " said the boss to his secretary.
   老板对秘书说："把这只手表包成礼品，寄给我的儿子。"

6. **make a note of** 记下来，写下来
   Make a note of everything I say, or you'll be sorry.
   把我讲的话一一记下来，否则你会不好过。

7. **distinguish A from B** 区别 A 与 B，使 A 有别于 B
   distinguish [dɪsˈtɪŋɡwɪʃ] *vt.* 使有别于
   Knowledge enables us to distinguish right from wrong.
   知识使我们明辨是非。

8. **personalize** [ˈpɜsn̩ˌaɪz] *vt.* 把个人姓名标示在（物品）上

Mom bought a whole set of linen napkins and had them personalized with our family's surname.

妈妈买了整套的麻制餐巾,并把我们的姓标示在上面。

9. **upscale** [ˈʌpˌskel] *a.* 生活水平高的, 上流的

After working hard for many years, the Andersons sold their small house and moved into an upscale neighborhood.

奋斗多年后,安德森一家卖掉他们的小房子,搬入高级住宅区了。

10. **compliment** [ˈkɑmpləmənt] *n.* & [kɑmpləˌmɛnt] *vt.* 恭维, 称赞

compliment + 人 + on + 事 称赞某人某事

Be careful not to take flattery as a compliment.

小心不要把谄媚的话当作是恭维。

11. **incompetent** [ɪnˈkɑmpətənt] *n.* 没有能力的人

本字原为形容词, 表"无能的", 亦可作名词, 尤用于下列短语中:

a hopeless incompetent 无可救药的无能者

Peter is a hopeless incompetent when it comes to women; he is so awkward that no girl wants to be seen with him.

说到追女人,彼得毫无能力;他笨拙得没有一个女孩子愿意跟他在一起。

12. **count** [kaʊnt] *vi.* 重要(= be important)

There is indeed nothing special about outer beauty; it is inner beauty that counts.

外在美没什么了不起;重要的是内在美。

13. **poise** [pɔɪz] *n.* 沉着处世的能力(不可数)

Elsa has such poise; although she is only 16, she is as confident as a young woman in her 20s.

艾尔莎沉着处世的能力真好;虽然她才 16 岁,却拥有 20 多岁女人的自信。

Lesson 32

Professional Telephone Etiquette

职业电话礼貌

Reading 阅读

"(ring...ring...ring...) Hello?"

"Uh, excuse me, but is this Dragon Mountain Trading Company?"

"Who's calling?"

"Well, I'm Mr. David Parker, and I...."

"What do you want?"

"I'd, uh, like to speak with your manager."

"He's busy. Call back later. (click)"

Unfortunately, some companies still have not trained their employees in the professional use of the telephone. The above telephone conversation is not only discourteous, but also hurts business prospects. If Mr. Parker is calling to speak with a number of companies in order to build business relationships with them, he is not very likely to call Dragon Mountain Trading

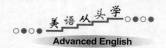
Company again. To prevent this from happening, those who are responsible for the conduct of business over the telephone should keep a few simple but important points of telephone etiquette in mind.

The first and most important point concerning the professional use of the telephone is the attitude towards any caller. The telephone is the lifeline of the company with the outside world, and those who call in should be considered potential business prospects. However, customers are not nameless, faceless voices; they are people who enjoy being and deserve to be treated courteously and fairly. Everyone who uses an office telephone should remember that a friendly, helpful, and efficient call can make the difference between success and failure with the caller. Once this is appreciated, a business office can operate at its full potential.

How can all office workers put the above principle into practice? Several tips on the successful use of the office telephone have been collected from many companies over the years. This advice is timeless and covers all manner of businesses. Companies whose employees use the following telephone etiquette are more likely to keep their clients and attract new customers.

When answering the phone, all employees should identify the company and themselves. In the above hypothetical conversation, the office worker should have answered the call with, "Dragon Trading Company, Janice Wang, speaking." rather than force Mr. Parker to inquire whether or not he had dialed the company telephone number correctly. In some companies, employees will further identify their position within the company, such as "Kodak, Michael Chou, sales representative, speaking." or "Great Light Sports Equipment, Frances Chang, personnel director, speaking. May I help you?" and so on. Of course, in larger companies which have automated dialing or an operator, it is often unnecessary to state the name of the company (that has been done already on the tape or by the operator), but self-identification continues to be helpful, and, thus, important.

As with Frances Chang above, a simple "May I help you?" is enough to invite the caller to state his or her business with the company. However, it is always important to listen carefully to the caller's request. It is possible, for example, that the callee is not the right person for whom the caller is looking; by listening carefully, the callee can respond to the needs of the customer on the line. Treating callers as routine or even annoying interruptions to one's work is a mistake. If someone outside the company has taken the time to call in, someone inside the company should take the time to respond to it.

If the caller is looking for someone not presently in the office, a message should be taken and then repeated over the phone to make sure all the information is correct. If a product or service is unavailable, the caller should be told

what possible substitute is available or when the desired item will be back in stock. Every effort should be made to please the caller. This extra effort makes a lasting impression, the kind of impression that often results in repeat business. In our conversation above, the callee should have told Mr. Parker when the manager would return to take his call, or offered to take a message for him. Hanging up on the caller is the best way to lose business.

After information has been given or help offered, the call should not be considered finished. Each call is an opportunity to further the interests of the company, as with "We have other fine products. I'd be happy to send you our catalogue." or "Our company can offer additional services. My manager or I would be happy to make an appointment with you to discuss them." Above all, end each conversation with a genuine "Thank you for calling. It's been a pleasure serving you." or other lines to make the customer feel he or she is not being discarded as just another business obligation. Successful calls make customers feel welcome to call again.

Today's world of business is highly competitive. People have not changed, however. They still like to be treated in a friendly and helpful way, even over the telephone. A genuinely friendly and helpful attitude on the phone, identification of company and callee, offers of help or message taking, promotion of further business opportunities, and leaving the caller with the feeling that he would like to call again seem like insignificant matters. Added up, however, they can make the difference between a company's success and failure in our high-tech but still human world.

"(铃……铃……铃),喂？"

"呃,对不起,这里是龙山贸易公司吗？"

"你是哪一位？"

"我是大卫·帕克先生,我……"

"你想要干什么？"

"我想跟贵公司经理谈谈。"

"他正在忙。待会儿再打过来。"(咔,挂电话声)

很遗憾地,还是有些公司未能训练员工职业的电话礼貌。以上的电话交谈不但粗鲁,也损失了商业机会。如果帕克先生打电话是要与若干公司聊聊以建立商业关系,很可能就不会再打电话给龙山贸易公司了。为了防止类似的事情发生,负责使用电话洽商的人士应牢记一些有关电话礼仪的简要重点。

有关职业电话礼貌首要重点就是对来电者的态度。电话是公司对外联络的生命线。任何来电者都应被视为潜在的未来商业顾客。不过,来电的客户可不是没有姓名和没有脸孔的声音而已;他们是喜欢被并也应被礼貌且公平对待的人。每位公司电话使用者皆应牢记,一通友善、热心又有效率的电话会决定与来电者关系的成败。一旦了解这点之后,公司便可全面发挥潜能运作了。

公司所有员工要如何履行上述原则呢？多年来不少公司累积了有关成功运用公司电话的若干提示。这些提示不受时间限制且涵盖所有的行业。员工若能遵行下列电话礼仪,公司便可能留住老客户也能吸引新客户。

所有员工在接电话时,应报出公司的名称以及自己的姓名。在上述的模拟电话交谈中,那位员工就应向来电者作这种的回应:"您好,这里是龙山贸易公司,我是贾尼斯·王。"而不是迫使帕克先生询问自己是否拨对了公司电话号码。有些公司的员工会进一步地表明自己在公司的职称,如:"这里是柯达公司,我是业务代表迈克尔·周。"或是"这里是巨光运动器材公司,我是人事主任弗朗西丝·张。我能为您效劳吗?"诸如此类。当然,规模较大的公司设有自动转接电话系统或总机时,通常不需要报出公司的名号(电话录音或总机就已提供这些讯息了),但是自我介绍仍是有所帮助的,所以是很重要的一个环节。

上述范例中,弗朗西丝·张简单的一句:"我能为您效劳吗?"就足以让来电者愿意表明他或她与公司的商务关系。不过,仔细聆听对方的需求永远是最重要的。举例而言,接话者可能不是来电者所要寻找的对象;只要仔细听,接话者就能在电话中响应对方的需求。将来电者当作例行公事般来应付,或将之视为中断自己工作的困扰,这样的态度是不对的。公司外的人若拨冗来电,公司员工理应拨冗应对。

如果来电者找寻的人目前不在公司内,应请对方留下口信并重复内容确定无误。如果公司无法提供现货或服务,应将可以替代的现货或指定产品的进货日期告诉来电者,必须尽心地来满足来电者,这种尽心会留下难以磨灭的印象,并往往带来不断的商机。在上述的对话中,接话者理应告诉帕克先生经理何时会返回公司回电,或是主动为他留话。失去商机最快的途径莫过于向来电者挂电话了。

提供讯息或服务后,并不表示这通电话就结束了。每通来电都是促进公司利益的机会,譬如我们可以说:"本公司还有其他不错的产品。我很乐意把公司产品目录寄给您。"也可说:"本公司还可提供其他的服务,经理或我本人很乐意与您约个时间见面谈一谈。"尤其重要的是,每次的电话交谈结束前别忘了献上诚挚的一句:"谢谢您的来电。很荣幸能为您服务。"或者其他一些话语,让顾客感到他或她没有仅被看成是履行工作职责而抛弃。成功的电话交谈会使客户感到开心而愿意继续来电。

今天商场上的竞争非常激烈。但是,人的基本习性还是没变。每个人都希望自己被善待,即使是在电话上也是一样。在电话中展现出真诚友善及助人的态度,先行介绍自己和公司,提供对方协助,为对方留口信,为公司争取其他商机,以及让对方觉得很开心而愿意继续来电等,这些看似微不足道的小事,在我们这个高科技却仍以人为主导的世界中,却是公司成败的关键。

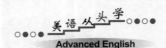
2   *Vocabulary & Idioms* 单词短语注解

1. **discourteous** [dɪsˈkɜːtɪəs] *a.* 不礼貌的（courteous 的反义词）
   Anyone that is rude and discourteous is certainly looked down upon wherever he is.
   粗鲁无礼的人走到哪儿都会被人瞧不起。

2. **prospects** [ˈprɑspɛkts] *n.* 希望，前途（恒为复数）
   "Never marry a boy with no prospects like John，" said the father to his only daughter.
   父亲对其独生女说：“万万不要嫁给像约翰这样没出息的人。”

3. **prevent...from** 阻止……免于……
   prevent [prɪˈvɛnt] *vt.* 阻止
   Most parents prevent their minor children from smoking.
   大多数父母禁止未成年子女抽烟。

4. **keep...in mind** 将……牢记在心
   = bear...in mind
   While traveling overseas, keep in mind, "When in Rome, do as the Romans do."
   在国外旅游时，牢记这句话：“入乡随俗”。

5. **etiquette** [ˈɛtɪkɛt] *n.* 礼仪，礼节（不可数）
   International etiquette is what a successful diplomat should master.
   成功的外交家应精通国际礼仪。

6. **attitude** [ˈætəˌtjud] *n.* 态度
   该词通常与介词 to、toward 或 towards 连用
   What's your attitude toward life? 你对人生抱什么态度？

7. **make the difference between A and B**
   在 A 和 B 之间造成不同，是 A 与 B 的关键
   If you wear a jacket while hiking, it will make the difference between your catching a cold and staying well.
   远行时你是否穿上夹克，是决定你感冒还是健康的关键。

8. **put...into practice** 把……付诸行动

Julia is such a hypocrite; she never puts her words into practice.

朱丽叶真是个虚伪的人；她从不履行她的诺言。

9. **identify** [aɪˈdɛntəfaɪ] *vt.* 辨识，辨认

The police could not identify the badly decomposed body in the lake.

警方无法辨认湖里那具严重变形的尸体。

10. **hypothetical** [ˌhaɪpəˈθɛtɪkl̩] *a.* 假设的，臆想的

If I were a millionaire, I would buy you a house and a car, but pitifully this is only a hypothetical situation.

我若是百万富翁，就会买房子和汽车给你，不过遗憾的是，这只不过是假设的状况罢了。

11. **automate** [ˈɔtəˌmet] *vt.* 使自动化

It can be very costly to have the office automated, but it is worth it.

办公室自动化会很花钱，但却是值得的。

12. **routine** [ruˈtin] *n.* 日常作息，例行公事 & *a.* 例行的

In our daily routine, we are likely to run into many setbacks.

在日常生活中，我们常会遇到许多挫折。

13. **substitute** [ˈsʌbstəˌtjut] *n.* 替代者 & *vi.* 代替（与介词 for 连用）

Honey can substitute for sugar when cooking certain European dishes.

当烹煮某些欧洲食物时，蜂蜜可以代替糖。

14. **hang up on sb** 挂某人电话

The girl hung up on her boyfriend after sensing that he had told a lie.

女孩发现男友对她撒谎时，便挂他电话了。

15. **discard** [dɪsˈkɑrd] *vt.* 丢弃

Please discard your used box lunches in the trash cans around the park.

请将诸位用过的饭盒丢到公园四周的垃圾筒里。

16. **obligation** [ˌɑbləˈgeʃən] *n.* 义务

be under an obligation to + V 有义务

= be obliged to + V

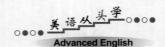

Parents are under an obligation to educate their children.

父母有义务教育他们的小孩。

17. **competitive** [kəm'pɛtətɪv] *a.* 竞争的

The computer industry is highly competitive; many companies try to be the first to make the same product.

计算机行业竞争很激烈；很多公司都设法抢先生产同样的产品。

Lesson 33

Did You Remember Your Tickets?

旅游行前准备

1   *Reading* 阅读

Robert and Michael leave their apartment in a rush and find a taxi to take them to the airport. After paying the driver, Robert turns to Michael and says, "That was close! I thought we'd be late for sure. Come on, now, we have to take our luggage into the terminal and check in at the counter." "Right," responds Michael, "did you bring the tickets and our passports?" "No," answers Robert, "I thought you did!"

This scene could be from a TV sitcom or real-life. Every traveler's nightmare is forgetting something major like tickets, ID, passport, or money. This is needless worry, however, if travel plans are made early and organized efficiently. Since travel for education, business, or pleasure is more and more common, knowing how to prepare for worry-free travel is both important and beneficial. This lesson will help the novice or experienced traveler avoid potential travel problems, allowing for a pleasant journey.

Unless there is an emergency, travel plans should be

made well in advance. Never wait till the last minute to try to reserve airline tickets or hotel rooms. They may not be available, or you may be forced to choose an inconvenient or unnecessarily expensive flight or accommodation. The best day to book travel or lodging arrangements is the day you decide to go.

After all travel arrangements have been secured, the next step is to make sure your travel documents are in order. Is your passport valid? Remember that some countries do not accept passports which have less than six months' validity remaining. Do you need an overseas driver's license? These can be applied for at certain government or travel agencies or associations. Leave enough time to process any paperwork that is required. A travel agent or experienced friend or colleague can inform you of what steps need to be taken and how best to take care of them.

Preparing for packing is next. Even if the proposed trip is a month away, certain items should be readied at once. The most important of these is, of course, the luggage itself. Do not wait for a last-minute sale on the suitcase of your choice; be ready with enough good-quality luggage long before you leave for the airport or train station. In choosing baggage, make sure that it is within regulations, especially for air travel. Oversize suitcases or carry-on baggage can be a great headache later.

The rule of thumb for packing is pack less, not more.

Most travelers buy at least some items on the road, and some buy quite a few souvenirs or personal items, so leave enough room for them. Keeping a toiletry kit permanently in a piece of luggage is a smart idea. In this way, you will never have to worry about whether your razor or deodorant has been packed. Casual clothing, including footwear, should be placed into bags or suitcases the night before. Formal wear can be packed in the last-minute to reduce wrinkling. Don't worry about taking reading or writing material for pleasure; newspapers and magazines are widely available, as is stationery.

The day before leaving, reserve a cab for the day of departure if needed. This is also the best time to ask a friend or relative for a wake-up call for those leaving early on the day of departure; this is even better than one's own alarm clock. Leave a copy of the itinerary with lodging telephone numbers with a family or friend. Place all travel documents into one briefcase or folder rather than in several places for ease of checking. After packing each piece of luggage, put it near the door for easy exit. These simple advance steps will help reduce stress on the day of travel.

On the day of departure, the only steps remaining should be to pack one's formal clothing and to recheck one's travel documents and money. Whether for business, education, or pleasure, travel can be an unforgettable experience. Whether you want to remember that experience fondly or try to forget it depends on the few simple steps outlined above. Bon voyage!

　　罗伯特和迈克尔匆忙离开寓所，找了辆出租车送他们到机场去。付了司机钱后，罗伯特转向迈克尔说："好险哦！我还以为我们肯定赶不上了呢。动作快点，我们必须立刻带着行李进入航站楼到柜台办理登机手续。"迈克回答说："说的是。我们的机票和护照你带了吗？"罗伯特回答说："没有。我还以为你带了呢！"

　　这种场面可能会出现在电视情景剧中或现实生活中。每位游客的梦魇就是忘了某些重要的东西，像机票、身份证件、护照或钱财等。然而，如果你能事先有效率地筹划好你的旅游计划，上述这些就用不着担忧了。由于留学、经商及观光日趋普遍，懂得如何安排一趟无忧无虑的旅游不仅重要，也是件好事。本课将协助旅游新手或老手避免旅游可能发生的问题，进而享受一趟愉快之行。

　　除非状况很紧急，否则旅游计划应事先做好。千万不要拖到最后关头才预订机票和旅馆房间。否则，你可能订不到机票或住房，要不就是你可能被迫要选很不方便或贵得离谱的班机或住房。你决定旅游的当天就是预订机票和住宿最恰当的时机。

　　旅游计划安排妥当后，下一步就是确定你的旅游文件是否已准备齐全。护照是否有效？记住有些国家是不接受有效期间剩下不到六个月的护照。你需要国际驾照吗？这些证件都可在特定的政府机关、旅行社和协会办理申请。要预留足够的时间来处理必要的文书作业。旅行社和有经验的朋友或同事均可告诉你应采取哪些步骤及如何妥善完成这些步骤。

　　整理行李是接下来应做的事。即使离拟定旅游的日子还有一个月之久，若干物品也应立即准备妥当。这些物品中最重要的当然就是行李箱了。千万不要等到最后一刻才去选购你的行李箱；早在你赶往机场或火车站前就要把足够数量且质量不错的行李箱准备好。在选购行李箱时,要确定它们符合规定,尤其是符合航空旅游的规定。过大的行李箱和随身行李都会成为后来令人头痛的事。

行李打包大致的原则就是要带得少而不是带得多。出门的人大都会在旅程中至少购买些物品,有些人甚至会买一大堆纪念品或个人用品,因此要预留足够的空间装这些东西。始终在行李中准备一套私人的盥洗用品是个上策。这样的话,你就永远不用担心是否已将刮胡刀或身体芳香剂装进去了。休闲服,包括袜子等,应该在旅游的前一晚就放进行李袋或行李箱里。正式场合要穿的服装可以在出发前再打包以降低弄皱的机会。不必担心要不要携带消遣性的书报或文具;报纸杂志到处都买得到,文具亦然。

旅游的前一天,如有必要,应事先预订一部出租车以应出发当天之需。出发当天要提早出门的话,可在前一天要友人或亲戚来电叫醒你;这样的做法甚至比自己的闹钟更棒。记得复印一份旅游行程及住宿地方的电话号码给家人或朋友。把所有的旅游文件放在同一个手提箱或皮包里而不是散放在行李箱里,这样的话,查看这些文件就很方便。所有的行李整理完毕后,应该把它们放在门边以便于携带。这些简单的先前作业有助于减轻旅游当天的紧张和压力。

出发当天依然要做的就是将正式场合穿着的衣服打包并再次检查旅游文件和钱财。不管是出差、留学或观光,出门旅行都会是个难忘的经历。你想要个难忘之旅或是想忘掉这趟旅行就取决于上述所列的几个简单的步骤了。祝你一路顺风!

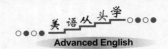

2   *Vocabulary & Idioms* 单词短语注解

1. **in a rush** 匆匆忙忙地
   = in a hurry
   John finished his essay in such a rush that it was full of mistakes.
   约翰匆匆写完文章,因此错误百出。

2. **sitcom** [ˈsɪtˌkɑm] *n.* 情景喜剧(一种连续单元喜剧, 是 situation comedy 的缩写)

3. **worry-free** [ˈwɜɪˌfri] *a.* 无忧无虑的
   注意
   此为复合词,作形容词用,乃由 free from worries (免于忧虑的)化简而成。类似的复合形容词还有:carefree(无忧无虑的)、duty-free(免税的)、sugar-free (不含糖的)等。

4. **beneficial** [ˌbɛnəˈfɪʃəl] *a.* 有益处的
   Sunshine and moisture are beneficial to plants.
   阳光与湿气有益于植物。

5. **novice** [ˈnɑvɪs] *n.* 新手 (= rookie [ˈrʊkɪ])
   I know a great deal about painting, but when it comes to music, I am a novice.
   我很精通画画,可是说到音乐,我就是个新手了。

6. **potential** [pəˈtɛnʃəl] *a.* 潜在的 & *n.* 潜力
   Only under healthy investment conditions can enterprises develop to their full potential.
   只有在健全的投资环境下,企业才能完全发挥实力。

7. **allow for...** 体谅 / 顾及……
   = take...into consideration
   Allow for his age before asking the old man to lift the box.
   你要这位老先生抬箱子之前,先要考虑到他的年龄。

8. **in advance** 事先,预先
   The movie is too long; tell me the ending in advance, please.

这部电影太长了，请先把结局告诉我吧。

9. **secure** [sɪˈkjʊr] *vt.* 获得，弄到手；确保……的安全

   John succeeded in securing the information he wanted for his paper.

   约翰成功获得他论文所要的资料。

   We secured our house by locking all the windows and doors before the typhoon struck.

   在台风来袭前，我们锁上所有的门窗来确保房子的安全。

10. **valid** [ˈvælɪd] *a.* 有效的

    validity [vəˈlɪdətɪ] *n.* 有效性

    The concert ticket is valid for half a month.

    这张演唱会的入场券半个月内有效。

11. **inform sb of sth** 告之某人某事

    inform [ɪnˈfɔrm] *vt.* 告知

    She informed her parents of her safe arrival.

    = She informed her parents that she had arrived safely.

    她向双亲报告她已平安抵达。

12. **ready** [ˈrɛdɪ] *vt.* 将……准备妥当 (= prepare)

    The students readied themselves for the speech contest.

    学生努力准备演讲比赛。

13. **rule of thumb** 根据经验的做法

    As a rule of thumb, you should leave a tip after having a meal at a restaurant.

    根据经验的做法，在餐厅用餐后应留小费。

14. **reserve** [rɪˈzɝv] *vt.* 预订

    = book

    = make a reservation for

    Could you reserve a table for me at the new restaurant?

    你能帮我在那家新餐厅订个位子吗？

15. **fondly** [ˈfɑndlɪ] *adv.* 深情地

The lonely old man murmured fondly to his dog.

这位孤独的老先生深情地对着他的狗喃喃低语。

16. **outline** [ˈaʊtˌlaɪn] *vt.* 将……写成大纲

We all like Professor Jenkins because he always outlines his lecture on the blackboard at the beginning of each class.

我们都喜欢上詹金斯教授的课，因为他总是在上课开始时把他的讲课大纲写在黑板上。

Lesson 34

English Small Talk Topics: What Is OK and What Is Not?

慎选英语闲聊话题

1 *Reading* 阅读

"When in Rome, do as the Romans do." What may be perfectly acceptable to talk about in one culture may offend or even shock others when in a different culture. Accordingly, it is important to know what topics are "safe" to discuss with strangers or acquaintances from a different background. Topics which can be discussed freely within a culture are referred to as "small talk."

As with any other language, English has its own stock of non-offensive topics. Among these are the weather, occupation, immediate conditions, family and family life, and school or work. Topics in English which should never be broached include one's personal life, physical appearance (unless complimentary), income, and age as well as religious, sexual, or political views. Each of these topics — both approved and taboo — will be discussed in more detail later.

Small talk is extremely useful when first meeting others. Actually, one purpose of small talk is not to find out the

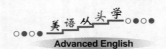

answers to questions like "How are you?" or "Nice day, isn't it?" but rather to gauge whether the person is the sort whom one would like to know better. While talking about essentially unimportant matters such as the weather, life in the office, or how many children — if any — one has, each speaker has the opportunity to determine whether the other is cooperative, interesting, potentially useful or friendly, etc. If a person answers the inquiry about the weather with a grunt or "I hate sunny days," no further energy need be wasted!

Another purpose of small talk, once a speaker is satisfied that the other person is worth talking with, is to explore possible areas of interest or cooperation. By tactfully going through "safe topics," some information may be revealed which leads the speaker(s) into a deeper discussion, especially when a topic is a shared hobby or interest. Talking about the weather may reveal that one speaker enjoys recreation like camping or hiking. Shooting the breeze about one's family may disclose similar shared family hobbies like board or card games or barbecues and picnics. In other words, small talk may serve as probing of the other person's personality and lifestyle.

"Everybody complains about the weather, but nobody ever does anything about it," so goes an old saying. Perhaps the safest of all small talk topics is the weather. Whether good or bad, a comment about the temperature or sky condition (sunny day, cloudy day, rainy day, etc.) never offends. Commenting on the crowded traffic or the late bus, or high prices in the department store (immediate conditions) is also always appropriate. Similarly, most people do not mind talking about their work, family, or school life, either, since for most people these are experiences held in common. Even so, asking whether someone is married or not crosses over into personal information and therefore should be avoided. If the speaker happens to mention that he or she has children or is married, however, it is all right to pursue the topic.

Asking such questions as "How much do you weigh?" "How old are you?" or "How much do you earn?" are taboo in English, at least as starters for conversation. Only when friends are close would they ask such questions of each other. Likewise, for most people, religious or political convictions or sexual mores are considered private matters. These should not be discussed until one speaker offers his opinion first. It is not necessary, though, to respond in kind. The other speaker can change the subject to show that this is a taboo subject.

Foreigners are usually "forgiven" the "indiscretion" of asking others offending questions. Still, it is not a good idea to wear out one's welcome. When a subject has been turned down, only a tactless person would pursue it. Being sensitive to others' feelings and sense of privacy will win more friends and influence more people than a reckless line of questioning. When curiosity seems to be getting the upper hand, remember that "Silence is golden."

　　"入乡随俗"在某文化里可以完全被接受谈论的话题,在另一个不同的文化里可能就会得罪人,甚至可能会吓着对方。因此,了解什么话题可以"安全地"跟不同文化背景的陌生人或熟识的人交谈是件很重要的事。在同一文化中可以高谈阔论的话题我们就称之为闲聊。

　　就如所有其他的语言一样,英语里也有一些不会得罪他人的闲聊话题。这些话题包括了天气、职业、目前个人的状况、家人与家居生活、学校或者是工作。英语中禁忌的话题则包括了个人生活、外貌(除非是赞美的话)、收入、年龄以及宗教信仰、性观念或政治观点等。这些被允许的以及禁忌的话题将容后逐一详细说明。

　　与人初次见面时,闲聊是非常管用的。事实上,闲聊的目的之一并非要如何回应"你好吗?"或"天气不错吧,是不是?"等这类问题,而是判断对方是否是我们想进一步认识的那种人。在谈论一些无关痛痒的话题时,如天气、办公室生活或是对方有多少小孩(若对方有的话),就有机会判断对方是否合作、有趣、有所帮助或友善等等。谈到有关天气的问题时,对方嗯了一声敷衍了事,或说:"我讨厌艳阳天,"那就甭再浪费唇舌了。

　　闲谈的另一目的就是,一旦满意对方且了解对方值得交谈后,谈话人就要探究彼此可能感兴趣及合作的范畴。透过巧妙运用"安全的话题",便可获知一些信息进而促使双方作更深一层的谈论,尤其是话题与彼此爱好或兴趣有关的时候。谈论天气透露对方可能喜欢露营或远足等休闲活动。而闲聊家庭的话题则可显露彼此相似的家居爱好,如下棋、纸牌游戏、烤肉及野餐等。换言之,闲聊可用来探知对方的个性和生活方式。

　　俗话说:"人人怨天气,无人管天气。"因此,或许天气可说是最安全的闲聊话题了。谈论气温或天气(晴天、阴天、雨天等),评语不论是好是坏,永远都不会得罪人。至于交通拥挤、公交车迟到或百货商店的物品售价太高等(临时发生的话题),也是很适合的。同样地,大多数人也不介意谈论他们的工作、家庭或学校生活,因为对大多数人而言这些都是大家共同的生活经验。即使如此,若是询问对方是否已婚时则就涉及私人问题,因此就应避免提及。对方若不经意提及自己有小孩或已婚时,追着这个话题发挥就无妨了。

"你多重?"、"你几岁?"或"你收入多少?"等的问题在英文里是个禁忌,至少不可用作闲聊的开场白。只有熟识的朋友才会彼此问这样的问题。同样地,对大多数人而言,宗教信仰、政治立场及性观念等话题也都属于个人隐私。除非对方先发表他的看法,否则不应谈论这些话题。不过,你也不用跟着回应你的看法。对方可能会改变话题,以表示这个话题是个禁忌。

外国人在闲聊时如果不慎提及禁忌的问题通常是会被原谅的。但是,因此而损及对方对你的好感也是不明智的。当对方已拒谈某个话题时,只有不上道的人才会追着这个话题谈下去。敏感察觉对方的感觉及对隐私的注重,要比胡乱问一连串问题能使你赢得更多的朋友,也影响更多的人。当好奇心蠢蠢欲动时,切记这句话:"沉默是金。"

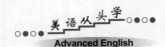
2　*Vocabulary & Idioms* 单词短语注解 ✍

1. **offend** [əˈfɛnd] *vt.* 触怒，得罪
   When Allen asked Mrs. Patterson about her age，he offended her.
   艾伦问到帕特森太太的年纪时,触怒了她。

2. **acquaintance** [əˈkwentəns] *n.* 认识的人
   make one's acquaintance 认识某人
   He is no friend of mine；he's just a nodding acquaintance.
   他不是我朋友,他只是点头之交。
   I made his acquaintance long before I went to college.
   我早在念大学之前就认识他了。

3. **refer to A as B** 把 A 称作 B
   You can refer to a Toyota as a car，but you cannot refer to a car as a Toyota.
   你可以称丰田是一辆车,但却不能把任何车称为丰田。

4. **broach** [brotʃ] *vt.* 提及，谈到 (= talk about)
   At the meeting，Gary broached the subject of salary raises to the boss.
   在会议中,盖瑞向老板提到加薪的话题。

5. **taboo** [tæˈbu] *n.* 禁忌
   Marriage is regarded as a taboo to monks and nuns.
   对和尚和尼姑来说结婚是一种禁忌。

6. **in detail** 详细地，巨细无遗地
   When writing a proposal for your boss，you have to write down everything in detail，or he won't consider it.
   你向老板提出建议案时,必须详细写下每个细节,否则他是不会考虑你的建议案的。

7. **grunt** [grʌnt] *n.* 咕噜声；怨言
   We could hear a fierce grunt of pain as the deer was shot down by the hunter.
   当那只鹿被猎人射倒时,我们可听到一阵凄厉的惨叫声。

8. **tactfully** [ˈtæktfəlɪ] *adv.* 圆滑地
   tactful [ˈtæktfəl] *a.* 圆滑的，技巧的（反义词为 tactless）
   Jack is tactful in dealing with people. 杰克与人相处很圆滑。

9. **shoot the breeze** 闲聊，鬼扯
   The young men were sitting on their motorcycles and shooting the breeze; they obviously had nothing to do.
   那些年轻人坐在他们的摩托车上瞎扯；显然是无事可做。

10. **probe** [prob] *vt. & vi.* 探索，探究
    = explore [ɪkˈsplɔr] *vt.*
    The mayor instructed the police to probe thoroughly into the case.
    市长指示警方彻查本案。

11. **"...," so goes an / the old saying.**
    俗话说："……。"
    "Honesty is the best policy," so goes the old saying.
    = As the old saying puts it, "Honesty is the best policy."
    = As the old saying goes, "Honesty is the best policy."
    俗话说："诚实是上策。"

12. **comment** [ˈkɑmɛnt] *vi. & n.* 评论（皆与介词 on 连用）
    comment on... 对……加以评论
    = make a comment on...
    I don't feel that I should comment on Helen's transgressions.
    我觉得我不应对海伦的过错加以评论。
    Don't make comments on matters which don't concern you.
    不要评论和你不相关的事。

13. **indiscretion** [ˌɪndɪsˈkrɛʃən] *n.* 言行不检（可数或不可数皆可）（为 discretion 的反义词）
    indiscreet [ˌɪndɪsˈkrit] *a.* 言行失检的，不谨慎的（为 discreet 的反义词）
    The politician was forced to step down because of his indiscretions.
    这名政客因行为不检而被迫下台。

14. **reckless** [ˈrɛklɪs] *a.* 鲁莽的；不顾一切的

A reckless driver is likely to get caught in a traffic accident.

鲁莽的司机很可能会发生车祸。

The soldiers are fighting against the enemy, reckless of danger.

战士们正不顾危险地与敌人战斗。

15. **get the upper hand** 占上风

Our basketball team got the upper hand in the second half.

我们的篮球队在下半场中占了上风。

Lesson (35)

Hot Animals Around the World: The Panda

世界热门动物：熊猫

1   *Reading* 阅读   📖

Some countries have adopted an animal as a kind of national mascot. The bald eagle is often thought of as representing the United States, for example. New Zealanders proudly display their kiwi, a native flightless bird. Australians cannot seem to make up their minds whether the koala or the kangaroo should represent them. China also has two animals which often stand out in everyone's mind: the dragon and the giant panda. As the dragon is a mythological animal, that leaves the giant panda as the only real animal representative of China.

Although dragons have been associated with China for thousands of years, the panda's inclusion into the Chinese psyche is far more recent. The giant panda was not even discovered until 1869; it was already a rare animal at that time, living in the high bamboo forests of Sichuan province and neighboring parts of Tibet. Its more plentiful cousin, the lesser panda, is also referred to as the cat bear or bear cat; however, zoologically speaking, it is neither. The lesser panda

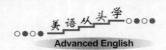
is a member of the raccoon family, whereas the giant panda's classification is still a dilemma: some authorities consider it a member of the bear family while others maintain that it belongs to the raccoon family, too.

The giant panda is well named. Reaching a length of 1.5 meters and 160 kilograms, this gentle omnivore is among the largest land animals of China. Subsisting on a diet of bamboo and other plants, and even small animals, it can consume as much as 30 kilograms of food a day. Now that's a giant appetite! Its distinctive markings — broad, white bands of fur alternating with black, and small black circles around the eyes — have endeared the giant panda to animal lovers everywhere.

People may want to hug this huge "teddy bear," but giant pandas prefer to live a solitary life. This may account for their scarcity; these pandas are on all official lists of endangered animals. Estimates of the wild panda population are difficult due to the rugged terrain they live in, but most experts agree that fewer than 1000 remain free. As they give birth to only one or two cubs when mating is successful, the giant panda's survival in the wild is anything but a foregone conclusion. The Chinese government has set aside 11 nature preserves where pandas are known to exist, hoping to protect them from the rapid encroachment of man. Though poaching is still a problem, strict laws have reduced this senseless carnage.

Pandas in captivity number less than 100, the largest

share, of course, in China. Those in Western zoos are treated as royalty and are the object of intense scientific interest and care. Recently, veterinarians have given male giant pandas Viagra, hoping to increase the animals' reproductive efficiency. Results are thus far inconclusive. Though births have been reported, they are few and far between. It seems the panda's chance of survival is razor-thin.

Its extinction would be a sad day for all of mankind. These playful and gentle creatures never fail to amuse adults and children alike lucky enough to observe them in zoos. Every plant and animal that leaves the world due to human intervention and encroachment of habitat diminishes the world we live in. The richness of the Earth's original biodiversity is being attacked. Will future generations of humanity be left with only a few species of food plants, and zoos exhibiting cockroaches and rats?

Hopefully, men will learn the excesses of their ways and strive to protect the remaining natural habitats as an investment not only in the flora and fauna remaining but in the quality of life, present and future, of all those on this planet. "Extinction is forever" and "There is only one world" need no longer be heard if one becomes conscious of preserving the beauty of the natural world around us.

若干国家已选择某动物作为国家的吉祥物。例如,美国就选择秃鹰作为它的象征。新西兰人则骄傲地展示他们的几维鸟,一种不会飞的鸟。澳大利亚人似乎无法决定应该选择树袋熊或袋鼠来代表他们的国家。中国也有两种大家都知道的动物——龙和大熊猫。由于龙是神话里的动物,因此大熊猫就成了真正代表中国的动物了。

虽然龙和中国的渊源已有数千年之久,大熊猫融入中国人的心灵却是近几年的事。大熊猫直到 1869 年才被发现,在当时,它已是生活在四川省高山林区和邻近西藏地区的稀有动物。比它数量多的表亲是体型较小的小熊猫,有人称之为猫熊或熊猫;但是,就动物学的观点来说,它既不属于熊科动物也不属于猫科动物。事实上,小熊猫是浣熊科的一种,而大熊猫的归属至今则仍无定论:有些专家认为它应属熊科,有些则认为它亦应属浣熊科。

大熊猫的命名蛮贴切的。大熊猫个性温顺,属杂食性动物,身长 1.5 米,体重达 160 公斤,是中国最大的陆地动物之一。它以竹子和其他植物及小动物为食,一天可摄取多达 30 公斤的食物。真是好大的胃口啊!它全身黑白色相间的宽条纹以及小小的黑眼圈,是它最明显的标识,也因而受到各地动物爱好者的喜爱。

大家都想抱抱这只庞大的"泰迪熊"。但大熊猫性喜独居,这可能是它们数量稀少的原因;熊猫已被列入濒危动物的所有官方保护名单之中。野生熊猫数量很难估计,因为它们都住在崎岖不平的地区。但专家大多认为野生熊猫的总数不到 1000 只。熊猫若成功受孕,每胎也只能产下 1 到 2 只小宝宝,因此,野生大熊猫的存活率根本无法遽下结论。中国政府已经设立了 11 处已知有熊猫出没的自然保护区,希望能保护熊猫免于人类快速的侵害。虽然偷猎仍是个问题,但严格的法律已使滥杀减少。

动物园饲养的熊猫数量目前不到 100 只,其中大多数当然是在中国。西方国家动物园内饲养的熊猫被视作皇族看待,也引起科学界强烈的兴趣及关爱。近来,有兽医给雄性熊猫服用药物,希望增加它们的繁殖力。截至目前为止,尚未有具体结果。虽然已有小熊猫诞生,但数量少之又少。熊猫的生存机会似乎很渺茫。

熊猫如果灭绝将是全人类的悲哀。这些活泼、温和的动物总是逗得有幸在动物园内观赏到它们的大人及小孩开心。任何一种植物或动物如果因为人类对它们栖息空间的侵犯和介入而使它们从地球上消失的话,也将会使得人类生活的空间变得越来越小。地球丰富原生物的多样化正遭到破坏。将来人类留给未来子孙的东西是否只剩下几种食用植物和只有展示蟑螂及老鼠的动物园呢?

但愿人们能从人类放肆的行为中汲取教训,努力维护现存的自然栖息环境,不仅为现有的动植物设想,也为地球上我们这一代及后代子孙的生活质量设想。如果人人都能了解保护我们外围自然生态美的重要性,就不必再听到"物种一旦灭绝便永远灭绝了"及"我们只有一个地球"这样的警语了。

② *Vocabulary & Idioms* 单词短语注解

1. **adopt A as B** 采用 A 当作 B

   adopt [əˈdɑpt] *vt.* 采用

   Our school has adopted blue and orange as our school uniform colors.

   我们学校已采用蓝色和桔色作为校服的颜色。

2. **be thought of as...** 被视为……

   = be regarded as...

   = be looked upon as...

   = be viewed as...

   = be seen as...

   = be thought to be...

   = be considered (to be)... （* 非 be considered as... ）

   John is so naive as to be often thought of as a moron.

   约翰太天真,因此常被人视为蠢蛋。

3. **stand out** 突出, 杰出

   There were many fine performances, but Alice's singing stood out among them.

   很多的表演都很好,但是爱丽丝的歌唱却是其中最杰出的。

4. **be representative of...** 代表……

   representative [ˌrɛprɪˈzɛntətɪv] *a.* 代表的

   The Eiffel Tower is representative of modern architecture rather than classical architecture.

   埃菲尔铁塔是现代建筑物的代表,而不是古典建筑物的代表。

5. **be associated with...** 与……有关联, 被与……联想在一起

   associate [əˈsoʃɪˌet] *vt.* 把……联想在一起

   Bullfighting is associated with Spain.

   人们常会把斗牛和西班牙联想在一起。

   注意

   associate 亦可作不及物动词, 亦与 with 连用, 表"与……交往。"

272

None likes to associate with one who is selfish and snobbish.
谁都不喜欢与自私而又势利的人交往。

6. **dilemma** [dəˈlɛmə] *n.* 左右为难

be in a dilemma 处在两难的情况中

Sean was caught in a dilemma; should he invite Gabriella or Janice to the dance?

西恩处在两难的情况中；他该邀请加布里拉还是贾尼斯参加舞会呢?

7. **subsist on...** 靠……为生

subsist [səbˈsɪst] *vi.* 生存

When I was a student, I subsisted on bread and tuna fish every day.

我还是学生的时候，每天以面包和金枪鱼为生。

8. **alternate with...** 夹杂着……

alternate [ˈɔltərˌnet] *vi.* 轮流，交替

Red stripes alternate with white stripes on the flag of the United States.

美国国旗是红色条纹夹杂着白色条纹。

9. **endear A to B** 使 A 受到 B 的喜爱

endear [ɪnˈdɪr] *vt.* 使喜欢

Miss Aller's good mood, conscientious work, and open-mindedness endeared her to all her students.

艾勒老师的好脾气、尽责的工作态度和开朗的个性使她备受她所有学生的喜爱。

10. **account for...** 说明……，解释……

Hard work accounted for John's success in business.

努力是约翰经商成功的原因。

11. **give birth to...** 生下……

Theresa gave birth to a healthy baby girl last Thursday in the hospital.

特蕾莎上星期四在医院生下一个健康的女宝宝。

12. **be anything but + 形容词 / 名词** 绝不是……

= be by no means + 形容词 / 名词

= be not + 形容词 / 名词 + at all

John is anything but a good student; he goofs around all day.

约翰绝不是个好学生;他整天混日子。

13. **foregone conclusion**

事情尚未结束就可预料的结论,笃定的结果

There is only one candidate in the election, so his winning is a foregone conclusion.

这次的选举只有一位候选人,因此他笃定当选。

14. **intense** [ɪnˈtɛns] *a.* 强烈的

It is intense pain that erodes a cancer patient's will to live.

真正剥蚀癌症病人的生存意志的是剧痛。

比较

intensive [ɪnˈtɛnsɪv] *a.* 密集的

The coach put his team into intensive training before the game.

教练让他的球队在赛前做密集训练。

15. **be few and far between** *少之又少*

Nowadays, people like that good old man are few and far between.

当今像那位老好人的人少之又少。

16. **razor-thin** [ˈrezəˌθɪn] *a.* (机会)渺茫的

注意

razor [ˈrezə] 原指"刮胡刀片", thin 则为形容词,表"细薄的"之意。razor-thin 表"薄得像刀片般",引喻为"渺茫的",多用以修饰 chance (机会)。

His chance of winning the election was razor-thin.

他选举获胜的机会很渺茫。

17. **never fail to V** 总是……,一定……

A filial son never fails to take good care of his parents.

孝顺的儿子一定会好好照顾双亲。

18. **encroachment** [ɪnˈkrotʃmənt] *n.* 侵犯,侵占

encroach [ɪnˈkrotʃ] *vi.* 侵犯，侵占（与介词 on 连用）

Man has encroached on much of the habitat of the wildlife.

人类已大大侵占了野生动物的栖息地。

19. **strive to V** 努力要……，尽力要……

strive [straɪv] *vi.* 努力

三态为：strive、strove、striven。

The students strove to pass their upcoming tests by studying day and night.

这些学生日夜苦读，努力地想通过即将来临的考试。

20. **be conscious of...** 意识到……

conscious [ˈkɑnʃəs] *a.* 有意识的

Only in the 20th century have people become conscious of the fragility of nature and thus have started to conserve resources.

直到 20 世纪人们才意识到大自然的脆弱，因而开始节约自然资源。

Lesson 36

Vancouver: Asia's Newest City

温哥华——亚洲的新都市

1 Reading 阅读

What? Wait a minute! Did I read that right? I thought Vancouver was in Canada, not in Asia. Why is the title of this article "Vancouver: Asia's Newest City"?

Relax, everyone. Yes, Vancouver is still in Canada, North America's largest country, not in Asia. Over the past twenty years, however, Asians from China, Taiwan, Hong Kong, Thailand, the Philippines, and other countries across the ocean have flocked into this largest city on Canada's Pacific coast. By some accounts, as many as 30% of households in Vancouver speak Mandarin or Cantonese, making the Chinese there the largest minority by far. Just what is the attraction of this English-speaking city, however?

A visit to Vancouver quickly reveals her charms. Situated on the ocean and possessing a fine, deep-water port, British Columbia's largest city faces Vancouver Island to the west and mountains to the east and north. Most of the city is relatively new, having been rebuilt after a great fire in 1886. The completion of the Panama Canal in 1915 during World War I helped spur growth all along the West Coast of North America, as products from the western states of the United States and the western provinces of Canada could be profitably shipped to Europe. By the 1930s Vancouver had become Canada's third-largest city, a position it maintains today. Lumber from the extensive forested areas within the province, minerals, seafood, and assorted industries, including tourism, give the million-plus residents of metropolitan Vancouver a high standard of living.

The city itself is comfortable and attractive. A large central park called Stanley Park includes a zoo, gardens, arboretum, and aquarium! The University of British Columbia and Simon Fraser University are located in the greater Vancouver area, as are many small and quaint farming and fishing villages within a few hours' drive. Scenic, unpolluted, and prosperous: who could ask for anything more?

Certainly not the Chinese. Although limited immigration from the Far East began as early as the 19th century, it was not until the 1970s that immigration to both Canada and the United States began to increase significantly. By the 1980s, the steady stream had become a flood. Today, Vancouver's Chinatown is said to be North America's second largest. Given the large numbers of Chinese living in the much larger cities of New York, Toronto, Los Angeles, and San Francisco, that represents astronomical growth.

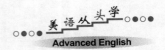

Vancouver's Chinatown is located within walking distance of the downtown area, as are most Chinatowns in North America. Here one can find both traditional Chinese herbal stores and fresh food markets as well as small retail and service businesses. From mid-May to September, Friday to Sunday evenings from 6:30 to 11:30, both Chinese and "foreign" visitors to this area might mistake themselves as being in Shanghai or Hong Kong. For daytime visitors, the Dr. Sun Yat-Sen Classical Chinese Gardens is a must, offering beautifully landscaped floral gardens. The nearby Chinese Cultural Center conducts walking tours of the historic district and even a slide show revealing the historic development of the area.

Of course, Vancouver has much more to offer its residents and out-of-town and overseas visitors. Though — or perhaps because — it lacks the manic energy of East Coast cities of North America or those of modern Asia, Vancouver continues to attract new residents with its serene, safe, and, well, sane lifestyle.

咦？等一下！我没有看错吧？我认为温哥华是在加拿大，而不是在亚洲的。为什么这篇文章的标题却是："温哥华——亚洲的新都市"？

各位读者，不要紧张。没错，温哥华仍位于北美洲最大的国家加拿大境内，而不是在亚洲。然而，过去 20 年中，来自中国、台湾、香港、泰国、菲律宾以及其他亚洲国家的各路人马大批涌进这个位于加拿大太平洋海岸的最大城市。根据若干统计，在温哥华多达 30% 的家庭说普通话或广东话，使得当地华人成为人数最多的少数民族。然而，这个说英语的都市到底有什么吸引力呢？

到温哥华走一趟很快就会发现它的魅力了。这个英属哥伦比亚的最大城市坐落在太平洋岸上，拥有一个很不错的深水港，西临英属温哥华岛，东边和北边则是群山环绕。温哥华大部分地区是在 1886 年大火之后重建的，所以整个市貌看起来相当新。1915 年第一次世界大战期间，巴拿马运河完工，使得美国西海岸几个州和加拿大西部几个省的产品可运往欧洲销售牟利，整个北美洲的西海岸得以蓬勃发展。20 世纪 30 年代，温哥华就已成了加拿大第三大城市，至今，这个地位还没改变。该省内广大林区所生产的木材、矿产、海鲜及各式各样的工业，包括旅游业在内，为这个人口超过百万的大温哥华地区带来很高的生活水平。

温哥华本身就是一个舒适又具有吸引力的都市。史坦利公园是座大型的中央公园，内有一座动物园，数座花园，一座植物园和一个水族馆。英属哥伦比亚大学和西蒙·弗雷泽大学则位于大温哥华区，区内还有许多别具特色的小渔村或小农村，开车只要几个钟头就可到达。风景优美，无污染而且繁荣：还有什么可求的呢？

对中国人而言，的确没什么可求的了。虽然来自亚洲远东地区的移民早在 19 世纪就开始了,不过数量有限,直到 20 世纪 70 年代,前往美加两国的移民数量才开始剧增。到了 20 世纪 80 年代,这股稳定的移民潮才像洪水般涌入。今天,温哥华的中国城据说已是北美洲第二大中国城。与住在纽约、多伦多、洛杉矶和旧金山等更大城市的华人人数相比,这样的增长算是非常快速的了。

温哥华的中国城离市中心很近,步行就可到达,这情形就如同北美地区的大多数中国城一样。在中国城里您可以找到传统的中药店和新鲜市场、零售店及服务业。每年 5 月中旬到 9 月间,中外游客如果在星期五到星期天晚上 6 点半到 11 点半这段时间造访中国城,不论是中国人及"老外",都很可能会误以为自己是身处在上海或香港。对白天的游客来说,孙中山中式古典花园是必游之地,它提供了非常美丽的花园景观。邻近的中国文化中心会举办古迹徒步旅游,甚至还举办幻灯片展,展示中国城的发展史。

当然,温哥华还有更多的东西值得居民、外地人及海外观光客游览。虽然温哥华缺乏北美东海岸都市或亚洲现代都市的狂热活力,但或许正因如此,温哥华不断地以它特有的宁静、安全、富裕以及理性的生活方式吸引着新移民。

2 *Vocabulary & Idioms* 单词短语注解

1. **flock** [flɑk] *vi.* 群集；涌入
   Shoppers flocked to the department store during its year-end sale.
   购物者在年终大甩卖期间涌入这家百货商店。

2. **reveal** [rɪˈvil] *vt.* 展现，流露
   Mary smiled at the sight of John, revealing that she was very much in love with him.
   玛丽见到约翰时微笑起来，流露出她很爱约翰。

3. **be situated in / on...** 坐落在……之内 / 之上
   = be located in / on...
   = lie in / on...
   = stand in / on...
   My hometown is a small village situated deep in the mountains.
   我老家是个坐落在深山里的小村落。

4. **relatively** [ˈrɛlətɪvlɪ] *adv.* 相当地
   Indonesia is a relatively populous nation, but it has only one-sixth the population of China.
   印度尼西亚是个人口相当稠密的国家，但是它的人口仅有中国的六分之一。

5. **spur** [spɝ] *vt.* 激动，刺激
   Low taxes and good infrastructure spur a nation's growth.
   低税率和完善的基础设施能激励国家的成长。

6. **assorted** [əˈsɔrtɪd] *a.* 混合的
   My boyfriend gave me a box of assorted chocolates on Valentine's Day.
   情人节时，我男友送了我一盒什锦巧克力。

7. **astronomical** [ˌæstrəˈnɑmɪkl̩] *a.* 巨大的；天文学的
   Many computer companies have experienced astronomical growth in the past ten years.
   过去 10 年中，许多计算机公司的成长速度惊人。

8. **be within walking distance of...** 离……走路就到了

The post office is within walking distance of where I live.

邮局离我的住处走几步路就到了。

9. **landscape** [ˈlændskep] *vt.* 将……作景观美化 & *n.* 风景

The city government had the dump landscaped and changed into a beautiful park.

市政府将垃圾场造景,把它变成一座美丽的公园。

10. **manic** [ˈmænɪk] *a.* 狂躁的;疯狂的

Life in Hong Kong is manic compared to the simple life of agricultural villages.

与农村的纯朴生活相比,香港的生活算是喧嚣的了。

11. **serene** [səˈrin] *a.* 宁静的

After he retired, Peter led a serene life in the country.

彼得退休后,就在乡下过着宁静的生活。

Lesson 37

The Germanic Languages

日耳曼语系

1 Reading 阅读

Most people have heard of the Tower of Babel story in the *Bible*. According to this story, long ago all people spoke the same language. Later, however, they were punished by speaking a great number of different tongues. Today, there are literally thousands of different languages (defined as mutually unintelligible tongues) around the world, though many are related to one another. Indeed, the two largest language families, the Indo-European (the language family with the largest number of speakers) and Sino-Tibetan (containing the Chinese languages, Thai, Vietnamese, and Tibetan) include hundreds of languages with over half the world's population.

Because there are so many languages within the above two super-categories of language families, linguists have further divided these linguistically rich and geographically diverse families into sub-groups, one of which, the Germanic language group, has the second-largest number of speakers (Chinese being first). Within this group of over 500,000,000 speakers is the world's foremost international language, English, foremost in terms of its geographic spread and

number of second-language users. German, spoken by just over 100,000,000 people, is one of the world's ten-largest languages in terms of population. As English and German speakers constitute the majorities in several of the world's most economically, militarily, and technologically developed countries, it is important to be familiar with this particular language grouping.

Linguists further divide the Germanic languages into three groups, two extant and one extinct. East Germanic languages are no longer spoken; Gothic is an example of this small and historic grouping. Afrikans, Dutch, English, Flemish, and German are the more important languages within the West Germanic grouping. The Scandinavian languages of Danish, Icelandic, Norwegian, and Swedish comprise the North Germanic grouping. Though these languages cannot be easily understood among their different speakers, the similarities in vocabulary are striking.

Take for example the two largest languages with this group, English and German. The word Haus in German is house in English, with nearly the same pronunciation. Some names of German family members are instantly recognizable to English listeners and readers: Mutter, Bruder, and Onkel for the English mother, brother, and uncle (all German nouns are capitalized in print). Other German family members are easily learned: Vater, Schwester, and Tante for the English father, sister, and aunt. Thus, those who know English and want to study German find their first year of learning vocabulary to be relatively easy. The same is true, of course, for those who want to learn Dutch or Danish from an English or German background; these many similarities are due to the single common parent language of all the Germanic tongues, even though this "grandfather" language no longer exists.

Speakers and writers of the Germanic languages account for a great deal of the world's output in everything from economics to literature to military to science and technology. Hardly an aspect of modern life does not benefit from the contributions made by those using these languages, as in the Internet, Hollywood entertainment, Dutch (Phillips) and Scandinavian consumer goods design (Ericsson, maker of cellular phones, is a Swedish company, as are Volvo and Saab), and even the Nobel prizes (awarded by both Norwegian and Swedish institutes). More than one-third of the world's economic production originates in these countries, too.

For any speaker of a language outside the Germanic language group preparing to choose a useful second language for the future, English is probably the best bet. German, too, is very useful in the fields of medicine, economics, military, and science and technology. Being able to communicate with others in this far-reaching linguistic group will offer the user immeasurable benefits.

大多数的人都听过《圣经》中巴别塔的故事。故事里说很久以前，人们说的是同一种语言。但是，后来人们遭受惩罚，而开始说各种不同的语言。今天，全世界真是有好几千种不同的语言（此处指的是彼此无法相通的语言），虽然其中语言彼此都有所关联。的确，这两个最大的语系，印欧语系（最多人使用的语系）和汉藏语系（包括中文、泰语、越南语和西藏语），涵盖了几百种不同的语言，使用者也超过了全世界半数的人口。

就因为有太多的语言涵盖于上述的两个超级语系，语言学家就进一步的把这两种语言丰富、地理涵盖范围非常广的语系再区分为几种不同的次级语系，其中的一个就是日耳曼语系，使用这个语系的人数在所有语系中排名第二位（第一位为中文）。在这个有 5 亿多人口使用的语系中，包括了世界最重要的国际语言，那就是英语。英语之所以称得上是最重要的语言是因为英语使用的地区很广，而且把英语当作第二种语言使用的人口也很多。有 1 亿多人说德语，故就人口而言，德语是世界十大语言之一。由于使用英语和德语的人口在几个经济、军事和科技先进的国家中占绝大比例，因此熟悉日耳曼语系的来龙去脉是很重要的。

语言学家又进一步地把日耳曼语系细分成三个支系，其中两个支系至今仍然存在，另一个支系，也就是东日耳曼语，因无人使用而已不复存在，歌德语就属于这种使用者不多但历史悠久的语系。南非荷兰语、荷兰语、英语、佛兰芝语及德语则属西日耳曼语的几个重要语言。丹麦语、冰岛语、挪威语及瑞典语等北欧语系则属北日耳曼语系。虽然这些不同语言使用者彼此不易沟通，不过词汇的相似之处却很明显。

就拿日耳曼语系中英语及德语两大语言来说吧，德文的 Haus

就是英文的 house，发音几乎完全相同。一些德语家庭成员的称呼如：Mutter、Bruder 和 Onkel，懂英语的人很快地就知道这些词指的就是 mother、brother 和 uncle（德文的名词一律大写）。其他有关家庭成员名称的德语说法也很容易学：像 Vater、Schwester 和 Tante 在英文里指的就 father、sister 和 aunt。因此懂英语而想学德语的人，会发现初学词汇的第一年是很容易的一件事。当然，具有英语和德语背景的人要学丹麦语和荷兰语也同样很容易。这些相似处乃因所有日耳曼语系皆源自共同的母语，尽管这个"爷爷级"的语言已不复存在。

全球凡是经济、文学、军事乃至科技等方面的产品，有很多都是使用日耳曼语系的人所生产的。现代生活几乎各方面无不受益于这些人的贡献，譬如互联网、好莱坞娱乐事业、荷兰(飞利浦公司)和北欧的消费品设计(生产手机的爱立信公司就是瑞典的一家公司，沃尔沃及萨博汽车亦是瑞典的公司)，甚至诺贝尔奖(由挪威及瑞典学术机构颁发)。全世界的经济生产量有超过三分之一也是源自这些国家。

对于那些不使用日耳曼语系的人而言，为了前途而准备要选修第二种语言时，英语很可能是最佳的选择。在医学、经济、军事和科技方面，德语也是一样管用。日耳曼语系影响深远，若能使用这种语言与该语系的人沟通将会带来莫大的好处。

2 *Vocabulary & Idioms* 单词短语注解

1. **literally** [ˈlɪtərəlɪ] *adv.* 确实地，不夸大地
   A conscientious reporter should write any news story literally as it happened.
   有良知的记者应确实根据事实发生的原委写新闻。

2. **unintelligible** [ˌʌnɪnˈtɛlədʒəbḷ] *a.* 口齿不清的，听不懂的
   intelligible [ɪnˈtɛlədʒəbḷ] *a.* 口齿清晰的，可听得懂的
   The little boy burst out crying after murmuring something unintelligible.
   小男孩叽哩咕噜说了一些话之后就放声大哭。

3. **category** [ˈkætəˌgɔrɪ] *n.* 类别，种类
   People may fall into three categories: introverts, extroverts, and ambiverts.
   人可分三类：内向、外向及中间型。

4. **divide...into...** 将……区分为……
   divide [dəˈvaɪd] *vt.* 区分
   It is a good method to divide a class into groups when you teach English conversation.
   教英文会话时，把一个班级分成小组是个好方法。

5. **diverse** [daɪˈvɝs] *a.* 不同的，多样的
   A great many diverse opinions were expressed at the meeting.
   许多不同的意见在会议中被表达出来。

6. **in terms of...** 就……而言
   Cakes and pies are delicious, but in terms of health, they are not very good for us.
   蛋糕和派都很好吃，但就健康而言，它们对我们的健康是不好的。

7. **constitute** [ˈkɑnstəˌtjut] *vt.* 构成
   = make up
   = form

His action constituted a breach of the law. 他的行为构成了犯罪。

8. **extant** [ɪkˈstænt] *a.* 现存的(= still existing)
The cockroach is the oldest extant winged insect, dating back more than 300 million years.
蟑螂是现存最久的有翼昆虫,已有三亿年的历史了。

9. **extinct** [ɪkˈstɪŋkt] *a.* 绝迹的,绝种的
The dinosaur is an extinct animal, and so is the dodo, a clumsy bird native to the Island of Mauritius, which became extinct in the 1600's.
恐龙是绝种的动物,产于毛里求斯岛的渡渡鸟亦然,这种笨拙的鸟于17世纪就绝迹了。

10. **comprise** [kəmˈpraɪz] *vt.* 构成
= compose
= make up
Fifty states comprise the United States. 美国由50个州组成。
= The United States is comprised of fifty states.

11. **similarity** [ˌsɪməˈlærətɪ] *n.* 类似之处
Though they are twins, they have no similarities in terms of personality.
虽然他们是双胞胎,可是个性却完全不同。

12. **striking** [ˈstraɪkɪŋ] *a.* 明显的,醒目的
The cover of this book is striking, but its contents are only platitudes.
这本书的封面很醒目,但是内容平平。

13. **benefit from...** 从……获益
benefit [ˈbɛnəfɪt] *vi.* 得益
It's despicable to benefit from others' misfortunes.
利用别人的不幸去获取利益是件卑鄙的事。

14. **originate in...** 起源于……
Many Western literary works originated in Greek mythology.
有很多西方文学作品源自希腊神话。

15. **far-reaching** [ˌfɑrˈritʃɪŋ] *a.* (影响)深远的

There is no denying that the influence of computers on modern life is far-reaching.

不可否认,计算机对现代生活的影响很深远。

16. **immeasurable** [ɪˈmeʒərəbl] *a.* 无可限量的

A mother's love for her children is immeasurable.

母亲对孩子的爱是无限的。

Lesson 38

Learning How to Apologize

道歉之术

1   *Reading* 阅读

What are the hardest words to pronounce in English? It seems that "I'm sorry" are the two most difficult words for most people to say. Perhaps this difficulty lies in the so-called "losing of face"; when a person apologizes, he lowers himself before another. Yet no one is perfect; everyone makes mistakes. After making a mistake, people should apologize to set things straight with others.

Two phrases in English often confuse non-native users of this language. These phrases are "I'm sorry" and "Excuse me." The latter is used to ask for information, as in "Excuse me, (but) do you have the time?" or "Excuse me, (but) can you tell me whether there is a post office near here?" "Excuse me" is also used when it is necessary to disturb others, as when one person interrupts two others speaking: "Excuse me for interrupting, (but) I have to leave now." Another example of the proper usage of this phrase is when, as a stranger, you want to point something out of benefit to someone, as in "Excuse me, (but) I believe you dropped something out of your wallet." Another common instance of using "Excuse me" is in crowded

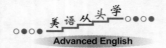

elevators, stores, or lines when a person needs to get through or get out. "Excuse me, (but) this is my floor" is a very handy phrase to learn when in crowded elevators. In all these cases, "Pardon me" may also be used; however, it is more often used in British than in American English.

When is "I'm sorry" used? For more serious incidents. Stepping on someone's toes on a crowded bus, though not intentional, should elicit an immediate "I'm sorry." Bumping into someone even on a crowded street where it is difficult not to also calls for "I'm sorry." Careless or late work in school or in the office requires our apology to teachers, colleagues, or employers. Being late for meetings or dates needs both an apology and often either a reason for the tardiness or an explanation of what course of action will be taken to eliminate any future possibility of recurrence. No one likes to be wronged, intentionally or otherwise. Saying "I'm sorry" can go a long way towards rectifying an awkward situation.

Even more importantly, saying "I'm sorry" is necessary when intentional harm has been done. The borrowing of an item without first informing the owner — who later discovers the "theft" — can be quite embarrassing. A simple but sincere "I'm sorry" might repair the damage done. Careless comments or insults which offend others may be ameliorated with that simple phrase, though sincerity in voice and gesture make all the difference. Similarly, young lovers, often exasperated in unrequited love, may purposefully hurt each other, only later to profoundly regret what they had done. At these times, a heartfelt "I'm sorry" may redress the pain of the one inflicted by love's arrows. Even better, "Please forgive me" may be used, as it is considered a stronger expression of remorse.

Learning to apologize in another language does not excuse speakers from practicing the same good manners in their mother tongue. So many people lament the coldness of modern society; human relationships have been worn thin from constant urban pressures. Part of this problem seems to be that people no longer use such simple words as "please," "thank you," and "I'm sorry." They cost nothing, but can bring a wealth of pleasure or relief to those who hear them. They require little effort, yet these few syllables can enliven someone else's day. So, why not use them whenever possible?

英文最难发音的词是哪些呢？对大部分的人而言，"I'm sorry"（对不起）这两个字似乎是最难的字眼了。也许其困难处就在于所谓的"有失面子"；当一个人道歉的时候，他要在对方面前放下身段。不过，没有人是完美的；人人都会犯错。我们犯错以后，就应道歉，把事情向对方说清楚。

英语中有两句话常让母语非英语的人士搞混，这两句话是"I'm sorry"（对不起）及"Excuse me"（对不起）。第二句话是用来请教他人的，如"对不起，现在几点了？"或是"对不起，能否告诉我这附近有邮局吗？"当我们得打扰他人时，亦可使用"Excuse me"。譬如要打断两个人的对话时，就可说："对不起打断诸位的谈话，我现在得离开了。"适当运用这句话的另一例就是当你与某人素昧平生而出自善意，想向对方指点时，就可说："对不起，我想你的钱包里有东西掉出来了。"使用"Excuse me"的另一常例就是在拥挤的电梯间、商店内或排长龙时，有人要从中穿过或走出来的时候。在拥挤的电梯间内，学会这句话"对不起，我的楼层到了"是挺管用的。以上各例中，亦可使用"Pardon me"（对不起）；然而，"Pardon me"在英式英语用的几率要比美语多。

什么时候才用"I'm sorry"（对不起）呢？"I'm sorry"用于事态较严重的情况。在拥挤的公交车上踩到别人的脚，虽是无心之过，也应立刻说声"I'm sorry"。在拥挤的街道上撞到别人时，即使是情非得已，也必须向对方说声"I'm sorry"。在学校或在公司内，我们表现粗心或迟缓，都必须向老师、同事或老板表示歉意。开会或约会迟到不但要致歉，而且要解释迟到的原因，或说明自己将采取哪些措施，不再让类似的情况发生。没有人喜欢被误解，不管这个误解是有心还是无心的。说声"I'm sorry"对尴尬场面的改观大有帮助。

更重要的是，当造成的伤害是有心时，就有必要说声"I'm sorry"。借东西却未事先告知其所有人，而对方事后发现时，会是相当难为情的。一句简单却诚恳的"I'm sorry"也许就可弥补已经造成的伤害。无心得罪他人的批评与侮辱，用这句简单的话或许就可以改善情况，不过语气及肢体动作的诚恳则是非常关键。同样地，年轻的情侣陷入在单恋的痛苦中时，往往会故意伤害彼此，事后却深深后悔自己的所作所为。在这些时候，真心的一句"I'm sorry"也许就能减轻被爱的利箭所刺伤的一方的痛苦。我们甚至可以使用更好的一句"Please forgive me"（请原谅我），因为一般认为这句话更能强烈表达悔意。

学习用另一种语言表达歉意跟使用母语一样，应注意我们的礼貌。太多人感慨现代社会的冷漠无情；人际关系因都市生活不断的压力已变得越来越淡薄。这个问题的部分症结似乎是因为人们不再使用"请"、"谢谢你"和"对不起"等简单的用语。说这些话花不了一文钱，却为听者带来无比的快乐和舒畅。这些话不费吹灰之力就可学到，可是这几个简简单单的音节却能让别人一天都觉得很开心。因此，可能的话，何不多多使用这些话呢？

② *Vocabulary & Idioms* 单词短语注解 ✎

1. **lie in...** 在于……

   = consist in...

   = hinge on...

   Luck has nothing to do with Albert's success; his success lies entirely in his diligence.

   艾伯特的成功与运气无关；他的成功完全是努力使然。

2. **apologize** [ə'pɑlədʒaɪz] *vi.* 抱歉，赔不是

   apology [ə'pɑlədʒɪ] *n.* 抱歉

   I apologized to Mary for standing her up last night, but she just wouldn't accept my apology.

   我昨晚对玛丽爽约，向她赔不是，但她就是不接受我的道歉。

3. **set things straight** 将事情理清，把话说清楚

   I guess you've wronged me; let's now set things straight from the start.

   我想你冤枉我了；咱们现在就把事情从头说清楚吧。

4. **disturb** [dɪ'stɜb] *vt.* 打扰，干扰

   The mosquitoes disturbed the baby's sleep and made it cry.

   那些蚊子干扰到这个婴儿的睡眠，并且把他弄哭了。

5. **interrupt** [ˌɪntə'rʌpt] *vt.* 打断，中断

   The ringing of the telephone interrupted our conversation.

   电话的响声中断了我们的谈话。

6. **handy** ['hændɪ] *a.* 方便的，管用的

   come in handy 派上用场

   Take an umbrella with you; it may come in handy.

   随身带把伞吧；它随时会派上用场。

7. **intentional** [ɪn'tɛʃənl] *a.* 有意的，故意的

   I don't think Sarah's dropping her books in front of Eric was an accident; I think it was intentional.

   我认为莎拉在埃里克面前掉落书本不是意外的；我认为她是有意的。

8. **elicit** [ɪˈlɪsɪt] *vt.* 引出

The teacher tried to elicit conversation among his students by letting them choose their own topics.

老师让学生们自己挑选话题以引起他们的交谈。

9. **tardiness** [ˈtɑrdɪnɪs] *n.* 迟到

tardy [ˈtɑrdɪ] *a.* 迟到的

John slept late quite often; his tardiness eventually led to his being fired.

约翰常常晚起,他的迟到终于使他被炒鱿鱼。

10. **eliminate** [ɪˈlɪməˌnet] *vt.* 消除;淘汰

The computer engineers are trying to eliminate the software bugs, but it is not an easy job.

这些计算机工程师想要清除软件上的漏洞,但这不是件易事。

11. **recurrence** [rɪˈkɜəns] *n.* 再发生,(疾病的)复发

recur [rɪˈkɜ] *vi.* 再发生

More care in the future will definitely prevent recurrence of the mistake.

以后小心点,这个错误肯定就不会再发生了。

I'll go crazy if my headache recurs.

如果头痛再犯的话,我就要抓狂了。

12. **go a long way toward + V-ing** 对……很有帮助

Reading a short English article on a daily basis will go a long way toward learning English.

每天看一篇英文短文对学英文大有帮助。

13. **rectify** [ˈrɛktɪˌfaɪ] *a.* 改正,矫正

The little boy admitted his mistake and was willing to rectify it at once.

小男孩承认错误,愿意立刻改正过来。

14. **ameliorate** [əˈmilɪəˌret] *vt.* 改善(= improve)

His disappointment at not getting the promotion was ameliorated with a large raise.

他没有升职的失望因为大幅加薪而改善了。

15. **exasperate** [ɪgˈzæspəˌret] *vt.* 激怒

Margaret was exasperated by her teenage daughter's unruly behavior at school.

玛格丽特被她正值豆蔻年华的女儿在学校不守规矩的行为给激怒了。

16. **unrequited** [ˌʌnrɪˈkwaɪtɪd] *a.* 无回报的（尤与 love 连用）

unrequited love 单恋

Knowing that his love for Mary was an unrequited love, Peter left her immediately.

彼得知道他对玛丽的爱是单相思时，便立刻离开她了。

17. **heartfelt** [ˈhɑrtˌfɛlt] *a.* 诚挚的

"Please accept my heartfelt apology, " Peter begged before his girlfriend.

彼得在女友面前央求道："请接受我真心的道歉。"

18. **lament** [ləˈmɛnt] *vt.* 哀悼，为……悲伤

The two brothers lamented the passing away of their favorite uncle, who used to take them out fishing and camping when they were young.

这两兄弟为他们最敬爱的叔叔的逝世而悲伤。叔叔生前在他们还小的时候会带他们去钓鱼和露营。

19. **a wealth of +** 不可数名词 大量的……

I take pride in my teacher because he seems to have a wealth of knowledge.

我老师似乎有满肚子的学问，因此我以他为荣。

英式 IPA 音标与美式 K.K. 音标对照表

序号	IPA	K.K.	Key Words
1	ɪ	ɪ	bit
2	e	ɛ	bed
3	æ	æ	cat
4	ɒ	ɑ	hot
5	ʌ	ʌ	cut
6	ʊ	ʊ	put
7	ə	ə	about
8	i	ɪ	happy
9	u	ʊ	actuality
10	iː	i	bee
11	ɑː	ɑ	father
12	ɔː	ɔ	law
13	uː	u	tool
14	ɜː	ɝ	bird
15	eɪ	e	name
16	aɪ	aɪ	lie
17	ɔɪ	ɔɪ	boy
18	əʊ	o	no
19	aʊ	aʊ	out
20	ɪə	ɪr	beer
21	eə	ɛr	hair
22	ʊə	ʊr	tour
23	uə	ʊə	actual
24	iə	jɚ	peculiar

Notes:

1. K.K.音标取自美国两位语言学家 John S. Kenyon 和 Thomas A. Knott 两人姓氏的第一个字母。其特点是按照一般的美国读法标音。

2. 本列表所用的 IPA 音标是英国 Jones 音标的最新修订形式。

3. K.K.音标除辅音中[ŋ]、[l]与IPA音标[n]、[l]符号不同外, 其余基本一致。

4. 美式和英式发音的不同点之一是卷舌音。如果单词的字母组合含有 r, 该组合一般会发卷舌音。例：four [fɔː]（IPA）；[fɔr]（K.K.）。